TH
STUDI

MAPPING TIME AND SPACE:

HOW MEDIEVAL MAPMAKERS VIEWED THEIR
WORLD

THE BRITISH LIBRARY
STUDIES IN MAP HISTORY
Volume I

Mapping Time and Space:
How Medieval Mapmakers Viewed Their World

Evelyn Edson

THE BRITISH LIBRARY

First published 1997
This paperback edition published 1999
by The British Library
96 Euston Road
St Pancras
London NW1 2DB

British Library Cataloguing-in-Publication Data
A CIP record is available from The British Library

ISBN 0-7123-4536-1

Designed by John Mitchell
Printed in England by Henry Ling, Dorchester

Frontispiece
This annus – mundus – homo diagram shows the harmonies existing among space, time and the human body. See pp.43–4 for further discussion. Isidore, *De natura rerum*. BL Harl. MS 2660, f.37, twelfth century.

CONTENTS

Preface

Until the recent revolution in the history of cartography, medieval maps were looked upon as quaint, amusing, and quite simply WRONG.[1] They might be studied to gain insight into the benighted medieval mind, but for maps *qua* maps one should consult the latest products of the most modern technology, such as satellite photography. The map, according to this view, is hardly to be distinguished from nature itself, and the history of mapmaking is a simple linear progression from darkness and error into the light of modern high-tech correctness.

When the first volume of the *History of Cartography* was published in 1987, the editors, J. B. Harley and David Woodward, put forward a view which had gradually been gaining adherents in the field. Maps, said Harley and Woodward, are human documents, artifacts, with all the limitations and interesting qualities which those terms imply. Maps are not natural, self-evident 'statements of geographical fact produced by neutral technologies'.[2] The hand of the mapmaker is guided by a mind located in a certain time and place and sharing inevitably the prejudices of his or her surroundings.

For a simple example, one may take the question of names. What are places called? The mapmaker must choose, and in the early sixteenth century mapmakers discarded the native American names for names in their own languages and traditions. At a stroke of the pen Indian villages and populations disappeared, replaced by comfortable, familiar (to the European) English villages and populations.[3] By 1506 the continent of South America was labelled 'Land of the Holy Cross', which would have been an unwelcome surprise to most of its inhabitants, had they been informed of it. Recent bitter controversy over the names of Macedonia and Palestine demonstrate the continuing partisan nature of geographical naming.

Few questions concerning maps are neutral. How about orientation? Is the map arranged so that north is 'on top'? If so, does this imply that northern countries dominate those of the south? What colours are used? Are the countries ruled by the British Empire all coloured red?[4] How are the cities chosen to be included, by size of population or by their political or historical or religious importance? What political boundaries are drawn and where? The choices made by the makers of maps impose meaning, whether consciously or unconsciously. Unless one can produce Lewis Carroll's proposed map of the world, which is the same size as the world itself, one inevitably eliminates or emphasizes, privileging some features over others. With a certain measure of humility about modern maps, one can turn with a more open mind and greater interest to the maps of the Middle Ages.

When seeking the meaning and purpose of medieval maps, one cannot assume that maps were used then for the same purposes or had the same meaning as they do today. The differences in structure and content are clues which lead us to imagine how medieval makers and readers of maps saw the world. Another place to look is the context in which maps appear, for a majority of surviving medieval maps appear in books, surrounded by written works and other diagrams. These accompanying materials can tell us much about the role of maps in medieval thought and society.

The founders of the discipline of the history of cartography were mostly geographers, who did pioneer work in deciphering the geographical knowledge available to the Middle Ages and classifying, according to various rules, the maps which survive. However, most of these scholars did not pay the same diligent attention to the rest of the codex. In the most authoritative catalogue of medieval world maps, that of Marcel Destombes, there are misattributions which must be reviewed and corrected if one's purpose is to understand the context in which the map was prepared.[5]

The thesis of this work is that a study of the context of medieval maps in books reveals that many were designed to encompass concepts of time as well as space. Such an idea has already been broached by the German scholar Anna-Dorothee von den Brincken. Looking at the maps themselves, particularly the larger world maps, she says their goal is 'to portray the course of universal history together with totality of historical space'.[6] Von den Brincken's theory helps to explain the persistent inclusion of places from the past on medieval maps. The city of Troy, the Garden of Eden, and the route of the Israelites from Egypt to Canaan were as consistently shown as physical features, such as the Pyrenees, or places of contemporary significance, such as the city of Rome. It also helps explain why some medieval maps were referred to by their makers as 'histories'.

In this book I will be concentrating on the various ways in which time as well as space is the subject of medieval world maps. My study branches out from the content and structure of the maps themselves to the written work or works which accompany them. Several cautions are in order. The first of these is the loss of the majority of books from the earliest period. Do we know that those which we now possess were typical of the whole? Another is that very old manuscripts have been rebound, even reorganized, at least once in their long lifetimes, and their pages may no longer appear in the original order. In addition they have sometimes been pillaged of their pages, particularly the illustrated ones, so we cannot assume that there was never a map in works which do not now contain one. Another problem is that medieval books were not necessarily meant to stand alone and to be completely self-explanatory. Books used for teaching were read not in isolation but with the teacher present, explaining more fully than the text alone can do. Many scientific books, for example, contain complex diagrams and tables which are briefly titled and explained, if at all. Clearly the reader was meant to receive live human assistance in his efforts to comprehend the work.

With these limitations in mind, this book begins with the examination of maps which appear in history books, works which deal with the passage of time in human terms and in earthly space. Some of these were universal histories which ranged over the entire earth from the beginning of time to the present day. Others were primarily chronicles, year-by-year records of events with a local focus, but sometimes set within a larger context. Next we will look at maps in Easter and calendar manuscripts, a rather surprising but common place to find them, along with other diagrams describing the structure of the universe and its motion in time. Then we will look briefly at maps which are histories in themselves. These are mostly found as individual items, outside books, but occasionally there is a book which seems to have been designed to explain them, such as Gervase of Tilbury's *Otia Imperialia*, which may have been intended to expound on the Ebstorf map. And lastly we will look at maps which were designed to illustrate theological concepts, including one of the most studied and most interesting of all map cycles, those in St Beatus's *Commentary on the Apocalypse*. His work draws together many of the themes of space and time, spiritual and physical, followed throughout the present book.

The medieval world maps studied here range from the earliest ones we possess, from the eighth century, to maps of the end of the thirteenth century. The later years of this period saw the culmination of the medieval mapping tradition in the great wall maps of Hereford and Ebstorf. The next century was to bring some technological innovations and new influences on European mapping, including the first of the voyages of discovery, which were to alter maps in interesting and complex ways. In time, maps came to narrow their focus to physical space and eliminate other dimensions, such as religious meaning and history, which were so important to the medieval world map. The story of this transition is another book.

My thanks for good advice and a generous sharing of information go to scholars in the field of history of cartography. Surely a more open-minded and welcoming collection of scholars never existed. The reigning goddess of this group is Catherine Delano Smith, who, in addition to her own considerable scholarly work, tirelessly organizes events to bring scholars together and to encourage productive communication among them. Special correspondence and assistance also came from Marcia Kupfer, who participated in several panels with me and commented on my papers; Patrick Gautier Dalché, whose erudite and pointed remarks were always enlightening; and John W. Williams, my former teacher, who selflessly shared his expertise on the Beatus manuscripts. My readers for this manuscript were Peter Barber and Paul D. A. Harvey, whose perceptive remarks were invaluable.

Librarians are next on my list, from those of Piedmont Virginia Community College, my own college, who patiently ordered books with unpronounceable titles on Interlibrary Loan, to the University of Virginia, which generously extends its wide-ranging services to fellow college teachers throughout the state. Corpus Christi College, Oxford, was my home for six delightful months in 1991–2, and while there I was privileged to work in the many libraries of Oxford, including that of St John's College and the Geography Library. Other libraries which opened their marvellous facilities to me include the Bibliothèque Nationale in Paris, the Biblioteca Nacional in Madrid, the Pierpont Morgan Library in New York, the Library of Congress, the Newberry Library and the Adler Planetarium Library in Chicago, the Huntington Library of San Marino, California, the University Libraries of Montpellier and Valladolid, the Biblioteca Medicea Laurenziana of Florence, the Biblioteca Apostolica of the Vatican, the Vatican Microfilm Library of Saint Louis University, and, above all, the British Library, particularly the Manuscript and Map Rooms. I have an especially warm memory of the small city library of Albi, where the kindly librarian seated me at a table overlooking a garden with lemon trees and handed me their priceless eighth-century manuscript.

Several timely grants provided necessary support for research time and journeys. Piedmont Virginia Community College gave me a sabbatical, then an unheard-of innovation in the Virginia Community College System, in 1991–2, and another half-year leave in 1996, while I was working on this book. A Virginia Community College System research grant gave some released time in 1995 and funds to travel to London to participate in the 'Maps and Society' lecture series. A travel grant from the National Endowment for the Humanities paid for an airline ticket to Spain in the summer of 1993, where I visited sites related to the Beatus manuscripts. And the Andrew Mellon Foundation financed a three-week research visit to the Vatican Microfilm Library at Saint Louis University in the spring of 1996.

To friends and family I owe thanks for their patience and warm-hearted support. My husband, Andy Wilson, has read a good deal more about medieval maps over the past several years than he would ever have imagined possible, and his thoughtful comments have been most valuable. My dear friend, Pryor Hale, also read parts of the manuscript and managed to combine her excellent critical sense with a friend's kind encouragement. The members of Springtree Community have cheerfully watched me disappear upstairs to the computer while they were busy canning tomatoes and hauling firewood. My children, Meredith Cole and Ben Edson, have been understanding and encouraging, as has my stepfather, David H. Gould, and my mother, Margery Edson-Gould, all of whose children are above average. This book is dedicated to the memory of my father, Arthur Lewis Edson, who was a writer and a great lover of books of all kinds.

ABBREVIATIONS

Bib. Laur.	Biblioteca Laurenziana, Florence
Bib. Marucell.	Biblioteca Marucelliana, Florence
Bib. Mun.	Bibliothèque Municipale
Bib. Nac.	Biblioteca Nacional, Madrid
Bib. Naz. Univ.	Biblioteca Nazionale Universitaria, Turin
Bib. Riccard.	Biblioteca Riccardiana, Florence
Bib. Roy.	Bibliothèque Royale, Brussels
B.L.	British Library, London
B.N.	Bibliothèque Nationale, Paris
Bodl. Lib.	Bodleian Library, Oxford
C.C.C.	Corpus Christi College
O.N.	Osterreichische Nationalbibliothek, Vienna
Vat. Bib. Apos.	Biblioteca Apostolica Vaticana, Rome

CHAPTER 1

Introduction to Medieval Maps

The story of medieval maps is a story of survival and of loss. We cannot begin to know how many have disappeared in proportion to those that remain to us. War, accident, decay, and deliberate destruction have all taken their toll, a significant part of which has occurred in our own century. We need look no further than the bombing of Hanover in 1943 and the loss of the Ebstorf map, the largest and, once, the best preserved of medieval *mappaemundi*.[1]

Maps bound in codices or books were better designed for survival than large, unwieldy wall or roll-up maps. Few of the rotuli or rolls mentioned in medieval library catalogues are extant today. As for those made of precious materials, such as King Roger of Sicily's silver map, they were all too easily melted down and converted to money. In contrast, the codex was compact, protected by its covers, and could be carried by fugitives or, in more peaceful times, transported for lending and copying. Its relatively small size made for less detail, of course, on any maps which might be pictured within. We have several medieval maps in books which are almost surely copies of larger wall maps, but equally certainly they have been edited to fit their smaller format.[2]

In addition to the accidents of survival, there are the hazards of copying. The almost total disappearance of maps from the classical era means that we see what was chosen to be copied by a later period. We must speculate, though we can know little, about how works were selected, altered perhaps, neglected or destroyed. The encyclopedists of the fourth and fifth centuries, such as Macrobius and Martianus Capella, made drastic decisions as they reduced the abundant heritage of classical knowledge to abridged versions, adapted to the impatient tastes of their readers. These works were copied again and again in the Middle Ages and appear in numerous libraries, while the originals on which they were based mouldered away to dust. Not many works survived that narrow passage of several centuries marked by invasions and disorders between the fall of the Roman Empire in the West and Charlemagne's consolidation of his power. While there were moments of peace conducive to scholarship – Northumbria in the time of Bede or Visigothic Spain in the days of Isidore –

these periods ended in confusion and flight and the invariable loss of books, as well as lives. Charlemagne, however, established himself as the patron of copyists and enlisted the monasteries of his empire in the work of preserving what remained. Most of our copies of classical texts date from no earlier than the ninth century.[3]

The text of many classical works has been well established by comparing surviving versions and making surmises about the errors copyists were likely to make, but illustrations are a greater problem. Looking at works known to have been copied from one another, one can see variations of detail and style in the pictures where the text is more faithfully reproduced. All the maps which now accompany classical works of history, such as Sallust and Lucan, may have been glosses of the energetically glossing early medieval period rather than diagrams which accompanied the original texts. Or, if the original authors did provide maps, they may have been altered over time.

CLASSIFICATION SYSTEMS FOR MEDIEVAL MAPS

What do medieval world maps look like? There is no single model, but a great variety of forms, degrees of detail, and selection of places to be included. It is interesting to note that there was no word which exclusively meant 'map' in the Middle Ages. The word *mappa* meant 'cloth', and *carta*, used in some languages today, was translated 'document', *Descriptio*, frequently attached to medieval maps, could also mean a textual description, as is true of both *carta* and *mappa*. *Pictura* and *figura* could be any diagram or drawing. This imprecision of language indicates to us that the visual representation of physical reality, so highly prized by ourselves, was perhaps less important to people of an earlier era.

Considerable scholarly energy has been expended in the last century on the task of classifying medieval world maps in different ways. The most obvious is by shape (rectangular, round, almond-shaped), but others have concentrated on the theory of the world they present (spherical, disk shaped) or the divisions thereof (quadripartite, tripartite, seven climates, or five zones).

One of the most influential systems, proposed by Michael Andrews in 1925, and adopted by Marcel Destombes in his monumental catalogue of early medieval maps, allowed for four main categories:

Type A. schematic maps of the *ecumene* (inhabited world) without geographic configurations;

Type B. maps which show a fourth continent outside the known world;

Type C. maps which preserve the idea of Greek geographers that the earth is divided into five zones;

Type D. maps, Type A in form, but having extensive nomenclature and geographic configurations.[4]

These types were modified by Destombes to be more specific. For example, he divided the Type A map into a number of subcategories, an A3V map showing continents surrounded by the winds, and an A3L map being one on which the southern continent was called Libya instead of Africa.

There are many problems with these categories, which are far from watertight. For example, a zone map may be quite detailed, if it is large enough, and include geographic configurations. Also, a map that shows only the *ecumene* does not mean that its author did not believe there was no fourth continent or land on the other side of the earth. In the recent *History of Cartography* David Woodward tackled the problem again and suggested these categories:[5]

1. Tripartite. These maps include the three known continents, separated by the traditional boundaries of the Mediterranean Sea, the Nile River, and the Black Sea/Don River. These maps may be simple or complex, containing many names.

2. Zonal (Destombes Type C). These may or may not include a fourth continent in the southern hemisphere.

3. Quadripartite. Woodward sees these maps as having characteristics of both the above – a tripartite ecumene in the northern hemisphere and a fourth continent in the south.

4. Transitional. These are maps drawn in the late medieval period, the fourteenth and fifteenth centuries, which incorporate the increasingly geographically accurate nautical maps of that time and anticipate changes that are to come in the great Age of Discovery. Without the geographical consciousness these maps display, the Age of Discovery probably would not have been possible. There are several excellent examples of impressive scale and accuracy in the few years just before the voyage of Columbus.

All these studies have been helpful in sorting out the chaos. First, it is important to remember that the variant forms of the world map do not represent exclusive theories. The same person might draw any one or more of these forms, depending on the purpose. Many manuscripts have more than one form among their pages; for example, the famous Anglo-Saxon world map appears in a manuscript which also contains a zone diagram of the earth, both probably done by the same hand and part of the overall plan of the manuscript.[6]

Next, it is now clear that nearly all medieval scholars conceived of the earth as a globe.[7] Its size was estimated according to one of two measurements of its circumference inherited from the Greeks, either 180,000 stades according to Posidonius and Ptolemy, or 252,000 stades according to Erastosthenes. A stade, six hundred Greek feet, is variously estimated to be equivalent to 517 to 607 feet by modern authors. If the former, Erastosthenes's figure for the earth's circumference is only 50 miles off from the modern one. These two numbers survived side by side throughout the Middle Ages and were still coexistent in Columbus's day. The smaller figure drastically overestimated the size of the inhabited, known world, or *ecumene*, in relation to the whole, and was greatly preferred by Columbus, who set out to cross a correspondingly smaller ocean.

For the purposes of this work, which is to consider the context and purposes of maps, rather than the map form alone, I propose yet another classification, which is based on the amount of detail rather than on the form of the maps, and is described below.

The T–O map

The simplest medieval maps show only the known world, or *ecumene*, often imagined as a circle divided into the three known continents. The most common is the T–O or O–T map, named from its configuration, a circle divided into three parts, with Asia twice the size of Europe and Africa. A less common variant, the Y and O map, shows the continents of equal size. The T–O form is of great antiquity, possibly being the type of map ridiculed in the fifth century BC by Herodotus in the *Histories*: 'I cannot but laugh when I see numbers of persons drawing maps of the world without having any reason to guide them; making, as they do, the ocean-stream to run all round the earth, and the earth itself to be an exact circle, as if described by a pair of compasses. . . .'[8] It is a good question whether in its simplest form the T–O should be called a map at all. It seems to have been used as a symbol, a shorthand reference, functioning in manuscripts like illuminated initials, to guide the reader to the desired chapter.[9] However, as the T–O became elaborated, with the addition of cardinal directions, the winds (four, eight, or twelve), the bodies of water which form the boundaries between continents, it evolved into something like a map. The T–O structure is used in some, but far from all, of the larger, more detailed medieval maps as a framework.[10] Sometimes the three continents are filled with descriptive text, such as the allotting of each to one of Noah's three sons or an account of the division of humanity after the Tower of Babel was destroyed. The happy inspiration of iden-

1.1. T–O map from Book XIV.2 of Isidore's *Etymologies*. 'The earth is divided into three parts, one of which is called Asia, another Europe, and the third Africa. Asia extends throughout the east from south to north, Europe from north to west and Africa from east to south. Whence it is evident that two, Europe and Africa, cover half the circle, while Asia alone covers the other half.' The map follows this text in most manuscripts. BL MS Royal 6.C.1, fol. 108ᵛ, tenth century, diameter 63 mm.
Courtesy of the British Library Board.

tifying the initials as signifying *Orbis Terrarum* or 'circle of lands' seems not to have appeared until the fifteenth century, in a geographical poem composed by the Dati brothers of Italy.

The idea of the T as a crucifix superimposed on the spherical earth, symbolizing its salvation by Christ's sacrifice, is an earlier one. Inscriptions accompanying a group of wall-paintings at the abbey of St Riquier (at Centula in north-eastern France) in the mid-ninth century by the monk Micon revolve around the theme of the symbol of the cross. One of the paintings is a world map, conceived of as a continuation of the theme. The map, sixth in a series of seven paintings, is described:

Hic mundi species perituri picta videtur
Partibus in ternis qui spatiatus inest,
Quarum Asia primumque locum hinc Europa secundum
Possidet extremum Africa deinde suum.

(Here appears a painted image of the mortal world; which is spread out, and divided into three parts, of which Asia occupies the first place, Europe the second, and Africa the last.)[11]

The most spectacular example of a crucifix on a map appears later in the thirteenth-century Ebstorf map, which shows the world imposed on the body of Christ with head, hands, and feet emerging from the edges. As far as development goes, however, the T–O form appeared first, in the ancient period, and was thought of as a crucifix only by Christians who could hardly look at two crossed sticks without thinking of the cross of Christ.

The T–O schema is occasionally replaced by an almost identical figure with a squared outline. Here the three continents are divided either by two lines forming a T, or by a triangle. The aim is the same: to show the division of the world into continents. In Isidore's *Etymologies* both forms are sometimes shown, with the circular T–O containing the names of the continents and the triangle-in-the-square having the names of Noah's sons.[12]

The list map

A second type of map, closely related to the T–O, I will call the list map. Here the basic cartographic frame, usually a T–O, is used as the space for a list of places in each region, most often a list of provinces. In its simplest form, it is just another way of presenting text, but the places are occasionally grouped in a geographically suggestive way, and there are transitional forms which move towards the more 'geographical' map.

1.2. Modified T–O, from Book XIV.2 of Isidore's *Etymologies*. The surrounding Ocean and the divisions between the continents are added to this map (the Nile, the Mediterranean, and the Tanais, or Don) with the additional refinement of the Sea of Azov (Meotites Palus, here: the lake or swamp of Maeotis). This feature is mentioned by Isidore in XIV.4, and in the diagram forms an elbow or Y shape. The scribe has also included the cardinal directions and the names of Noah's three sons, as well as a small cross in the east. This diagram appears for the first time in a pair of Spanish manuscripts from the ninth century. BL MS Harl. 2660, fol. 123ᵛ, twelfth century, diameter 90 mm.

Courtesy of the British Library Board.

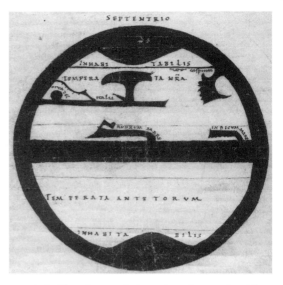

1.3. List map, from a manuscript containing computus and astronomical papers, charts, and diagrams. The manuscript contains an English version of Isidore's *De natura rerum*, though here patriotically attributed to Gildas. The map is separated from the text by several pages and is introduced by a passage on the preceding page describing the division of the earth among the sons of Noah. The provinces or countries in each continent are listed on the map. An oddity of this diagram is the reversal of Africa and Europe. BL Cotton MS Vitellius A.XII. fol. 64^r, tenth century, south-western England, diameter 110 mm.
Courtesy of the British Library Board.

1.4. Zonal map. Oriented to the north with 'septentrio' above, this diagram shows the two frigid zones ('inhabitabilis') and the two temperate zones, while a coloured band indicates the middle torrid zone. The two temperate zones are labelled 'temperata nostra', our temperate zone, and 'temperata antetorum', the opposite temperate zone, though 'antetorum' appears to be a made-up word. The northern temperate zone contains several geographical features, including the Orkney Islands, the Caspian Sea, Italy, the Red Sea, and the Indian Ocean. From Macrobius, *Commentary on the Dream of Scipio*, Book II, ch. 9. BL MS Harl. 2772, fol. 70^v, ninth century. Diameter 120 mm.
Courtesy of the British Library Board.

A diagram of this type might have served as a memory aid, the visible form helping the student to sort out and recall the list of names.

The zonal map

A third type of medieval map is the zonal map, derived primarily from manuscripts of Macrobius's *Commentary on the Dream of Scipio*, but transported into other, surprising places, such as Virgil's *Georgics*. The diagrams in Macrobius's work must have been original with him, as the text specifically calls for figures which are well integrated with the work, illustrating the points he makes in his description of phenomena in the heavens and on earth. The zonal map presents in pictorial form the ancient Greek thesis, attributed to Parmenides,

c. 515 BC, that the globe is divided into five zones: two frigid at opposite poles, two temperate, and one torrid zone at the equator. Only the temperate zones were habitable, and, though there might conceivably be people living in the southern temperate zone, they were beyond reach due to the killing heat in the intervening torrid belt. The quadripartite maps, according to Woodward's classification, reflect this thesis in their depiction of a fourth continent, presumably in the southern hemisphere. These divisions persisted, even though in the early Middle Ages fuller knowledge of the northern frigid zone, which included part of Britain, made it quite clear that it was habitable – or at least inhabited. The zonal maps often have very little geographical detail, as the ecumene is crammed into a fraction of the circle. There are only a few places to indicate the limits of the zones, such as the Orkney Islands in the north-west and Meroe in the south, but occasionally the form is adapted to a map with a larger number of places.

A variant of the zone hypothesis is the division of the inhabited world into seven climates, based on latitude. This classification, originally developed by Hipparchus in the second century BC was employed by Ptolemy for his map four centuries later. The concept was known in the Middle Ages – the climates were described by Bede, who took them from Pliny – but it is rare to find a map based on them until later in the Middle Ages in the works of Sacrobosco (John of Holywood) and Pierre d'Ailly. Climate maps are more commonly found in the medieval Arabic tradition.[13]

The detailed map

The fourth type is the map which comes close to satisfying our modern idea of what a map should be: a wealth of place-names with cities, seas, mountains, regions, nomadic peoples all located, however bizarrely, in accordance with some idea of spatial organization. This is similar to Woodward's Transitional Type, but it includes early maps, such as the Vatican map of 800 AD, the Albi map of the eighth century, and the Anglo-Saxon map of the eleventh century. Relatively few surviving world maps fall into this category. When they were asked to represent the world within the confines of a codex, the overwhelming nature of the task seems to have induced medieval mapmakers to prefer one of the simpler forms above. Of 1106 maps in Destombes's catalogue, only 103 are of this description (his Type D), and a mere eight of these date before 1200.[14]

The variety of format among medieval maps of the more detailed type is considerable. A few stemmata have been worked out, for the maps accompanying St Beatus's

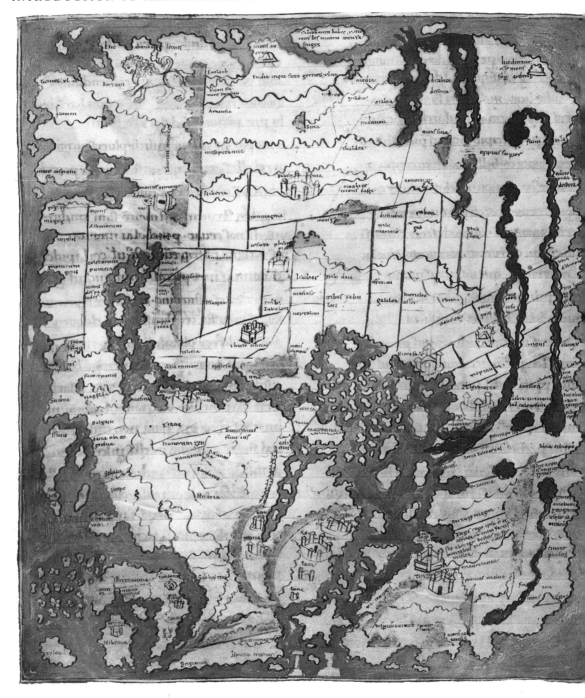

1.5. Anglo-Saxon map; an example of a detailed world map. The compiler of this map made a serious effort to present the inhabited world in a realistic manner. The use of irregular shapes and wavy lines make it especially convincing to a modern viewer. It is called 'Anglo-Saxon' because it pre-dates the Conquest and the manuscript contains several works in that language. The manuscript contains computus materials and one other map, a zonal type. BL Cotton MS Tiberius B.V.1., fol. 56ᵛ, c.1050, English. Size of map 210 × 170 mm.
Courtesy of the British Library Board.

Commentary on the Apocalypse for example,[15] but other maps appear as one-of-a-kind originals, both in form and in content, and still other maps migrate from one text to another with alacrity. One of the reasons for lack of standardization was that the idea of using longitude and latitude as a basis for location had died with the loss of Ptolemy's *Geographia*. Neither the concept nor the necessary data were available to the medieval mapmaker. In the thirteenth century Roger Bacon proposed the idea of using coordinates and perhaps even made a map of this type, but it does not survive. Al-Idrisi at the court of Palermo in the tenth century made a very Ptolemaic-looking map, but his fellow Arabs generally made maps as abstract as European ones. The Arabs maintained charts of the locations of cities by latitude and longitude, but for centuries used these for horoscopes, rather than for mapmaking.[16] It took the conjunction of the concept of the locational grid and the data to transform mapmaking in the later Middle Ages.

SOURCES OF INFORMATION FOR MAPMAKERS

Mapmakers were largely dependent on textual description for their mapping information – that is, when they did not have a physical map to copy; and since most of these descriptions were somewhat impressionistic, no wonder the maps vary. The reader may experiment by taking Orosius's brief description of the world in *Seven Books Against the Pagans* and trying to draw a map which reflects it. Konrad Miller, the great German cartographic scholar in the early 1900s, undertook this exercise for several medieval geographic descriptions, including that of Orosius, with problematic results.[17] Even Ptolemy's more exact descriptions in the *Geography* produced at least two quite different versions when transmuted into graphic form in the later Middle Ages.[18]

Geographic statements in the Bible, while few, were an important concern for Christian mapmakers. Such expressions as the 'waters above the earth' in Genesis 1.6 caused intense soul-searching by St Augustine,[19] and lesser men mirrored his concern. If the Bible was an infallible source, what could the reasoning of mere mortals do? Among other problematic biblical statements was that Jerusalem had been placed in the centre of the lands (Ezekiel 5.5). When, in the later Middle Ages, this was interpreted literally as the centre of the earth, it caused a reorganization of maps. In general, however, the Bible was vague on physical geography, and the so-called Christianization of the map was more a matter of the selection of places of spiritual significance than a reorganization of the map's structure.

In addition to bookish sources, medieval mapmakers were not averse to using travellers' accounts or their own experiences. The fact that so many of the scribes producing the codices were sequestered in monasteries meant that personal experience was likely to be severely limited, but still the home monastery, at the very least, crops up on numerous maps, such as the convent of Ebstorf on the Ebstorf map and the monastery of Saint-Sever on the map made for its abbot. When the Crusades got under way, medieval geographers and historians tried to include incoming information about the all-important Holy Lands on their maps, while maintaining allegiance to their textual authorities.

A few mapmakers seem to have decorated their works with some freely chosen symbols, setting down a city here, a river there, a picturesque tower over there.[20] Others worked within a structure (such as, east at the top, Paradise, the four rivers emanating from it, the three continents with their boundaries) and embroidered on it with a free hand. Others seem to have worked with a painstaking concern for the accurate representation of spatial relationships, taking into account distances, in the form of days' journeys, and relative position. But the data they had to work with were limited, and without a system of coordinates a high degree of accuracy was impossible.

THE ROMAN MODEL

If there was a single authoritative map made in the Roman world, a sort of Rand McNally of the Empire, such as we imagine Marcus Agrippa's map in Rome to have been, it does not appear to have been inherited intact by the medieval world. Certainly no world map has survived to our own time from classical antiquity. Two cartographic works which survive are the Peutinger scroll, an itinerary map of the Empire which is an twelfth- or thirteenth-century copy of a fourth-century work, and the Madaba floor mosaic in a sixth-century church in Jordan, which might have been a map only of the Holy Land. Scholars have selected various maps as reflecting the hypothetical model of the Roman world map (for example, the St Sever manuscript of Beatus),[21] but the reasoning is circular: 'this is an excellent map, therefore, it must be based on a Roman model'. The use of classical names, such as Roman provinces, shows us only that classical texts and perhaps place-name traditions survived, not necessarily a map.[22]

Agrippa's memorial was erected in the Porticus Vipsania (now the Via del Corso area) in Rome after his death in 12 BC, and has generally been assumed to have taken the form of a map. In the *Natural History* Pliny makes repeated references to dimensions of various provinces and distances which derived from this work on public display. The idea that an agent of Augustus would undertake a survey of the known world after the foundation of the principate seems reasonable, and a recent work connects it with other organizational and propaganda projects of the time.[23] More recently Kai Broderson has doubted that Agrippa's memorial was a map at all, asserting that it was more likely a lengthy geographical inscription. He reproduces wildly contradictory reconstructions of the alleged map and presents one after another the various suppositions that have been made about it. It was a mosaic, a wall-painting, a bronze engraving, a marble carving. It was round, oval, rectangular. It was oriented to the east, the north, the south. It was an itinerary map, or a globe.[24] His questions make it abundantly clear that, whether there was a map or not, we have very little concrete idea about its appearance.

Since the Roman Empire did not disappear all at once, but dwindled and declined unevenly from place to place, even then continuing its existence for another millennium in Constantinople, it is likely that, whatever world maps the Romans made, some must have survived to influence the mapmakers of the Middle Ages. Certain common features of medieval maps can be traced back to very ancient times, such as the division of the *ecumene* into three continents with their traditional boundaries, and many geographic features, such as the triangular shape of Sicily. Whether these traditions were passed on by descriptive text or in pictorial form is unknown. In the history of cartography the status of the Roman map is, at present, as a missing link.

MAPS AS ILLUSTRATIONS

Why did an author or a scribe choose to include a map in his book? One wonders, as the maps are often not found in the texts which seem to call for them. Geographical texts, for example, are seldom accompanied by maps in the Middle Ages. Some scholars have suggested that this is because, to the medieval mind, the text was superior to the picture: if you had a verbal description of the world, a map was superfluous.[25] Others have noted that some descriptive geographical works seem designed to explain a large detailed map, which we now no longer possess, perhaps one of those tantalizing missing *rotuli* or wall maps. In other words, an in-book map would have been too small to serve the author's purpose. As an example, we still have Gervase of Tilbury's description which may have been designed to accompany the Ebstorf map.[26] The recently discovered Evesham map in the College of Arms in London was clearly made for display. Was there at one time an explanatory text which went with it?[27] Lecturing in front of a map was apparently common, as it is today. We have records of such lectures from Eumenes of Autun in 298 to Hugh of St Victor in 1130 to St Bernardino of Siena in 1427 – all involving maps which are now lost.[28] This suggests that the maps which survive in books are condensed in format and may represent other uses and ideas than the purely geographical.

Maps in codices range from scientific line drawings to sumptuous works of illumination. The works they accompany are relatively few, for a dozen authors make up the corpus of ninety per cent of our medieval maps in books: Isidore, Beatus, Sallust, Lucan, Bede, Macrobius, Virgil (*Georgics*), Gautier de Metz, Ranulf Higden, William of Conches, Lambert of St Omer account for most of the maps which appear in books with known authors. They are a diverse group, including three Romans of the late republic/early Empire, a Roman of the fourth century, and medieval writers ranging from Isidore in the early seventh century to Higden in the fourteenth. They are encyclopedists (Isidore, Gautier, Macrobius, Lambert), historians (Sallust, Lucan, Higden), a philosopher (William), a poet (Virgil), and a theologian (Beatus). They are pagans (Virgil, Sallust, Lucan) and Christians. Bede crosses several of these categories, being a historian, a theologian, and a scientist. The maps which accompany his *De natura rerum*, a scientific encyclopedia, or those appearing in manuscripts of his works on time, were probably not made by him, and no maps appear in his works of history and theology.

While maps are not present in every copy of the works mentioned above, and some are copied with no illustration at all, they do accompany a significant number, dating from a very early period. In some cases (Beatus, Macrobius, Higden, Lambert, Gautier, William) we have reason to believe the maps belong to the original edition. In others the maps appear about the time of the oldest manuscript we possess, but we do not know who put them there, or if they were copied from manuscripts still older (Sallust, for instance). Certain key phrases seem to cue up these illustrations, such as 'The earth is divided into three continents' (Sallust, Lucan) or 'There are five circles which make up the world' (Virgil, Bede). But other works which have these phrases do not have maps.

As for the works with maps which do not have known authors, those by 'Anon.', many are scientific compilations similar to the encyclopedias above, and others are calendar manuscripts, devoted at least in part to tables and texts which help determine the date of future Easters. These need to be studied further, as many contain a number of works and are difficult to classify. Sometimes the map is linked to a brief text, such as the poem on the twelve winds, which is part of a compilation on natural phenomena. Sometimes it is one in a series of diagrams illustrating astronomical principles. Sometimes the map appears to be a wanderer, detached from its original site and given a home in the nearest available manuscript. But such a conclusion should be reached only as a last (and temporary) resort. Historians are too quick to attribute things we do not understand to scribal error or random behaviour. Just because medieval reasons were different from our own does not mean their decisions were not rationally based, and a closer look at the context of each manuscript map will help us to move forward in understanding medieval ideas about maps. An example is the world map in the Vatican Library, MS reg. lat. 123, which was made at the monastery of Ripoll in the eleventh century as a separate bifolium and bound in a volume of works on cosmology and the *computus*. It is by no means a wanderer but part of the overall plan of the volume (see below, ch. 5). By asking questions about the presence of the map in a volume, we hope to come closer to understanding what maps were used for in the Middle Ages.

GEOGRAPHICAL INACCURACY

The concern with geographical blunders that so occupied the cartographic historians of the last generation was based on the assumption that the purpose of medieval maps was similar to ours – to represent the world by a physically accurate model, which would enable one to find one's way about. Perhaps this was true for some medieval maps, but these would have been regional or local maps and almost none have survived, if indeed many were made. In a society much less literate than our own, travelling was done with the assistance of human guides, and nautical pilots learned their trade through apprenticeship, just as Mark Twain was to do on the Mississippi River many centuries later. We do have a number of *periploi*, or textual descriptions of the coasts, which were made for sea travel, but no maps, until the very end of the thirteenth century, when they suddenly appear. These are the sea-charts or portolan maps. Looking at them in the library after a day of poring over earlier maps, it is as though one's glasses had suddenly come into focus. The Mediterranean and the Black Sea coasts leap into their proper and distinctive shapes, caught by the slender spiders' webs of the rhumb lines radiating out from the compass roses. Over a thousand place names appear, lining the coasts, while the interiors remain almost blank. Where did they come from? How long had they been in existence? Do they represent a vital sailors' culture, independent of our scholarly map artists? Or, as more than one author has daringly asserted, are they the survival of a tradition dating back to the Greeks or even the ancient Phoenicians?[29] Once they appear, it does not take long for the information on these charts to be integrated into the *mappaemundi* tradition: witness the Catalan Atlas of 1375, as highly decorated and pictorial as any in the Middle Ages, but encompassing a true portolan chart of the inner seas. (See Plate I.)[30]

Yet other types of maps continued to be made. Even in the first hundred years of printing one can find medieval-style maps little changed from the twelfth or even the tenth centuries. For example, an early printed Isidore is illustrated by a simple T–O, and another series, the popular Rudimentum Novitiorum, has what is really only a T–O list map, decorated by hill-shaped abstractions.[31] Since we can assume that the printers had access to maps of greater geographical sophistication, we can only infer that these maps had some other purpose. We can also assume that they did not look ridiculous to fifteenth-century readers and buyers of books.

While the Middle Ages produced pilgrims and travellers of truly heroic dimensions – Ibn Battuta and the Polo family come to mind – there was a group for whom travel was strictly limited. These were the cloistered religious, monks and nuns, who dreamed of pilgrimage, but remained at home. This *'Peregrinatio in stabilitate'* lent itself to a kind of geography of the soul, in which spiritual journeys led one to wonderful destinations. Seeking out relics and holy places, monastic dwellers consulted the maps in their libraries. Turning from St Jerome's list of locations in the Bible, to Adamnan's account of Arculf's actual journey to Jerusalem, to Beatus's 'Book of Fire', which showed the Apostles' journeys, poised between Creation and the Last Judgement, the would-be travellers could launch themselves in spirit at least, leaving the body behind.[32] When Burchard of Mount Sion described the frisson of holy terror he felt when beholding the place of the Crucifixion, he had without a doubt numerous stay-at-home readers who trembled along with him.[33]

PHILOSOPHICAL AND RELIGIOUS MAPS

Harley and Woodward proposed a new and more inclusive idea of a map in their study. The old definition had maintained that a map was a representation of the earth's surface or any part of it. According to the editors of the *History of*

Oriens

Sem accepit trā tēpē mɑ̃

asia

Iafeth trā frigi dam.
Europa
Septētrio

Kam trū calī dam.
Libia
Meridies

Deadīc

1.6. T–O map in a table of the ancestors of Christ. It appears next to Noah, showing the division of the earth among his sons after the Flood. Beatus, Commentary on the Apocalypse, prefatory pages. Rylands MS 8, fol. 8ᵛ, twelfth century, Spanish. Diameter, 7 cm.
Courtesy of the John Rylands University Library, Manchester.

Cartography: 'Maps are graphic representations that facilitate a spatial understanding of things, concepts, conditions, processes or events in the human world', including celestial and imagined cosmographies.[34] Such a broadened definition makes room for those medieval maps whose function was to organize physical space according to philosophical or religious principles. What was the meaning of physical space? How could it be described? The Christian concept of the world as a temporal phenomenon, derived from the simultaneous creation of time and space as described in Genesis, inspired a mapping which would show both dimensions. The division of the continents among the three sons of Noah is an example. The details of this legacy are far from clear in the Book of Genesis, chapters 9 and 10, and medieval mapmakers clearly superimposed their own tripartite formula on the existing three-continent schema. Three-part organization appealed to both the medieval sense of space/time relationships and the passion for classification. Tripartite divisions, while not as rich in associations as quadripartite ones,[35] bore a satisfying echo of the Trinity, and occasionally we meet with a trefoil world map instead of the more common T within the O. The idea that all the races of the world in their apparent diversity descended from Noah, the single just man and founder of the renewed human race, was also attractive. Little diagrams of the tripartite world sometimes appear in the genealogical charts, next to Noah and his wife, thus linking space and time, the division of the earth, and the descent of the human race.[36]

Another religious idea which was represented on maps was the presence of the earthly paradise in the east, at the top of the world, with the four rivers descending to water the lands. Just like the rivers, humanity had migrated west (down) from that point to populate the earth. The fact that the four original rivers had to perform considerable gyrations to reappear as the Ganges, the Nile, the Tigris, and the Euphrates was not a problem for the inventive map artist. Since it was believed that man would never re-enter the earthly paradise, this map was plainly not designed for travel, but for contemplation. How far – alas! – we have come, both in terms of time and space![37]

Maps were also meant to entertain. As one who has spent many happy hours poring over every picture and every inscription in the wonderful Hereford Cathedral map, it seems self-evident that its purpose was amusement as well as instruction. What wonders the earth contains! What enormous distances there are out there! Although the similarly constructed Ebstorf map claims that it will assist travellers, one certainly hopes that they remembered to ask directions from local inhabitants as they went from town to town. *The National Geographic Magazine* continues to publish travellers' maps in this delightful mode. Though conforming to our standards of the shape of the physical world, they are covered with pictures and snippets of text, detailing the sights that are to be found for the pleasure of armchair dreamers.

An ornament of some medieval maps which has excited much attention is a standard array of humanoid monstrosities, inherited as a group from the writings of antiquity and retailed in an illustrated collection entitled 'Marvels of the East'. Headless humans with eyes in their chests, Amazons, people who lived on the scent of apples, creatures with one leg, floor-length ears or dog-heads were a part of the variety of God's creation. Pliny, who was the source of many of these descriptions,[38] had located them in specific places: northern Scythia (one-eyed people), the Himalayas (people with their feet on backwards), India (dog heads and one-legged folk), but on the larger medieval maps of the thirteenth century most of them were neatly arranged on the southern edge of Africa, a suitably remote place. Monster-sightings or at least rumours of such continued to liven up travellers' tales for some centuries yet, right up to the Loch Ness monster and the Abominable Snowman. On the maps these served to fill up embarrassing empty spaces in unknown regions, a custom which went back to Roman times and forward to the sixteenth century, when drawings of ships and sea monsters appeared on the oceans of world maps.[39] A higher purpose of the monsters, however, was to illustrate the many wonderful possibilities of God's creation. As the author of the Book of Job had marvelled at the great size and power of the Leviathan – 'Behold, Leviathan, which I made as I did you' –[40] the medieval map-maker showed that God, unfettered by human limitations, could truly make any amazing thing He chose. (See Plate II.)[41]

A WORLD MAP SURVEYED

Let us conclude this chapter by conducting a tour of a medieval map, the so-called Anglo-Saxon map, made in England around 1050 (fig. 1.5.). First, we need to know that the map is oriented with east at the top, as the term implies. This is true of most European maps until the sixteenth century. Only the three continents of the known world are shown. Although people were well aware that the *ecumene*, or inhabited world, covered only about one-quarter of the globe – and some maps were drawn accordingly – this map limits itself to Asia, Europe, and Africa. The immense surrounding ocean is reduced to a narrow border. The Mediterranean/ Black Sea complex occupies the centre, with Europe to the left and Africa to the right. Cartographic conventions include drawings of fortresses or castles to represent towns, while borders between provinces and countries are straight lines. Mountains are green and lumpy. Rivers meander, usually from their mountainous sources to the sea.

Red is used for the Red Sea and the Persian Gulf, but here, too, for the various configurations of the river Nile. This troublesome river is shown several times: once, flowing from a source near the Red Sea into the delta and on to the Mediterranean at Alexandria. The other Nile rises in the African desert, flows west, and disappears in the sands, only to reappear for a short run. The course of the Nile was to remain a puzzle until late in the nineteenth century. The Red Sea is severed to show the important moment of time when its waters were parted to allow the Hebrews to pass through, escaping from the Pharoah's army.

Unlike some larger medieval maps which are covered with paragraphs of text, the Anglo-Saxon map, relatively small and bound in a book, limits itself mostly to place-names. Only around the interesting edges of the map, in areas largely inaccessible to the English of the eleventh century, are there more extended notes. In Africa we read that there is a mountain which is perpetually burning and that, while the country is fertile, it is full of beasts and serpents. In the far north-east is a drawing of a lion, an exotic animal. Additional notes in the north indicate the presence of the Biblical monsters Gog and Magog, as well as classical griffins. At the top or east is the island of Taprobane (Sri Lanka) and on the nearby coast a mountain of gold. These wonderful places and people were not invented by the Middle Ages, but inherited by them from the Bible or from highly respectable Greek and Roman writers, such as Herodotus and Pliny the Elder.

Closer to home the British Isles are easily recognizable to a modern contemplater of maps, with the Isle of Man between Great Britain and Ireland (Hibernia) and the Orkneys scattered to the north. Is its form a reflection of a centuries-old Roman survey, or a lucky guess on the part of the artist?

Once one is oriented and the various conventions are understood, one can begin to read the map. What were the mapmaker's chief concerns in presenting the world to his readers? How did the readers of the map interpret this picture and what use did they make of it? These are some of the questions to be considered in the pages that follow.

Illustrated Histories

THE CLASSICAL TRADITION

Maps in histories serve to establish the location of actions and the routes of armies, and to show the passage of time as events worked their changes on the countryside. The latter is most easily done by a sequence of maps, but if there is enough text on the map, or text accompanying it, the sequence of happenings can be made clear. The historical content of medieval maps has long been noticed by perceptive observers.[1] In fact, the great Hereford Cathedral map describes itself as an *estorie*, whose modern descendant is the word 'history,' and its lengthy inscriptions, which blanket its 2.23 square metres, tell a story indeed. Maps nowadays, except for historical atlases and tourist maps, tend to be resolutely spatial, but there was a time when they were conceived of quite differently.

Sallust

Two historical works from classical antiquity were copied and recopied throughout the Middle Ages, frequently accompanied by maps. The first was by the Roman historian Sallust (86–34 BC), who lived during the chaotic first century, in the extended death trauma of the Republic. A partisan of Caesar, he accompanied his hero to Africa, where the forces of Pompey were finally defeated in 47 BC at the battle of Thapsus, on the Tunisian coast. Caesar appointed him governor of Numidia. There he embezzled and extorted to such effect that he was able to retire in spectacular luxury to Rome, where he took to writing history. His big book, *The Histories*, covered his own time, and survives only in fragments, but his two shorter works were much cherished in the Middle Ages and many copies still exist, frequently appearing bound together. The first, *Bellum Catilinae*, dealt with the failed conspiracy of Catiline in 63 BC. The other, *Bellum Jugurthinum*, described the Jugurthine War of 118–105 BC, an event occurring before Sallust's time, but located in his former province of Numidia and glorifying Marius, the uncle of his patron Julius Caesar. Jugurtha, able and ambitious,[2] conducted a rebellion against Rome, which was ultimately suppressed, but only with great difficulty. Sallust, writing in 40 BC, used the occasion to

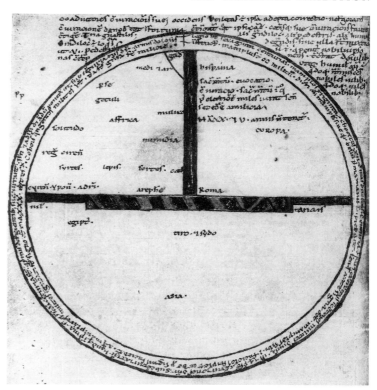

2.1. Sallust map. Oriented with west at the top, this map has a great deal of detail in Africa, as it was designed to illustrate Sallust's history of Jugurtha's revolt against Rome. In this manuscript, as is common, the *Jugurthine War* is bound with Sallust's account of the conspiracy of Catiline. What is less common is that the map appears in the Catiline section rather than in the Jugurtha text. A teacher's notes on the details of Roman military organization, taken from Cincius, *On Military Science*, appear on the rim of the map. Bodleian MS Rawl.G.44, fol. 17ᵛ, eleventh century, Flemish (St Pierre, Ghent). Diameter 110 mm.

Courtesy of the Bodleian Library, Oxford.

ruminate on the corruption of human nature and the venality of the Roman Senate. Peace and material prosperity, he thought, led only to corruption and civil strife.

This moralizing on history appealed greatly to the Middle Ages, and Sallust's theme found all-too-frequent confirmation in current events. Disgruntled ecclesiastics particularly enjoyed Jugurtha's contemptuously uttered line about Rome: the city where everything is for sale. The book was also used to teach Latin grammar and rhetoric, and some copies have come down to us scribbled over with the teacher's notes.[3] Sallust's style was so much admired that some of his speeches can be found in medieval histories, put in the mouths of latter-day kings and generals.[4]

After the dramatic opening events of his story, he pauses at the beginning of chapter 17 to reflect on the setting. 'My subject seems to call,' he says, 'for a brief account of the geography of Africa and some description of the nations there with which the people of Rome has had wars and alliances.'[5] He begins by discussing the tripartite division of the earth into continents, mentioning that some authors (he might have had Strabo and Varro in mind) thought of Africa as part of Europe, since Asia is so much larger than the other two

entities. Sallust does not pronounce a decision in this controversy, but goes on to describe the original inhabitants of
Africa and the immigration of the remnants of Hercules' army
there after their commander's death in Spain. These people,
originally Medes, Persians, and Armenians, were transmuted
into Mauritanians, or Moors, and Numidians or nomads. The
Phoenicians came next, but Sallust excuses himself for lack of
space to deal adequately with the history of great Carthage.
Then he goes on to mention some of the cities and other
features of the land before returning to his narrative in
chapter 20.

It is at the beginning of this digression in chapter 17 that
the world map most frequently appears. Birger Munk Olsen
lists 106 copies of the *Jugurthine War* in his catalogue of manuscripts surviving from the ninth to the twelfth centuries, and
over half of these contain a world map, usually as the only
illustration.[6] In half of these, the map is found in the text at
the relevant point. Others appear on the flyleaf at the end or
the beginning, in the margin, or even in one case in mid-
Catiline. Some are glosses, added later by the reader perhaps,
if not by the scribe. It is clear that, in the reader's mind as well
as the copyist's, Sallust was supposed to have a map.

Sallust maps are circular, divided into the three continents
of the known world in the form later called T–O, with Asia
the size of Europe and Africa added together. They are distinctive in that they call the southern continent Africa, which was
a Roman province, part of modern Tunisia, rather than Libya,
the more commonly used name in antiquity. The place-names
are taken from the accompanying text where twenty-one
places and eight peoples are named, nearly all in Africa. This
fidelity to the text, and the frequency of the map, would lead
us to think that it might have been part of the original work.
The oldest manuscript we have dates from the ninth century,
while the oldest manuscript with a map is from the tenth century.[7] In many of the maps, the drawing of the continents follows Sallust's suggestion that Egypt is part of Asia and that
the border between Africa and Asia is Catabathmon, 275
miles west of Alexandria (modern Salum), rather than the
Nile. Others have the more conventional medieval boundaries
between the continents: the Mediterranean, the Nile and the
Don (or Tanais) Rivers, the last two not mentioned by our
classical historian in his text. Other additions by creative mapmakers include Jerusalem (Asia is pretty bare otherwise), Tyre,
Sidon, Troy, and Rome. These additions appear mostly in
later manuscripts. Sallust maps may be simple T–Os with
nothing on them but the names of the continents,[8] or may be
more elaborate with as many as fifty names. Generally they
are oriented with east at the top, but there are exceptions.[9] A

few are highly decorated with drawings of towers and geographical features, but most are quite sober – just the names
and simple indications of mountain, river or boundary. In a
twelfth-century manuscript in the Vatican Library, which
includes also several saints' lives, the scribe felt impelled to
'Christianize' the map by adding Bethlehem, Jericho, and the
preaching sites of four Apostles.[10]

A tribute to the unique character of Sallust maps is their
identification as such in other texts. One which has not travelled far can be found in a volume containing Sallust's two
works, as well as items by Seneca and Cicero. The map
appears near the beginning surrounded by a text dear to
medieval hearts, equating the four parts of the earth to the
four gospels, Noah's ark to the Church, and pursuing a chain
of analogies involving angels, teachers, roosters, and gold
rings.[11] Sallust maps in manuscripts without Sallust include
several computus manuscripts (of which more anon),
Macrobius' *Commentary on the Dream of Scipio*, and a copy
of Juvenal's *Satires*.[12] None of these volumes contains texts by
Sallust, but they are identified as Sallust maps because of their
characteristic form and nomenclature.

Sallust taught 'the historian to study geography', wrote
Beryl Smalley.[13] This was not only physical but also human
geography, including the migration of peoples and how they
were shaped by their surroundings. By his example, the idea of
the utility of maps in history books was passed on to subsequent generations of historians. Like other history maps, it
shows something of the passage of time. Hercules's death in
Spain, which occurred in the legendary past, is usually
marked, frequently the only note cited in Europe. Dido's
departure from Tyre for Carthage, driven by her evil brother,
merits a note in Asia. Sallust does not mention this event, but
of course it would have been familiar to the schoolmaster
expounding on Africa with the aid of his book.[14] The Medes,
Persians, and Armenians, who made up Hercules's army,
appear on the map in north-west Africa, along with the people
they eventually became in Africa. Sometimes they are shown
also in Spain with Hercules and in Asia where they originated.
One version even shows the line of their travels.[15] The text
makes the sequence of these events clear, but on the map they
have a kind of simultaneity which we will encounter again in
the cartographic productions of the Middle Ages.

Lucan's Pharsalia

The struggle between Pompey and Caesar was the theme of
Pharsalia, an epic poem composed by Marcus Annaeus
Lucanus (39–65 AD). Lucan, the nephew of Seneca the

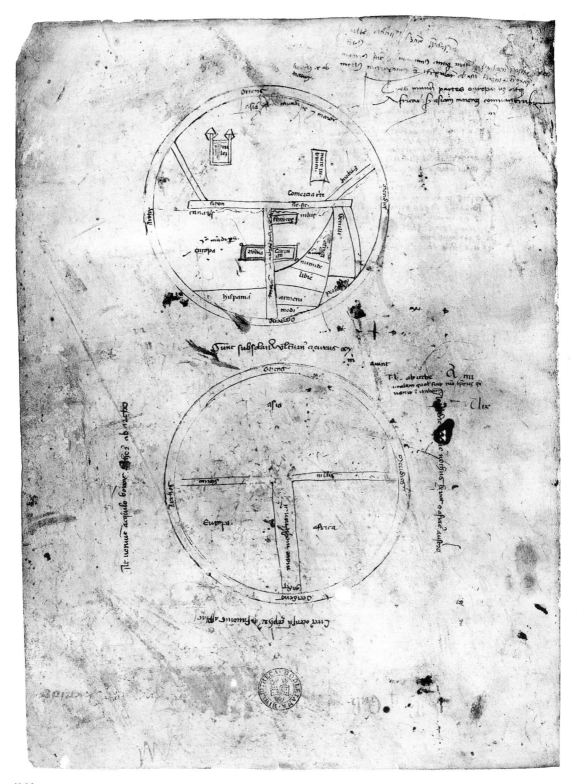

[22]

philosopher, was a precocious talent, first patronized by Nero, later envied and persecuted by that jealous emperor. He was eventually sentenced to death at the age of twenty-five for his participation in the conspiracy of Calpurnius Piso. A few lines in Book I, suggesting that the horrors of civil war were balanced by the joys of the 'everlasting dynasty' of the Caesars, is generally thought to be ironic and certainly did not save his life. The dramatic material of his work and his own tragic history made him a favourite in the Middle Ages, and Dante puts him with Homer, Horace, Ovid, and Virgil in the prestigious First Circle of the Inferno.[16]

Lucan manuscripts are heavily annotated from an early period, the most famous being a tenth-century manuscript now in Bern, Switzerland, Cod. 370. The Bern *scholia* or glosses, which accompany many subsequent manuscripts, include several maps.[17] These include a world map, a diagram of the harbour of Brundisium and another of Thessaly, where the decisive battle of Pharsalus was fought, as well as a sketch of the orbits of the planets and the constellations of the zodiac, all (usually) in appropriate locations in the text.

The world map is in Book IX, where the virtuous Cato finds himself soliloquizing in Africa and Lucan digresses from his narrative to speculate on the division of the continents. Like Sallust, he observes the great size of Asia and thinks that Africa and Europe ought to be considered as a single continent. The three boundaries he names – the river Don (Tanais), the Nile, and Gades or Cadiz – were to become standards of medieval geography. A special characteristic of Lucan is his emphasis on the winds, which are put forward not only as features in the story, where they cause sandstorms and the desert climate of Africa, but also as picturesque substitutes for the cardinal directions. In Lucan maps, which are usually simple T–Os with no more than ten geographical names, the winds are indicated around the rim.[18]

The other maps in Lucan's history are equally schematic. Brundisium (Book II) is a simple sketch of a harbour, sometimes ornamented with a lighthouse or a castle, doubtless to illustrate 'Brindisi's watchful tower'. Thessaly, a plain surrounded by mountains, is presented as a rosette with the mountains (Olympus, Pelion, Ossa, Pindus, Othrys) as petals (Book VI). The zodiac diagram appears in Book V, and the planetary orbits in Book X. Not all maps appear in every illustrated manuscript.

Lucan and Sallust maps sometimes change places. In a fourteenth-century manuscript of the *Pharsalia* in Oxford, a Lucan map and a Sallust map appear one above the other on the last page.[19] Munk Olsen in his catalogue describes a map in a Sallust manuscript which has an explanatory text from

2.2. Lucan map. This simple sketch is typical of Lucan maps in that it presents only the four cardinal directions, the three continents, and the features which divide them, including 'gades', or Cadiz. The text alongside describes the winds. This map is drawn on the last page of a heavily annotated manuscript below another, Sallust-type map. Bodleian MS lat.class.d.14, fol. 137ᵛ, fourteenth century. Diameter 85 mm.
Courtesy of the Bodleian Library, Oxford.

Lucan's work written over it.[20] Still another interesting document is a map described in the catalogue as '*un débris de charte carlovingienne*' bound upside down on the flyleaf of a ninth-century Lucan.[21] It has the three continents (though Africa rather than Libya), the winds and cardinal directions, as well as the Tanais, Nile, and Mediterranean.

Lucan's geography and astronomy became part of the medieval school curriculum and were the subject of numerous textual glosses as well as the maps. Isidore of Seville quoted him reverently and might have used him as a source of his map. Although the maps accompanying his work were simple, his text emphasized the physical setting of events and reinforced the importance of geography in history, which was to influence future historians.

Virgil

Aside from Sallust and Lucan, other classical histories which circulated in the Middle Ages generally did not have maps. An exception is Virgil. Although we think of him as a poet, this was a powerful occupation in both ancient and medieval times, when he was thought of as one of the truest of historians. The *Aeneid* was quoted as an authority not only on historical events, but also on such subjects as comets, the characteristics of the planets and the winds, lightning, and pestilence.[22] But the most important geographic work of Virgil was Book I of the *Georgics*, where he describes the division of the heavens into five zones and the reflection of these zones on earth. The entire passage is quoted piecemeal in the course of Isidore's influential work on the nature of things, and subsequently retailed throughout the Middle Ages. Virgil writes:

Idcirco certis dimensum partibus orbem
per duodena regit mundi sol aureus astra.
quinque tenent caelum zonae: quarum una corusco
semper sole rubens et torrida semper ab igni;
quam circum extremae dextra laevaque trahuntur
caeruleae, glacie concretae atque imbribus atris;
has inter mediamque duae mortalibus aegris
munere concessae divom, et via secta per ambas,
obliquus qua se signorum verteret ordo.
mundus ut Scythiam Riphaeasque arduus arces
consurgit, premitur Libyae devexus in Austros.
hic vertex nobis semper sublimis; at illum
sub pedibus Styx atra videt Manesque profundi.
(I, ll. 231–43)

(To this end the golden Sun rules his circuit, portioned out in fixed divisions, through the world's twelve constellations. Five zones comprise the heavens; whereof one is ever glowing with the flashing sun, ever scorched by his flames. Round this, at the world's ends, two stretch darkling to right and left, set fast in ice and black storms. Between these and the middle zone, two by grace of the gods have been vouchsafed to feeble mortals; and a path is cut between the two, wherein the slanting array of the Signs may turn. As our globe rises steep to Scythia and the Riphaean crags, so it slopes downward to Libya's southland. One pole is ever high above us, while the other beneath our feet, is seen of black Styx and the shades infernal.)[23]

This text travelled through the Middle Ages, often accompanied by Servius's Commentary, which expounded further on such topics as the existence of the Antipodes and further characteristics of the zones. A simple sketch of the round universe divided into five sections and crossed by the band of the zodiac accompanies the text in a number of manuscripts.[24] In his commentary on Cicero's 'Dream of Scipio' from the *Republic*, the fourth-century writer Macrobius goes to great pains to explain what Virgil leaves unclear: the relationship between the heavenly and earthly zones. Two more diagrams clarify his discussion.[25] Macrobius's work contributed further to the authoritative status of Virgil as an authority on geography, and sometimes his text was used as a gloss for the poem. The Riphaean mountains, a fictional marker for farthest north, appear on countless medieval maps. (See Plate III)

The power of the poet is due, not so much to his elegant and concise description of the universe, which after all is not very clear, but rather to his ability to think of the universe in terms of its meaning to the human race. He describes the construction of the universe as centred on human activities, particularly farming, and the book is full of portents which alert the farmer to changes of weather and seasonal timetables for various kinds of work. Although he makes frequent reference to pagan gods, such as Ceres and Jupiter, it did not take much imagination to alter these caring and consistent deities to the Christian Father of All. Coupled with his authority based on antiquity and his supposed prophetic powers, these qualities made Virgil one of the foremost sources on the place of the earth and its relation to the celestial bodies. The little drawing that sometimes accompanies the *Georgics* became part of the medieval corpus of maps.

Despite the admiration for Sallust and Lucan, their works were not the model for medieval historians. Rather than composing monographs, drawing wide conclusions about the human condition from a relatively restricted event, Christian historians of the Middle Ages favoured a broader, universal vision: a history from the beginning of the world to the Last Judgement, all ordered according to the Divine Plan. The sequence of events was structured into six ages, which paralleled the six busy days of creation, or, alternatively, into the sequence of four empires, moving from east to west. In each case the human race found itself in the last age, going down in a welter of sin and corruption to the final denouement, which could not be far off. Livy, with his broader brush and central theme, would, if he had been more generally available in the Middle Ages, have served as a better model.

Eusebius, Jerome, Orosius, and Augustine were the fathers of this type of medieval history. Eusebius (*c.* 260–340), bishop of Caesarea and religious adviser to the emperor Constantine, wrote a history of the church, a life of Constantine, and the *Chronicon*, a set of chronological tables, which melded biblical and classical history into a single time-line. The *Onomasticon*, a list of place-names from the Bible, was translated and expanded by Jerome (*c.* 360–420), who possibly added a map.[26] Eusebius's maps and diagrams included a map of Jerusalem and a plan of the temple, but they do not survive. It has been speculated that the sixth-century Madaba mosaic map on a church floor in Jordan is based on his work.[27]

The Jerome maps

Two maps in a twelfth-century French manuscript in the British Library accompany Jerome's version of the *Onomasticon*, *De situ et nominibus locorum hebraicorum liber* (Book of the location and names of Hebrew places) or sometimes simply the *Liber locorum*.[28] The text is an alphabetical listing of place-names organized under the headings of books of the Bible. The maps are usually described as being of Palestine and Asia respectively, and Miller thought that the latter had been cut from a larger world map.[29] The nomenclature is abundant: Asia has 278 names or legends and Palestine 195, with 66 of these common to both.[30] The map of Asia is oriented with east at the top, showing the Indian Ocean. Asia Minor is in the centre with Greece at the bottom and the northern part of the eastern Mediterranean coast at the right. It is confusing for modern map readers, because the map-maker has made the Mediterranean form a gulf here, stretching towards the east, and the north/south coastline is running east/west. The other, or Palestine, map has Palestine in the centre with Egypt at the right, the four rivers of Paradise at the top (east), and Constantinople and the entrance to the Black Sea at the lower-left-hand corner. The maps are relatively unadorned: simple towers suffice for most towns, rows of humps for mountains, and river sources indicated by circles. The only illustrative flights are the large circle for Jerusalem, the oracular trees and the columns of Hercules and Alexander, both curiously located together in the far east. On the Asia map there is a drawing of Noah's ark.

The content of the two maps is heavily biblical, which is not true of other early medieval maps. Eusebius, a native of Palestine, and Jerome, a long-term resident, have taken on the task of explicating its topography for Christian readers living elsewhere. There is far from perfect correspondence between the catalogue of names in *Liber locorum* and the map – though better than one thinks at first, as many names turn up in the catalogue, not as main entries, but in the explanations of other names – but it is clear that both serve the same purpose. 'Ararat, Armenia' begins the catalogue under the heading for the Book of Genesis. 'Because the ark is said to have come to rest in the mountains of Ararat after the flood, and vestiges of it are said to remain there today.'[31] On the Palestine map a mountain complex is labelled, 'The mountain of Armenia where the ark came to rest.' The Asia map has a drawing labelled 'Noah's ark' and 'Armenian mountain'. The devout Bible reader could browse back and forth, from scriptural text, to the list of names, to the map itself.

The text generally has more information than the maps. For example, the four rivers of Paradise are fully described: 'The river Fison which our sources call Ganges flows out of Paradise and through the regions of India, after which it discharges into the sea. Scripture also says that it circulates all around the land of Havilah where it produces gold, carbuncles, and lapis of outstanding quality.'[32] The rivers of Paradise are shown on the Palestine map, but with mundane sources in the mountains, and the Nile is firmly located in Africa. Paradise is not shown on either map, although Jerome comments under the listing for Eden: 'Eden, the place of holy paradise in the east, which means joy and delights.' Under the river Euphrates, he says, 'a river of Mesopotamia, rising in the East. Sallust, a most reliable author, says that the Tigris as well as the Euphrates are shown to have their sources in Armenia. We must differ from him, knowing of paradise and its rivers.'[33] The map, however, follows Sallust.

Other biblical sites include Hur (Ur), the homeland of Abraham, and the desert, 'where our Lord fasted'. Such notes

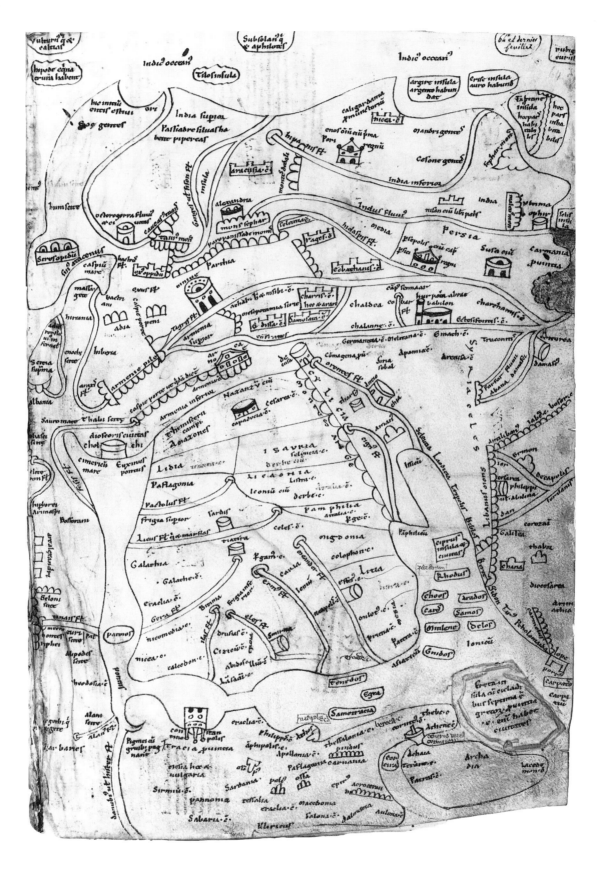

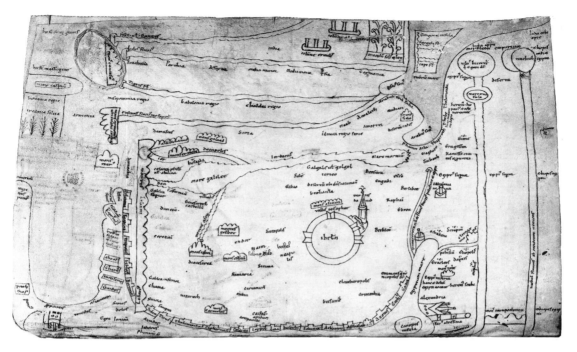

2.3. Maps from St Jerome, *Liber locorum*.
(a) Map of Asia, (on facing page) 356 × 230 mm. Subsolanus, or the east wind is at the top, but it is located in the Indian Ocean. The map does not hold to a consistent orientation – note that the coast of Palestine runs vertically (east-west?), with a gulf between Palestine and Asia Minor. Achaia (Greece) is at the lower right while Constantinople is the upside-down crown at the lower left. Jerome's catalogue of places is directed to Biblical explication rather than geography in itself. (b) Map of Palestine, (above) 356 × 230 mm. Oriented to the east, the map's most prominent feature is the large circle labelled 'Jerusalem', crowned by the tower of David. The coastal cities of Palestine are arranged along the lower edge, Constantinople is at the lower left, and the islands of the Aegean are above it to the right. Other features include the oracle trees consulted by Alexander in the far east. The rivers Ganges, Indus, Tigris, and Euphrates flow from Mount Caucasus and Armenia, rather than Paradise, while the Nile(s) appear as two parallel bodies to the south. BL Add. MS 10049, fols 64[r–v], twelfth century, French (Tournai).
Courtesy of the British Library Board.

took the reader back in time to important events in their spiritual history. Mount Gelboe, where Saul and Jonathan were slain, the desert hermitage of Sts Anthony and Paul in Egypt, Patmos where St John received the Revelation, and Cana (Chana) where Jesus performed his first miracle can all be found on the maps. There are also the various places visited by St Paul on his missions, from Tarsus, where he was born, to Iconium, where he was nearly lynched.

In addition to biblical names, the map includes the standard reference points for all classical maps (Tanais River, Catabathmon, Crete, the Black Sea) and a surprising number of mythological sites, such as the island of the Gorgons in the Red Sea. None of these is in the catalogue. The names on the map are consistent with a fourth-century date, which led Miller to surmise that the copyist was relatively faithful to an older original. The only exception is the indication of the Bulgarians settling in Moesia, which took place in the seventh century. Miller concluded the map is certainly Jerome's, made by him from Eusebius' work with the assistance of a secular map, but other scholars have noted that proof is lacking.[34] It is difficult to decide the matter, as the purpose of the map is to illustrate Jerome's (fourth-century) catalogue of places, but it is interesting to note that most of the additions (Tanais, Catabathmon, etc.) are consistent with an ancient source, whether it be Jerome or another. On the other hand, any map purporting to show Palestine in the twelfth century leads one to suspect the influence of the Crusades.

Eusebius and Jerome had seen the Christianization of the Roman Empire, following the conversion of Constantine. The Church and the Empire became linked in their minds, particularly for Eusebius who had been a close adviser of Constantine on church affairs. But with the sack of Rome by Alaric and the Goths in 410 AD a different prospect opened before the horrified eyes of the citizens of the Empire. Jerome, Augustine, and Orosius, working in the fourth and early fifth centuries, were conscious of the decline of the Empire and the end of classical civilization. It was a cause for mourning as well as rejoicing. Certainly Jerome was deeply ambivalent – he had a dream in which a celestial court ordered him to renounce pagan reading, and he tells us that he took up his beloved Cicero and Plautus only after tears and fasting. Augustine, if scornful of his classical education, profited fully from it, as is shown in his writings.[35]

What if the Empire were mortal? In *The City of God* Augustine tackled that important question, concluding that there were actually two cities: the city of man, currently represented by the Roman Empire, and the City of God, which was eternal. Though the city of man might fall, as previous empires had done, the Christian need not be concerned. His primary dependence should be on the City of God. But even Augustine, as bishop of Hippo, took over many of the functions of the Roman law courts. He might imagine that the world could come to an end, but until then it would probably be administered according to the limits and rules of the Empire.

Orosius

Paulus Orosius's *Seven Books of History Against the Pagans*
was commissioned by Augustine as a response to those who
blamed the sack of Rome on the Christians for undermining
traditional Roman values, a charge that was to be revisited by
Gibbon in the eighteenth century. *Seven Books*, written in
416–417, ranged through 5618 years of world history, showing that calamities a-plenty had dogged mankind long before
the advent of Christianity. 'You bade me discover from all the
available data of histories and annals,' wrote Orosius,
addressing Augustine,

> whatever instances past ages have afforded of the bur-
> dens of war, the ravages of disease, the horrors of
> famine, of terrible earthquakes, extraordinary floods,
> dreadful eruptions of fire, thunderbolts and hailstorms,
> and also instances of the cruel miseries caused by parri-
> cides and disgusting crimes.[36]

This engaging theme won Orosius instant popularity, and his
work survives in over two hundred manuscripts from the
Middle Ages.

Instead of inserting his geographical description into an
appropriate passage as a digression from the main theme,
Orosius began his work with a survey of world geography:

> ... viewing [events] as from a watchtower, first I shall
> describe the world itself which the human race inhabits,
> as it was divided by our ancestors into three parts and
> then established by regions and provinces, in order that
> when the locale of wars and the ravages of diseases are
> described, all interested may more easily obtain knowl-
> edge, not only of the events of their time, but also of
> their location.[37]

Here he set the stage for the events that were to follow. He
laid out a picture of the world primarily in terms of boundaries, making an outline map in words, with little topographi-
cal description or economic geography. For this reason, there
is not much correlation between his geographical chapter and
the places mentioned in the rest of the text as the sites of historical happenings. Yves Janvier, who has written perceptively
on Orosius's geography, believes he was looking at a map as
he wrote, based on the language he uses ('looking toward,
departing from,' etc.).[38] However, the text lacks any indication
that a map was provided for the reader, and there are very few
maps accompanying the many surviving Orosius manuscripts
– only four in Destombes's catalogue.[39] When a map, such as
the Hereford Cathedral map, indicates its dependence on
Orosius, it may be referring to his text rather than a (hypothetical) map.

The Albi map

The map found at the municipal library in Albi is the earliest and most detailed world map accompanying a text by Orosius.[40] The manuscript is a collection of extracts.[41] The map appears on fol. 57[v], followed immediately by a page listing the 25 seas and twelve winds of the world, then by the geographical chapter from Orosius, Book I. Several other brief geographical texts follow: Polemius Silvius's *Nomina omnium provinciarum*, the *Notitia Galliarum* which lists the provinces of Gaul and the cities therein, and *De nominibus Gallicis* which is an analysis of the meaning of French place-names.[42] Among these texts Orosius is placed nearest to the map which reflects his world view, though it should be noted that the map also shares a number of place-names with Polemius Sylvius (24 out of a total of 50).

The map is oriented with east at the top and shows the *ecumene* or inhabited world as a rectangle with rounded corners. Boundaries are indicated by straight lines, and not all provincial names in northern Europe are filled in. There are only two specifically Christian features, in contrast with the Jerome map above: a triangular Mount Sinai in the Arabian peninsula, and the configuration of the four rivers of Paradise in the east, though Paradise itself is not labelled. Neither of these is mentioned in Orosius's geographical chapter, nor are Judaea and Jerusalem, both on the map. The map follows Orosius in his description of the Caspian Sea flowing into the northern ocean, but this was a common bit of geographical misinformation in the Roman world. The mapmaker also tries in part to follow Orosius's confused description of the course of the Nile, having it flow between the Red Sea and the Mediterranean, but omitting its long detour to the West. The overall shape of the map, however, departs from Orosius in several significant respects: the tripartite division of the world he mentions is not emphasized in the drawing, the continents are not labelled, nor does the Tanais River, which he mentions several times as the boundary between Europe and Asia, appear. Spain is not a triangle, as Orosius states, and the islands of Hibernia and Taprobane (Ceylon) are omitted. The most notable errors of the map – the reversal of Sardinia and Corsica and the placing of the Cimmerian Sea north of Europe – cannot be laid to Orosius's charge.

Of the 50 names on the map, 41 come from Orosius's geographical chapter, which contains more than 300 names altogether. It could be that other Orosius maps were made that were too large to fit in the book and were stored separately in libraries on rolls.[43] Forty-nine of the 50 names on the map can be found in Isidore's *Etymologies*, Book XIV, as opposed to

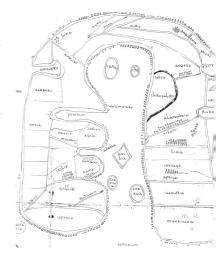

2.4. Albi map. This simple sketch map is one of the few maps to accompany Orosius's geographical text. On the facing page is a list of seas and winds, supplementing the names of cities and provinces which appear on the map itself. The Albi map is the oldest detailed world map that we have. MS 29, fol. 57[v], last half of eighth century, Spain or south-western France. Size 290 × 230 mm.
Courtesy of the Bibliothèque Municipale, Albi.

41 out of 50 from Orosius.

In at least one medieval version of Orosius's work the geographical chapter was edited to include local knowledge. This is the well-known Old English Orosius (ninth century), which has hallowed associations with King Alfred. The second chapter includes a revised description of northern Europe and reports by two seafarers, identified as Ohthere and Wulfstan. Janet Bately, editor of a modern edition of the work, notes that there are other geographical changes throughout the book. She discusses whether a *mappamundi* could have been used as a source for correcting Orosius's geography. 'Nowhere,' she concludes, 'is cartographical explanation the only one possible.' She also speculates on whether the Latin manuscript, from which the translation into English was made, could have contained a map, but notes 'Mappae mundi are surprisingly rare in extant MSS of Orosius. . . .'[44]

Since David Woodward's influential classification of early medieval maps into 'Orosian' and 'Isidorean', one may ask what an Orosian map is, since few co-exist with the text and those that do are not all that congruent with it.[45] Woodward lists six maps as Orosian, only one of which (the Albi map) accompanies an actual excerpt from the history. The others are the Hereford map, the Anglo-Saxon or Cotton map, the two Matthew Paris world maps, and that of Henry of Mainz. About these, he says: 'They usually emphasize the Mediterranean basin, and their coastlines are almost always generalized in undulating style.' While these features are common to the maps listed, there does not seem to be anything particularly Orosian about them. Since Orosius was so widely available in the Middle Ages, and so much copied, particularly by Isidore, almost any map after the fifth century could be Orosian.

John Williams has recently proposed an Orosian foundation for one branch of the Beatus world maps, based on their similarity to the Albi map in shape and content. His thesis downplays the significance of the 'fourth part of the world' shown on Beatus maps. He sees this as a mere addition to the Orosian model, along with the preaching sites of the apostles. Beatus maps as a group are quite schematic in form and thus do not fit at all into Woodward's group with their undulating coastlines. These hypotheses are thus incompatible but, as Williams observes, his thesis 'still implies the same mixture of Late Antique traditions, and essentially the same formula for capturing the earth's contours', whether the influential (and missing) map was Orosian or Isidorian.[46]

One of the most interesting features of Orosius's text is its archaism. Born in Spain in the late fourth century, he travelled to Africa, then through the desert to Alexandria and on to

Palestine, eventually returning to Africa via Minorca. Some of his writing may reflect his experience, such as his bemoaning the bad climate and extensive deserts of Africa and his description of the 'towering lighthouse' at Brigantia (Spain). In general, however, his geographical knowledge comes from books – he was particularly indebted to the *Chorographia* of Pomponius Mela of the first century AD – and the names of provinces predate the reforms of Diocletian two centuries earlier. In his native Spain the provincial names are even older, dating back to the days of the Republic. Orosius does not mention the division of the eastern and western Roman Empire, and he locates tribes of people in places long abandoned by them.[47] The Suevi, whom he was probably fleeing when he left Spain in 414, are still described as lingering in Germany. Of course, his intent was not to describe contemporary politics. Rather he meant his description to serve for a history of the world, and so he sought timeless names for his geographical framework, if such could be found in the flux of human affairs. In the upheaval of geographical names in our own time (Sri Lanka, Zaire, Cumbria, for example) we can understand his problem. As for the peoples, should he indicate where they came from or where they were in his day?

The enormous influence of Orosius helped to stabilize medieval ideas of geography around the Roman Empire as though it still existed in reality. The sack of Rome in 410 was a humiliation which lasted less than a week. Even the dethronement of Romulus Augustulus in 476 brought an end neither to the eastern Roman Empire nor to Latin culture and Roman law in the west.[48] The Church, structured on the dioceses and provinces of the Empire, picked up much of Roman law which was administered through its courts. Several events, the crowning of Charlemagne in Rome in 800 (the 69th emperor since Augustus) and that of Otto I in 962 (the 77th), were hailed as restorations of the Empire in a Christianized form.[49] Did this mean that the two cities at last were one? In 1313 Dante was still dreaming of the Empire as the only rational organization of humankind, with the power of the Church limited to spiritual matters.[50] 'When the throne of Augustus is vacant,' lamented the poet, 'the whole world loses its way.'

Governed by the theory that there was a succession of four empires in world history, moving from east to west as did the heavenly bodies, historians could not get beyond Rome, except to arrive at the end of the world. Nebuchadnezzar's dream of the giant figure with a head of gold, chest and arms of silver, middle and thighs of bronze, legs of iron, and feet of iron, and clay, had been interpreted by Daniel as a vision of this progressive degeneration of empires (Daniel 2). He proclaimed Nebuchadnezzar's empire to be the 'head of gold' (which had a poor effect on the royal character) and subsequent historians mulled over the identity of the succeeding regimes. Usually the near Eastern kingdoms, grouped together under the heading of Babylon, were succeeded by the Medes and Persians, with the Greeks (that is, Philip and Alexander of Macedon) coming next, and Rome at the end. Next, said Daniel, would come a kingdom established by God which would never be destroyed. One possibility in the medieval view was that this kingdom could be the Holy Roman Empire, with the universality of Rome sanctified by God. However, the realities of imperial politics when conducted by sinful human beings made it difficult for even the most credulous monastic chronicler to believe this to be true, except when located in the philosophical future, as it was for Dante.

Virgil, despite his paganism, never lost his popularity in the Middle Ages and even acquired some surprising new qualities as prophet, magician and proto-Christian. In the *Aeneid*, he had envisaged Jupiter looking down at the lands and seas of the world and decreeing of the Romans:

> *His ego nec metas rerum nec tempora pono;*
> *Imperium sine fine dedi.* (I, 278–9)
> (To these I place no boundaries of space or time;
> I have given them empire without end.)

When the medieval mapmaker put his hand to the task of representing the world, all these ideas must have revolved in his head, in addition to the fact that he must have worked, at least in the early days, from classical models of cartography. So here appear Roman provinces as well as a surprising array of mythological and classical sites: Calypso's island, Troy (from which almost everybody in Europe claimed their ancestors), the tree of the sun and the moon visited by Alexander, Crete with its labyrinth. In the corner of the Hereford map we even see Augustus Caesar enthroned, issuing an order with an impressive seal, assigning the mapping of the world to three geographers. (See Plate IV.)[51] The implication is that this is the map we now see, when thirteen centuries have passed.

CHAPTER 3

The Nature of Things

What is the nature of things? The Christian world had inherited from antiquity a set of scientific doctrines and speculations that needed to be refined and simplified, as well as converted to Christianity. The Church committed itself early on to a democratic, instructional role. Ritual was only part of a religious service – there was also a sermon, and some early practitioners prided themselves on their use of simple rustic language.[1] So, the complexities of Aristotle, the doubts and cynicism of Lucretius, and the mysteries of Plato had to be transformed into a simple, direct system which could be understood by people who were not well educated. First there were the priests, who needed practical handbooks with explanatory material. Then there were the monks, who had committed themselves to the religious life and valued study, but were not all intellectuals. Then there were the people, the growing Christian throng, which included slaves and barbarians, as well as more carefully educated Romans. Augustine makes it clear that, in the fourth century at least, a sophisticated convert such as himself was rare.[2]

Some of the simplification required had already been done by the Romans themselves. For example, Pliny's chatty *Natural History* pops up in excerpts in numerous manuscripts, and in the work of his follower, Solinus, who took all the sensational bits and put them into his *Collection of Marvels*. In the late fourth century Macrobius, a Roman government official who may or may not have been a Christian, wrote an extensive commentary on the Dream of Scipio. This poetical passage occurs at the end of Cicero's *De Re Publica* and bears more than a little resemblance to Plato's story of Er in his *Republic*. In Cicero's story Scipio Africanus the Younger is borne aloft in a dream to meet his dead adoptive grandfather, the Roman hero Scipio Africanus the Elder. As he looks down on earth, he is encouraged to reflect on the puny quality of human ambition. Such a theme was appealing to the Middle Ages, and the manuscript was copied many times – in fact, for centuries this was all we possessed of Cicero's great work. However, Macrobius's commentary, seventeen times the length of the original work, digressed freely into number symbolism, morality, the immortality of the soul, and astronomical theory. In fact, this book became one of the great authorities on astronomy in the Middle Ages.

One of Macrobius's merits was a set of diagrams he provided. 'Since our eyes often open the way to the understanding of a problem,' he wrote, 'it would be well to draw a diagram.'[3] He describes in detail how the diagrams were to be drawn, and they faithfully accompanied his work through the ages. One of the most important for our purpose was his zonal map, which showed the globe divided into five zones, with the *ecumene* crowded into the northern temperate space. This map showed also the ocean currents which Macrobius believed flowed out of the torrid zone toward the poles, colliding with great force and rushing back toward the equator, thus causing the tides. Both the map and the theory found a home in many medieval manuscripts.

After simplification, the second need of medieval science was to Christianize the classical inheritance. The Bible, a book which concentrates mostly on human behaviour and God's distress over same, has little to say about cosmology. The exception is the opening chapter of Genesis, which makes it clear that the creation of the universe (including stars, planets, sun, and moon) was a one-time event, preceded by an appalling void, in which God alone existed. Thus, cyclical theories of regeneration were ruled out (and a puzzling line from Ecclesiastes needed to be explained). With this exception, most classical ideas and observations on the functioning of the universe were perfectly compatible with Christian ideas. The orbits of the planets, the cycles of the sun and moon, the occurrence of eclipses, the phenomena of tides, winds, and weather offered no challenge to religious doctrine and passed more or less intact into medieval science. The only thing needing to be supplied was meaning.

Isidore of Seville rose to both challenges in the early seventh century. He was ideally suited to do so. The youngest son of an Hispano-Roman family, Isidore was probably born in Cartagena about 560. When the city was attacked by the forces of the Byzantine emperor Justinian a few years later, the family was forced to flee and found sanctuary in Seville, where Leander, the oldest brother, became a bishop and a royal councillor. The parents having died, Leander took on responsibility for the education of his three younger siblings to such effect that two of them became bishops and the other an abbess. Isidore was to succeed his brother as bishop of Seville, some time before the year 600.

By the time the barbarians got to Spain, they had passed through numerous other lands of the Empire, looting as they went. Among the loot was a certain amount of civilization, including conversion to Christianity. In Spain they switched their allegiance from Arian to Catholic Christianity, and under the Visigothic monarchs Spain enjoyed an Indian summer of classical learning. A survey of the books available to Isidore reveals a considerable gap between the riches of his library and that of a reasonably well-equipped monastery some three centuries later.[4]

Isidore was not a professional scholar. He was a busy bishop, involved in politics, both secular and ecclesiastic. He did have, however, a keen appreciation of learning for its own sake and the mentality of a teacher. In *De natura rerum* he took on the task of explaining the way things worked to (we assume) an admiring public. Certainly the book was widely and rapidly disseminated, and within a century it was available in Italy, Germany, and the British Isles, from which it permeated the western Christian world, where it continued to reproduce itself in library copies for centuries.[5]

ISIDORE'S DE NATURA RERUM

After a flattering (but justified) opening address to his cultured king, Sisebut (reigned 612–21), Isidore says that he will begin with the calculation of days and months, so that one may know the limits of the year, the succession of the seasons, and also the nature of the elements, and finally the course of the sun and moon and the properties of the stars with their presages of winds and weather, without omitting the position of the earth and the alternation of the tides. The book opens with the twin subjects of time and the cosmos, followed by the four elements of creation in descending order: the realm of fire (stars and planets), ch. 13–27; air, ch. 28–39; water, ch. 40–4; and earth, ch. 45–8[6].

'All this we have noted briefly,' he writes, 'presenting it as ancient writers have done and, even better, adding whatever one finds written in the works of Catholic men. This knowledge of nature is not mere superstitious learning, but rather should be considered as sane and sober doctrine. For if scientific learning were completely alien to the truth, that wise king [Solomon] would not have said: "For it is he [God] who gave me unerring knowledge of what exists, to know the structure of the world and the activity of the elements; the beginning and end and middle of times, the alternations of the solstices and the changes of the seasons, the cycles of the year and the constellations of the stars."'[7]

Let us begin with the day, writes Isidore, as the first of all visible things. His first seven chapters deal with various measures of time from the day and its parts through the year and its seasons. Then he goes on to describe the universe as a whole, beginning with the heavens, the planets, the sun, the moon, and the stars, pausing briefly to deal with those perplexing waters above the earth. After discussing some of the problems – why don't they fall down or spin off when the universe rotates? – he exclaims indignantly, 'But these sages will eventually cease to babble insanely and realize with embarrassment that He who could create all from nothing, could easily stabilize these waters in the heavens by giving them the solidity of ice.'[8]

He proceeds to cover meteorology: thunder, lightning, rainbows, snow, hail, winds, weather forecasting, and pestilences, brought on by atmospheric disturbances, or changes of climate. Then he moves on to discuss the sea, its tides, its saltiness, the river Nile, earthquakes, and Mount Etna. His first edition apparently ended here, in the infernal rumblings of the volcano with its foretaste of hell, but he later added a final chapter (XLVIII) on the parts of the earth, that is, the three continents and their boundaries, the cardinal directions, the relative size of the continents, and finally an estimate of the earth's circumference: 180,000 stades, the smaller of the two estimates inherited from classical antiquity.[9] It is this final chapter in the (slightly) longer version which is followed by a map, usually a fairly schematic one.[10]

Throughout Isidore's book he takes time to comment on the larger doctrinal significance of natural phenomena. Some of these interpretations come from Ambrose, Augustine, and Gregory the Great,[11] but others seem to be his own. Light and dark, day and night, we can see as the contrast between knowledge and faith, on the one hand, as opposed to sin on the other. Night, he says, has two meanings in Scripture. One is a time of trial and persecution and the other is a blind heart. In his etymology of the word for night, he says it comes from 'nocendo', injuring, because it 'hurts the eyes'. After a straightforward account of the seasons, he turns to allegory. Winter is a time of tribulation, battered by storms and whirlwinds. Summer is the persecution of religion, when Christian doctrine is parched by the dryness of unbelief. As for spring, it is the renewal of the peace of the faith which is restored to the church after the trials of winter. When the earth is covered with flowers, the church is ornamented by the gathering of its saints.[12]

The sky, understood in a spiritual sense, is the Church which, in the night of our life here below, shines with the virtues of the saints like the brightness of the stars. However, he warns us of Isaiah's prophecy that the heavens will vanish like smoke and the earth wear out like a garment, thus stressing the ephemeral nature of even the grandest element of the physical universe.[13] The sun is a symbol of Christ, and the moon is the Church, which shines by reflected light, waxing and waning as it receives more or less of Christ's teachings.[14]

Some of his metaphors are more strained, as when he compares the tides to the waters of baptism (he has just compared the moon to the Church), or when he says that the seven phases of the moon represent the seven graces of the Holy Spirit. But overall the comparisons are apt and telling, imbuing the entire physical world with an aura of divine purpose.

The names of the stars, being those of pagan gods and heroes, presented a problem, and the Church made several attempts to Christianize them, but without success.[15] He explains that these, being common names, are used even in the Bible so that people may understand, [Job 9.9 and 38.31–2] but suggests that we might think of the seven stars of the Great Bear as the church shining with seven virtues: four cardinal virtues (prudence, temperance, fortitude, and justice), which are works, and three spiritual virtues (faith, hope, and charity), which are faith. Thunder, he says severely, is a reproach from God and the voices of saints reminding us of our sins. As for the position of the earth, we learn in the Book of Job (26.7) that God suspended it in the midst of nothing, but maybe the air is thick enough to support it, or maybe it floats on water. Anyway, Isidore reminds us, that what is hidden from our mortal nature must be left to the power of God.[16]

To assist him in his exposition of the nature of things, Isidore included diagrams. We have reason to believe that at least seven of them were included in the first edition, and an eighth (the map) added in the second edition.[17] The text introduces nearly every diagram with a phrase, such as this one, for the rota, or wheel, of the planets: '*Quorum orbium atque stellarum positionem subdita demonstrat figura.*' (The figure below shows the position of the orbits and the stars.) The only diagrams not specified in the text are the map, which comes at the end of the longer edition, and the wind diagram, which nevertheless appears in nearly every manuscript, accompanying ch. xxxvii, '*De nominibus ventorum.*' An additional diagram of the seven phases of the moon seems also to be called for in the text, but could be less obtrusively located in the margin and is missing from Fontaine's exemplar.[18] Many early manuscripts also include a sketch of the mechanism of solar and lunar eclipses as well. Manuscripts without figures retain the wording and often the empty space for the illustrations.[19] The book was so well known for its circular diagrams that throughout the Middle Ages it was referred to as the *Liber rotarum*, or *Book of Circles*.

The group of diagrams includes the following:

1. A twelve-section *rota* (wheel) of the Egyptian months. The Egyptians used a lunar calendar with twelve thirty-day

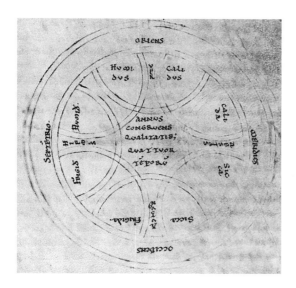

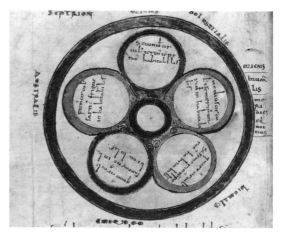

3.1. Annus communis or Annus mundus diagram, here Annus congruens (harmonious year). This simple diagram from ch. X of Isidore's *De natura rerum* illustrates his philosophy of the unity of time and space. The seasons (ver, estas, autumnus, hiems) are shown in relation to the cardinal directions (oriens, meridies, occidens, septentrio) and the physical qualities of humidity, heat, dryness and cold (humidus, calidus, siccus, frigidus). From a tenth- or early-eleventh-century manuscript, originating in south-western England. BL Cotton MS Vitellius A.XII, fol. 50ʳ.

Courtesy of the British Library Board.

3.2. Zones rota. Isidore's zone diagram is an abstraction rather than an attempt at simulating physical reality. After referring to Virgil's line, 'Heaven has five zones', Isidore says, 'Let us imagine them in the form of our right hand in such a way that the thumb is the arctic circle, cold and uninhabitable; the second finger is the zone of the summer solstice, temperate and habitable; the middle finger is the equator, torrid and uninhabitable; the fourth is the circle of the winter solstice, temperate and habitable; the little finger is the antarctic circle, cold and uninhabitable.' The celestial zones were projected on the earth with corresponding climates. Isidore's circular arrangement of the diagram has the effect of putting the two polar zones side by side. Around the edge are scattered other climatic terms: australis (south), solstitialis, oriens, brumalis (winter solstice), meridies (also south but on the opposite side of the diagram from australis), equinoctius, hiemalis (wintry), and occidens. This diagram comes from a ninth-century computus manuscript from the abbey of Fleury in France, which contains portions of Isidore's text along with his illustrations. BL MS Harl. 3017, fol. 90ᵛ.

Courtesy of the British Library Board.

months, and five intercalary days. Isidore's diagram shows when each month would have begun according to the Roman calendar; for example, the Egyptian July would begin on 7 Kalends July, or 25 June. The use of this arcane information is unclear. Probably Isidore wanted to show the source of his knowledge from the wise Egyptians, the fount of astronomical learning from early days through Ptolemy and the computists of the fourth century. The use of a circular diagram to represent cycles of time was to continue, with elaboration, throughout the Middle Ages.

2. *Annus* (year) diagram. This is a circle with a pattern of overlapping circles to show correspondences between the four seasons of the year, the cardinal directions, and the four qualities (hot, cold, wet, dry). For example, spring equates with the east and the qualities of heat and moisture. A more complex version of this diagram appears below as number 5. Here for the first time space (the directions) and time (the seasons) appear linked, with their circles literally superimposed.

3. Rota of zones. The purpose is to illustrate the five zones of the universe, as described by Virgil in the *Georgics* and quoted by Isidore, but the illustration is not very apt. Instead of representing the zones (two frigid, two temperate, and one torrid) as bands on the globe, Isidore shows each one as a circle, arranged like the petals of a flower. Thus the two frigid zones are not poles apart, but side by side. In most manuscripts there is an attempt to place the cardinal directions and/or the Greek names for the zones around the margin, making it even more confusing. Fontaine notes that he is omitting these notes because they make no sense.[20] It is this diagram which has caused several scholars to conclude that Isidore did not conceive of the earth as a globe, and thus could draw the 'circles' of the world only as circles on a flat disc. While the diagram is certainly odd, such a conclusion ignores Isidore's use of the world '*sphera*' in ch. XLVIII and his description of the earth as equidistant in all directions from the heavens – a phenomenon possible only for a sphere within a sphere.[21] In addition, he notes that the form of his diagram is based on the hand, with the thumb representing the northern frigid zone, and each of the fingers in turn representing the next zone. Any reader of medieval manuscripts will attest to the very wide use of the human body, particularly the hand, for all sorts of calculations.[22] This is an example of a diagram which acts as a memory device rather than being a graphic depiction of the phenomena which are its subject.[23]

4. Cube of elements. Here Isidore is discussing the four elements which make up the universe – earth, water, air, and fire – and their respective qualities – lightness, heaviness, bluntness, sharpness, mobility, immobility. The diagram attempts to show the shared qualities; for example, air and fire are both mobile and sharp, but fire is light, while air is heavy (according to the formula). Also on the figure is the note 'This figure is a solid according to the rule of geometry.' What this means is hard to say, but one idea is that Isidore is harking back to a Platonic theory, repeated by Boethius, that the four elements can be represented by four regular geometric solids: earth by a cube, fire by a pyramid, air by an octahedron, and water by a twenty-sided icosahedron. The cosmos as a whole was represented by the fifth regular solid, the twelve-faceted dodecahe-

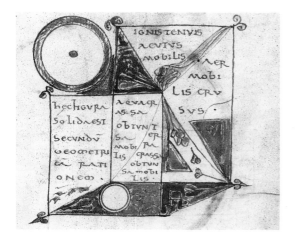

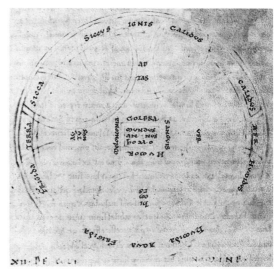

3.3. Cube of elements. This is another abstract diagram which reflects Isidore's thinking, as well as the rather arcane theory on which it is based. It shows the four elements of creation (fire, air, water, earth) with their qualities, unique or shared, in the form of a geometric figure. In this version fire is at the top and described as tenuis (slight or weightless), acutus (sharp), and mobilis. Air is below it, also 'mobilis', but 'crassus' (dense) as well. Water is dense, mobile, and obtusa (dull or dark) and shares a compartment with earth, which is dense, dull, and immobile. On the left Isidore tells us that 'This solid figure is according to the reasoning of the geometers.' This particular diagram is often glossed or altered in manuscripts in an attempt to make sense out of it. BL MS Harl. 3017, fol. 92^r.

Courtesy of the British Library Board.

3.4. Annus-Mundus-Homo. Isidore extends the rota shown in Fig.3.1 to include the humours of the human body and the four elements of creation which he has just discussed and presented in cubic form (Fig.3.3.). In the text he writes:

Siccus calidus ignis: aestas, cholera rubea.
Calidus humidus aer: ver sanguis.
Humida frigida aqua: hiemps, phlegma.
Frigida sicca terra: autumnus, melancholia.
(Dry hot fire: summer, red (or yellow, angry) bile.
Hot humid air: spring, blood (sanguine humour).
Wet cold water: winter, phlegm.
Cold dry earth: autumn, melancholy (black bile).)

Isidore, *De natura rerum*, ch. XI.3. This terminology is almost exactly repeated on the diagram. The correspondences, on which much of medieval medicine was based, can be traced at least as far back as Hippocrates in the fifth century BC. BL Cotton MS Vitellius A.XII, fol. 52^r.

Courtesy of the British Library Board.

dron.[24] Isidore seems to have created this diagram himself. It is the only one of which he says proudly, '*subiecta expressi pictura*' – 'I have represented by the picture below.'[25] Some manuscripts supplement this drawing with a clearer one, or replace it altogether.[26]

5. *Annus-Mundus-Homo* (The Year, the Universe, and the Human Being). To the simpler *annus* diagram above are added the four elements (air, fire, earth, and water) and the four corresponding humours of the human body (blood, yellow bile, black bile, and phlegm). These humours produce the four

basic temperaments: sanguine, choleric, melancholy, and phlegmatic. Above, in chapter IX, Isidore had noted that man is a '*minor mundus*' or world in miniature, and this figure shows the relationship. The human being experiences space in terms of the material body and time in terms of the annual cycle of the seasons, as well as in his own passage from birth to death. These are the coordinates of human existence. Here all three elements are drawn together in a diagram that was to be widely copied and elaborated. A common addition was the ages of man, which were linked to the seasons and the humours. Childhood, for example, was linked to spring and the sanguine humour, blood. Old age was identified with winter and the phlegmatic humour.

6. Planetary *rota*. We pass a number of pages (from ch. XI to ch. XXIII) with no pictures, until we arrive at a set of concentric circles illustrating the orbits of the planets, including the sun and moon, around the earth. Each ring has the name of the planet and sometimes its symbol and the number of years before it resumes its original place in the sky in relation both to the earth and to the stars.

7. Wind *rota*. In many manuscripts this diagram has a small T–O or world map as a centre, or the centre is labelled simply '*terra*'. Twelve sections or petals bearing the names of the twelve winds surround the centre. Sometimes it is elaborated by the Greek names, which are given by Isidore, and by the qualities of the winds. In one version the winds have speeches issuing from their mouths, cartoon-style. For example, Zephyrus or Favonius, the west wind, says, 'I adorn the earth with flowers.' Less amiable, Vulturnus or Calcias, blowing from the east northeast, says, 'I dry up everything.'[27]

8. World map. The world map appears at the bottom of the last page of the longer recension, usually a T–O in format. There is no reference to a drawing in the text, and, unlike the other diagrams, the legends on the map do not repeat information already given. In fact, the map serves as a last paragraph, with its information given in graphic form, discussing the peopling of the continents and the origins of their names. It reads, with some variation:

Asia. *Post confusionem linguarum et gentes quae dispersae fuerant per totum mundum, habitaverunt filii sem in asia de cuius posteritate descendunt gentes viginta septem et est dicta asia ab asia regina quae est tertia pars mundi. Regio orientalis.*

Europa. *Dicta ab europa filia agenoris regis libie uxore iovis ubi filii iaphet visi sunt terram tenere de cuius origine sunt gentes quindecim et habent civitates cxx. Regio Septentrionalis.*

Affrica. *Dicta ab affer, unum de posteris abrahae*

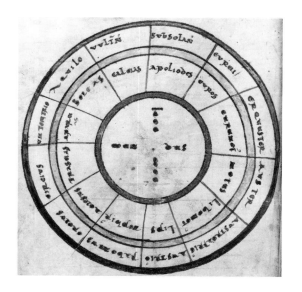

3.5. Wind rota. In ch. XXXVII of *De natura rerum* Isidore discusses the four primary winds and the eight subsidiary winds, which were not only natural phenomena but stood in for the cardinal directions. Here the Latin names for the winds are paired with the Greek names (example: subsolanus = apoliodes [Apeliotes], east). In the centre are the words mundus/kosmos, the Latin and Greek words for the universe. This space is, in some diagrams, occupied by a T–O map. BL MS Harl. 3017, fol. 128ᵛ.

Courtesy of the British Library Board.

3.6. World map from Isidore, *De natura rerum*. A diagram arranged in a simple T–O form appears at the end of the longer recension of this work. Unlike the other diagrams it is not described or introduced by the text, and the information it contains is in addition to, though on the same theme as, ch. XLVIII, 'De partibus terrae', which precedes it. The dispersion of the people of the world after the destruction of the Tower of Babel is here conflated with the division of the earth among the sons of Noah. Isidore cannot resist adding information on the derivation of each continent's name. The manuscript is from the second half of the ninth century, and originated in the Rhineland, reflecting the Anglo-German tradition. Vat. Bib. Apos. MS pal. lat. 834, fol. 90ᵛ.

Courtesy of the Vatican Library.

quem possiderunt filii cham de quo sunt egressae gentes xxx. Et habet civitates ccclx. Regio australis.[28]

(Asia. After the confusion of languages and the dispersal of people throughout the whole world, the sons of Shem lived in Asia and from his posterity descended twenty-seven peoples. And it is called Asia from Asia the queen, and is the third part of the world. Eastern region.

Europe. Named after Europa, daughter of King Agenor of Libya and bride of Jupiter. [Europe is] where the sons of Japhet were seen to hold land. From this ancestor came fifteen peoples and they have one hundred and twenty cities. Northern region.

Africa. Called by the name of Afer, one of the descendants of Abraham, which the sons of Ham possessed and from which came thirty peoples. It has three hundred and sixty cities. Southern region.)

This brief text gives identical information for each continent, including etymology, history, current population, and geographical position. It is a curious mix of classical and biblical information, and it suggests that the continents did not really exist in human consciousness or receive their names until after the multiplication of languages at the Tower of Babel, at which time the descendants of the sons of Noah scattered throughout the world. The same information can be found in the *Etymologies*, although in different words and spread over several locations.

With one exception (the cube of elements) the diagrams Isidore chose are circular, a model for the universe that was certainly of great antiquity.[29] The *rota* is used both for time and space separately and, with overlapping circles, for time and space together. In the T–O at the end of the work, one notes both temporal and spatial factors indicated upon it. Even in this simple sketch a pattern for medieval cartography is set – that it will deal not with space alone, but will incorporate temporal and even spiritual factors in its depiction of the world.

We do not know the source of Isidore's diagrams. Sources as diverse as Lucan, Chalcidius,[30] Aristotle, Plato, and Pliny have been suggested, but the lack of early manuscripts makes it hard to determine which came first. Such diagrams as the tripartite earth *rota* or the planetary orbits *rota* were probably quite ancient, dating back as far as ancient Egypt.[31] Certainly Isidore consulted Macrobius, but when it came time to draw his diagram of the five zones, he made up his own rather than copying Macrobius's more scientific drawing.

From this point forward, Isidore's diagrams will travel as a group, illustrating *De natura rerum*, of course, but also appearing in numerous other works and compilations of works designed to teach elementary science. Fanciful scribes might add their own embellishments, such as the talking winds. Indolent or ignorant scribes might confuse the data and reduce them to meaninglessness. But in general these simple graphic lessons retained their integrity as they were copied and recopied for hundreds of years, even appearing in early printed editions.[32]

TIME AND SPACE IN THE ETYMOLOGIES

While Isidore had tacked on his geographical chapter and diagram to *De natura rerum* almost as an afterthought, geographical information was to play a larger role in his big book, the *Etymologies* or *Origins*. The underlying principle of the work, he explained, was that the derivation of words was the key to knowledge. 'When you see where a name has come from,' he wrote, 'you understand its meaning more quickly. For everything is known more plainly by the study of etymology.'[33] The book was never finished, and after Isidore's death his friend and admirer, Braulius, divided it into chapters and rushed it into publication, medieval-style. Reynolds and Wilson call it 'at the same time the last product of the Roman encyclopedic tradition and the starting point for most medieval compilations. . . . This systematically arranged encyclopedia, packed with information and misinformation on every topic from angels to parts of a saddle, descends so often into false etymologizing and the uncritical parade of bric-à-brac that it cannot be read without a smile. But Isidore wins one's respect, and even affection, by his obvious appreciation of knowledge for its own sake.'[34] Even Ernest Bréhaut, whose opinion of Isidore is generally low, is forced to admit that without his work the Dark Ages would have been considerably darker.[35]

The material so tightly compressed in *De natura rerum* is greatly expanded and scattered throughout the twenty books of the *Etymologies*: astronomy in Book III, time in Book V, weather in Book XIII, and a detailed geography in Book XIV. He treats people and their languages in Book IX and cities in Book XV. Most manuscripts (and there are many) have very few illustrations: sketches of geometrical forms in Book III where geometry is explained, a diagram of relationships in which marriage was forbidden by the Church in Book IX, and a small world map in Book XIV. The relationships diagram shows six generations and appears in the form of a tree or a *rota*, or superimposed on the body of a human being.[36]

In the majority of manuscripts of the *Etymologies*, the map is a bare T–O, displaying the names of the continents only. (See fig 1.1 above.) Miller calls these *Kärtchen*, or maplets.[37] They appear at the beginning of the chapter 'De Asia' in Book XIV, sometimes accompanied by a small square divided into three by a triangle, giving the names of Noah's sons.[38] Some of these 'maps' are sketched in the margins, clearly added later. Others function like an illuminated initial, embedded in the text. It is interesting to note that there is no cross-over from the map found in *De natura rerum* with its text on the confusion of language and the dispersal of the human race.

If these simple sketches were all that was to be found, they could hardly establish an Isidorian map tradition. However, some manuscripts, of which the earliest is tenth-century, bear a slightly more elaborate drawing, which incorporates in a single illustration the sons of Noah and the borders between the continents, and introduces a distinctive elbow shape for the Meotides Paludes or Sea of Azov, where the river Don flows through marshes and sandy flats into the Black Sea.[39] (See fig 1.2 above.) Some of these drawings are further embellished. In two tenth-century Spanish manuscripts at the Royal Academy of History in Madrid appear identical maps. They show Paradise with its four rivers (fons Paradisi), the cardinal directions and about a dozen place-names, including Asturias, Spania, and Galicia in Spain. In addition there are notes on the number of provinces in each continent and the number of islands in the Mediterranean and the Ocean.[40] In the far north-west corner of Africa is a note that this is the '*terra de pedes latos*', land of the wide feet, which may refer to the Sciapods who use their single large foot to shade them from the unrelenting African sun.[41]

There is a handful of more detailed maps which appear with Isidore. One, on which much theorizing has been founded, is the world map in a late-eighth-century manuscript in the Vatican Library, lat. 6018. Since the manuscript has recently been examined and discovered not to be the *Etymologies*, that map must be re-evaluated (see below) and with it the entire mapping tradition known as Isidorian.

The skimpiness of the maps in the *Etymologies* is a striking contrast with Isidore's wordy description of world geography in Book XIV – 36 densely packed pages in Lindsay's edition. His descriptive phrases, even paragraphs, were used by later mapmakers, and ended up on maps, giving information about exotic animals, mineral deposits, and human populations. The eleventh-century Saint-Sever map in Beatus's *Commentary on the Apocalypse* is an example of the copious use of Isidorian inscriptions.[42]

In the text Isidore begins in Asia with the earthly Paradise and moves majestically from east to west, to Europe, Africa, the islands, peninsulas, mountains, and finally the world below. He speculates on the existence of a fourth continent in the southern hemisphere: '*Extra tres autem partes orbis quarta pars trans Oceanum interior est in meridie, quae solis ardore incognita nobis est; in cuius finibus Antipodes fabulose inhabitare produntur.*'[43] (In addition to these three parts of the world, across the interior Ocean to the south lies a fourth part, which is unknown to us due to the heat of the sun. In these regions, according to story, the Antipodes are said to dwell.) Along the way he gives the derivation of place-names, boundaries, rivers, mountains, and special features, such as the physical appearance or relative barbarity of the people, and the presence of spices or precious stones. He also includes some historical notes, most many centuries old: the desert condition of the area around the Pentapolis, which includes Sodom and Gomorrah, due to the sins of its people, the site of the battle of Marathon (490 BC) and the invasion of Hannibal (218–216 BC). There is more on Greece than on any other single country, and Isidore waxes rhapsodic over Attica, 'which is true Greece, where the city of Athens was, mother of the liberal arts and nurse of philosophy'.[44] He quotes Virgil and Homer as though they were contemporary authorities:

there are still tigers in Hyrcania and Asia Minor is a good place to raise horses.[45] The closest thing to current events appears in Book XV, which begins with a description of the cities of the world. In Spain Isidore notes the burial of Christian martyrs at Saragossa and tells us that Cartagena was overthrown by the Goths and reduced to desolation, an event of the fifth century.[46]

In harmony with his philosophy of knowledge, Isidore emphasizes place-names as a central fact of geography. Where possible he notes their derivation from history, mythology, or physical characteristics. He concludes that Libya must have been named before Europe, as Europa was the daughter of Agenor, a king of Libya. He also points out changes in place-names over time. Libya is now called Africa, but 'true Africa' is the area between Byzacium and Numidia, the old Roman province of that name. As for the name Africa, it could be derived from '*aprica* [sunny], because it is open to the sky or the sun, and there is no fear of cold weather'. But others say it is named for Afer, a descendant of Abraham, who led an army there.[47]

The Christian elements of his description are almost equally balanced by mythological information – Jason's voyage, the rape of Europa, the fall of Icarus. While he mentions the four rivers of Paradise, he describes them as merely watering the grove in Eden, not branching out through the whole world.[48] Jerusalem, he says, is the centre of its region (*umbilicus regionis totius*),[49] not of the world, and he makes no mention of the sacred events which occurred there. From the Old Testament, he mentions the place where Noah's ark came to rest on Mount Ararat, but he tells us also that, after the great flood of the classical tradition, the island of Delos was the first place to see the sunlight.[50]

It is probable that Isidore was looking at a map as he wrote,[51] though it would have been one of a number of sources, and not the most important one in his mind. There is no indication that he provided a map for his readers. That future historians, geographers, and mapmakers mined his work is certainly true, but what would a map look like that was based entirely or even mostly on Isidore's text? Again Miller experimented with this exercise in vol. VI of his work on medieval *mappae mundi*. Inevitably the narrative order of description of space translates with difficulty to a map. Arthur Robinson and Barbara Petchenik have observed that a map as a form of communication has little in common with language, which is especially unsuited to communicating about space, though rather better adapted to narrating events in time. The simultaneous presentation of information on a map is quite different from discursive or linear presentation in language.[52]

And, unless the map is very large, it cannot show the amount of information that a written text can. Isidore names hundreds of places in his text – far more than appear on any medieval graphic production.

Isidore's material on time is combined in Book V of the *Etymologies* with a treatise on law. Time and the law were already associated in the opening chapter of *De natura rerum*, where he had observed that, 'Mystically speaking, the day bears the image of the law. For as the brightness of the day illuminates the shadows of darkness, so law, showing the way to life, dispels the darkness of error, reveals the light of virtue and, clarifying what is good, leads the sinner to what is better.' The chapter continues with numerous parallels between events in time and the law. Fontaine, however, thinks this section of *De natura rerum* was a later addition, not by Isidore, as it appears only in a later recension. It might have been added by Braulius, who came across this appealing analogy while editing the *Etymologies* after Isidore's death and could not resist incorporating it into the relevant section of *De natura rerum*.[53]

After beginning with definitions of the words for time, he describes moments and hours, proceeding systematically through days, weeks, months, seasons, and years to centuries and eras, ending with a chronicle of the six ages of the world, from Creation to the present day. The material here is greatly expanded, compared to *De natura rerum*, while the allegorical interpretation is generally absent. Isidore does note the harmonies between the seasons (time) and the cardinal directions (space), and inserts a plea for a change in the days of the week from those which honour pagan gods, but in general his treatment is straightforward. His work on the date of Easter and the presentation of a ninety-five-year Paschal cycle can be found in Book VI, grouped with material on the Bible and the establishment of the canon. But, of course, it is difficult to draw conclusions about Isidore's organization in the *Etymologies*, since we do not know what liberties were taken by his editor.

THE WORK OF BEDE

The usefulness of a handbook on time and space was made manifest by Isidore's numerous imitators in centuries to come. Not quite a hundred years had passed before Bede (*c.* 673– 735 AD) wrote his own tract, dividing time and space into two separate works – *De natura rerum* and *De temporibus* – which, however, are often bound together. Born in Northumbria, Bede passed his entire life on the remote north-eastern coast of England (though this was far from an intellectual backwater in his day). At the age of seven he was sent to the monastery of St Peter, Wearmouth, where the abbot was the learned Benedict Biscop from Lérins, an island hermitage off the southern coast of France. In 682 he was transferred to a new monastery at Jarrow, ruled by abbot Ceolfrid. There is a story that the plague swept through the new monastery in 686, leaving only the abbot and a young boy (almost certainly Bede), who together maintained the rigorous programme of the divine office. Bede was indeed fortunate to serve under two able and educated abbots and to have access to a good library, partly imported from Rome. He also had access to material from Ireland, which had maintained an active tradition of learning throughout the preceding centuries.

Bede began to write in his twenties, and his life's work includes numerous commentaries on books of the Bible, the lives of the abbots of his monastery, a life of St Cuthbert, a martyrology or calendar of feast days, a history of the English church and people, as well as his works on time. *De natura rerum* and *De temporibus* were probably composed about the same time, in 703.[54]

In his *De natura rerum* Bede drew heavily on Isidore, following a similar outline and plundering his text freely for apt phrases. Almost as frequently, though, he uses Pliny's '*opus pulcherrimum*', as he called it, 'most noble work'.[55] The result is a concise account of the 'nature of things', generally without the allegorical flights favored by Isidore or the anecdotal padding beloved by Pliny. Four or five sentences suffice for most of the fifty-one chapters of the book. *De temporibus* is equally compact. In the first nine chapters he presents measures of time from moments to months to years, and the last six chapters are devoted to phenomena which relate to Easter (leap years, the nineteen-year cycle, the Christian era). In fact, these books were too short, more explanation was needed, and in 725 Bede produced a much longer work, incorporating material from them both. This was the *De temporum ratione* (On the calculation of time) which was to be the handbook of calendar scholars and the mainstay of libraries for centuries.[56]

Space and Time in the Computus Manuscript

De ratione temporum, on the calculation of time, was the title Bede gave to his master work of 725 on the *computus*. At its heart was the dating of Easter, putting in harmony human and heavenly time. Just as the winter solstice had been selected for the celebration of Christ's birth, so his resurrection corresponded with significant and symbolic astronomical phenomena. The feast should be celebrated by all Christian churches simultaneously, their prayers and psalms flowing upwards in a glorious world-wide chorus. The complexities of the calculations were very great, and medieval people put together increasingly weighty volumes of supporting materials, surrounding the basic Pascal tables and calendars with charts, diagrams, astronomical works, writings from Church fathers and the Bible, polemical letters, genealogies, world histories, even medical texts. Charles W. Jones, the great Bede scholar, estimates that by the tenth century 2500 separate items were circulating through western Christendom, from which the masters selected the contents of their computus manuscripts.[1] Our chief concern here is with the maps these documents occasionally contained, and why they were put there, but first some explanation of the computus and its history is necessary.

COMPUTUS AND WESTERN SCIENCE

Western science in the Middle Ages has been described as a backwater of religious dogmatism and mindless quotation of authority. Many works on history of science simply skip over the thousand-year period with a hasty chapter, in a rush to get to Galileo and Newton. However, medieval scientists, who were generally devoutly religious and often monks, were asking different questions from those asked by modern scientists, and in the modern mania for precursorism we miss the point of their work. For example, David Lindberg, in his excellent *Beginnings of Western Science*, has a single reference to computus in his index, and refers to Bede's seminal works as being simply about 'timekeeping and calendar control'.[2]

The focus of much of medieval science had to do with model-building, constructing a cosmological picture which harmonized with Christian theology, authoritative texts inherited from antiquity, and practical observation. This model had to satisfy not only the questions of what and how, but even more importantly the question of why: What was the meaning of it all? What was the role of humanity in the universe, from the whole course of human history to the moral choices of the individual? The model which they constructed was so complete and satisfying, and the role of humanity in the cosmos so well defined, that the overthrow of the model in the seventeenth century caused profound spiritual and psychological disorientation, from which we have yet to recover.[3] In particular the Cartesian separation of human consciousness and concerns from objective scientific observation has created a great gulf between ourselves and the scientific thinkers of the Middle Ages.

The model of the universe, originally Greek, postulated a planetary system with the earth at the centre. In substance the earth was dark, heavy, and material. In time, it was the place where things changed and decayed. The other bodies of the universe revolved in concentric orbits about the earth in ever-widening spheres, to each of which was assigned a musical tone, so that their revolutions created a celestial harmony. As one approached the outer spheres of the empyrean, the dwelling of the angels, and finally that of the prime mover, God himself, the radiance became more and more intense. In these realms of light, there was no change – no suffering, no death, no decay. In Dante's great work the model is most vividly described, from the dark, subterranean horrors of the Inferno, to the mount of Purgatory located in splendid isolation in the south Atlantic, to the heavenly spheres themselves, suffused with the light of pure spirit. It was no accident that Plato's cosmological work, the *Timaeus*, preserved through Chalcidius's commentary, was the best-known work of that philosopher in the early Middle Ages.

Within the model, every detail was fraught with meaning, every event symbolic of some greater truth, and here the medieval astronomers elaborated on their inheritance from the past. Modern readers may find the medieval writer's leap to allegory tiresome, but to the medieval scholar himself this was the important part. What was the meaning of the universe? This is a question scientists no longer presume to ask, much less dare to answer.

Central to the cosmology of the Middle Ages was the reckoning of time, carried on through the computus. 'Computus' originally meant any kind of calculation, but it came to mean specifically the measurement of time, and thus was intimately linked with the time-determining motions of the heavenly bodies. The chief task of the calendric computus was the calculation of the future dates of Easter and its dependent movable feasts, which were the heart of the Christian year. Easter was historically linked to Passover and the Jewish lunar calendar, but early on it became associated with the Julian solar calendar and ferial (weekday) cycles as well. By the time of the Council of Nicaea in 325 the church had decided that Easter must be celebrated by all Christendom simultaneously on the first Sunday following the first full moon after the spring equinox. This was a day of maximum light: twelve hours of daylight, followed by twelve hours of full moonlight. Its symbolic significance was made plain in a letter written in 710 by Abbot Ceolfrid of Jarrow in northern England:

> We are commanded to keep the full moon of the Paschal month after the equinox, so that first the sun may make day longer than night and then the moon may show the whole of her light face to the world, because first 'the Sun of Righteousness with healing in His wings', that is the Lord Jesus, overcame all the darkness of death by the triumph of His Resurrection and then, having ascended into heaven sent down the Spirit from on high and so filled His Church, which is often symbolically described as the moon, with the light of inward grace.

Whoever tried to celebrate Easter before the equinox, he warned, 'allies himself with those who believe they can be saved without the assistance of Christ's grace'.[4] The timing of Easter was in dramatic contrast, particular in northern latitudes, to the darkness of the world at the birth of Christ during the winter solstice.

The contemplation and understanding of the computus was spiritually rewarding. An African computist of 455 AD observed that the diligent scholar must not only read and re-read, but go through expiation, baptism and prayer, and then:

> at once the divine mercy shines forth and the light of knowledge glows, so that those things which seemed to him, seeking and desiring, to be obscured by clouds, lie open; all hidden things are uncovered for him, so that the motions of the moon are made clear in all their purity and the cycles of Easter are known together with the common and embolismic years, without any error from ignorance. The years of the *ogdoas* [eight-year cycle] and *endecas* [eleven-year], made by divine will, are understood, so that they are not unclear in any respect.[5]

The divine origin of the computus was further stressed by the tradition that its rules in the form of doggerel verse had been revealed to St Pachomius, a fourth-century Egyptian monk, by an angel.[6] Even long after the problem was solved, not only the calendars but also the rationale and supporting documents of the computus continued to be copied and studied well into the sixteenth century.[7]

The medieval computists had set themselves a difficult task, which was to bring into coordination three uncoordinated calendars: the lunar, the solar, and the seven-day week.[8] It took seven hundred years for a workable, repeatable cycle to be developed and generally accepted throughout the Christian world. The Easter problem surfaced again and again in the early Christian centuries, until the western Church was brought into conformity. Some of the dispute was based on honest differences in understanding (or misunderstanding) the astronomical questions involved, which were complex. Some was pure politics. Control of the calendar, as Julius Caesar had realized, gave one power over many human activities. As the various rivals to Christianity were eliminated and the Church itself became a power, the question of who controlled its agenda became more interesting. Among the various proposed cycles and tables and their supporting treatises appears a collection of unedifying forgeries and falsifications, which have generated a good deal of scholarly industry in the last century, and have made it rather difficult to trace the true history of the Easter controversy. As Charles W. Jones has noted, 'It relieves the often tedious study of ecclesiastical calendars to portray a stealthy Irish monk "forging" documents in the lonely quiet of his hermitage for the sole purpose of persuading the Irish and English Churches to his views.'[9]

Two periods of crisis stand out. One occurred in the mid-fifth century AD when the date of Easter, according to Alexandrian calculations, fell on 23 April (in the year 444) and 24 April (in 455), both of which were too late, according to Rome. A spate of anxious letters from Pope Leo and haughty replies from the Bishop of Alexandria resulted in Rome surrendering in the interests of unity.[10] At this point Victorius of Aquitaine was invited to resolve the Easter problem and compose a new cycle. His work created more problems than it solved, but he did stumble on the 532-year cycle, which was later adopted by Dionysius Exiguus. Dionysius, a Scythian monk, put together five new nineteen-year cycles, beginning (by coincidence) in the year 532. He also denounced the current use of the Diocletian era, in which events were dated from the accession of the emperor in 285, saying, 'I did not wish to preserve the memory of the impious persecutor in my cycles, but rather chose to denote the times from the birth of Our Lord Jesus Christ.'[11] Dionysius's work was continued by others and seemed to have inspired general agreement, but Gothic invasions and the disintegration of the administrative structure of the Empire led to several centuries of individual practice in various parts of Europe. In Spain, in Africa, in

parts of Gaul, and in Ireland, people quietly celebrated Easter in isolation from the rest of the church, probably without even knowing it.

In the seventh century, the situation came to a head in the British Isles. During the long dark night of Anglo-Saxon invasions, Celtic monks had maintained Christian institutions, including the 84-year Easter cycles which had been in vogue at the beginning of Britain's period of isolation. The Roman Church's mission in 597 to re-Christianize Britain found Christians already there, and considerably less easy to deal with than out-and-out pagans. While the pagans were allowed to keep their temples, once they were reconsecrated, and their holidays, once devoted to the newer usage, the customs of the old Celtic Church posed serious questions.[12] In 630 an Irish delegation was sent to Rome, and came home to report that their room-mates there – a Greek, a Scythian, a Hebrew, and an Egyptian – all celebrated Easter according to a schedule differing from 'the Britons and Irish, who are almost at the end of the earth'.[13] At the Synod of Whitby in 664 the issue was thoroughly discussed, and most of Britain came round, with the exception of the island of Iona, which was the last to capitulate in 716. This period generated another round of letters and documents, some spuriously dated to previous centuries and attributed to long-dead saints.

The work of the Venerable Bede put an effective end to controversy in his master work on time, *De ratione temporum* (On the calculation of time), which he completed in 725. He drew on classical sources, church documents, and some of his own observations, presenting with admirable clarity the knotty issues and the intricate reasoning behind the Church's solution. He only lost his temper occasionally.[14] No eighth-century manuscripts of Bede survive in England – the Vikings took care of that – but English missionaries had carried his work to the Continent (from which copies were later to return), and under Charlemagne the orderly science of computus became a cornerstone of the Carolingian Renaissance. As early as 789 Charlemagne had decreed that the computus be established in a correct form and taught in monastic schools. In 809 a conference on the subject was held at court.[15]

Numerous manuscripts survive from the ninth century, incorporating both of Bede's works on time and his *De natura rerum*, for good measure. These works, with their accompanying calendars, tables, and explanatory material, both written and pictorial, became the computus manuscripts of the Middle Ages.

4.1. St Pachomius and his monks receive the computus in verse form from an angel. The verse which appears below the dramatic illustration gives information on the beginning of Lent for each year in the nineteen-year cycle. The verses are older than the story, and neither is related to the actual St Pachomius, an Egyptian monk of the fourth century. From an eleventh-century computus manuscript of English origin. BL Cotton MS Caligula A.XV, fol. 122ᵛ.
Courtesy of the British Library Board.

A BRIEF COMPUTUS PRIMER

The computist's problem stemmed from the unevenness of the two celestial years: the solar year of $365\frac{1}{4}$ days and the twelve-month lunar year of 354 days. If Easter were celebrated according to the lunar calendar alone, as Moslem festivals are today, the date would continually recede in terms of the solar calendar and the vernal equinox would quickly be left behind. The Greeks had discovered that after nineteen years the sun and moon returned to the same respective positions (the Metonic cycle), but this short cycle omitted the problem of the recurrence of weekdays. Once it was decided that Easter must be celebrated on a Sunday, the Lord's Day, an additional twenty-eight-year cycle (taking leap year into account) had to be added to the calculations. After various experiments with 84-year cycles (3×28) and 95-year cycles (5×19), Victorius of Aquitaine in 457 was apparently the first to figure out that a 532-year cycle (28×19) was the only possible repeatable cycle which took into account all the variables. A version of this cycle was the one eventually adopted and promulgated by Bede.

In order to understand the Easter calendars and even to do the calculations oneself, a number of tools were developed. One of the most important items needed was the epact of the moon, or its age on a given date. In the Paschal tables this figure was given for 1 January, which enabled the phases of the moon to be determined throughout the rest of the year, or for the vernal equinox itself, the crucial observation in the prediction of Easter. Since the lunar cycle is approximately $29\frac{1}{2}$ days, the lunar calendar alternated between lunar months of 29 and 30 days, so called hollow and full months. The nineteen-year cycle consisted of 235 lunar cycles: 228 lunar months plus seven intercalated months of 30 days each plus $4\frac{3}{4}$ leap-year days. The years in which these intercalated months were placed were called embolismic, as opposed to common years. Each year in the cycle was assigned a number (the Golden Number), and years with the same number would have the same lunar epact and Paschal full moon. Table I was developed in the fifth century and is traditionally attributed to Cyril, Bishop of Alexandria. It was used by Dionysius Exiguus in 532 as the first nineteen-year cycle of his 95-year table.

In the first year shown on this table, the moon is new (epact = 0) on the vernal equinox, here reckoned to be 22 March, and therefore the first full moon will be fourteen days later, on 5 April. The next year's epact is 11, the moon being eleven days older (365-day solar year minus 354-day lunar year), and the first full moon after the equinox, Luna 14, is two days later, on 25 March. In the third year the epact is 22, so it

Table 1. The Easter Cycle of Alexandria					
Year	Epact (3/22)	Concurr. (3/24)	Golden #	Paschal full moon	Easter Sunday
513 (229)	0	I	17	5 April	7 April
514	11	II	18	25 March	30 March
515 B	22	III	19	13 April	19 April
516	3	V	1	2 April	3 April
517	14	VI	2	22 March	27 March
518	25	VII	3	10 April	15 April
519 B	6	I	4	30 March	31 March
520	17	III	5	18 April	19 April
521	28	IV	6	7 April	8 April
522	9	V	7	26 March	2 April
523 B	20	VI	8	15 April	16 April
524	1	I	9	4 April	9 April
525	12	II	10	24 March	30 March
526	23	III	11	12 April	19 April
527 B	4	IV	12	1 April	4 April
528	15	VI	13	21 March	28 March
529	26	VII	14	9 April	15 April
530	7	I	15	29 March	31 March
531 B	18	II	16	17 April	20 April

Notes to table:
Year is AD, adapted from original table of Cyril which used the era of Diocletian, which began in 285 AD. *B* = bissextile = leap year.
Dates changed from the Roman (Kalends, Nones, Ides) system.
Two columns of the eight-column table have been omitted here: that showing the indiction and the age of the moon on Easter.[16]

becomes necessary to add an intercalated month, or the epact would exceed 30 in the next year. This added month makes the fourth an embolismic year, and the epact will be 3. Columns 1, 3, and 4 (lunar epact, Golden Number, and Paschal full moon) will be the same in each nineteen-year cycle.

The third column, the concurrent, contains numbers from one through seven representing the days of the week, beginning with Sunday as one. Various systems were used for the concurrent, also called the solar epact. Here 24 March is the key date, chosen because it fell on the same weekday as 24 February. Instead of adding a twenty-ninth day to February, as we do now, the twenty-fourth day occurred twice in leap years. The term 'bissextile', used widely in computus literature, means a doubling of the sixth, or VI Kalends March = 24 February. The March date was useful because of its proximity to Easter. Bede had noted the useful fact that 31 March and 7, 14, 21 April would share the same weekday.[17] Medieval writers thought up various mnemonic verses to assist someone who wanted to know the weekday and might not have a calendar handy. The concurrents would occur in the same order every 28th year. For all the elements of the table to repeat itself exactly, a cycle of 532 years (28 × 19) was required.

An additional wrinkle is that, if the Paschal full moon fell on a Sunday, Easter had to be celebrated on the Sunday after, in order to avoid coinciding with the Jewish celebration of Passover. Such a celebration was a heresy, called the Quartodecimanist or Fourteener heresy, denounced in the second century.[18] In Table 1, note that on six of the nineteen years the full moon falls on a Sunday, and thus Easter will be celebrated a full week later.

Most Easter tables have still more information. The holidays dependent on Easter, such as the beginning of Lent, are also listed. Epacts or lunar ages on the first days of the months January through April, or even for the entire year, are a useful detail. The actual moon's age on Easter, ranging from fifteen to twenty-two days, would fill another column. The number of the indiction, a fifteen-year cycle widely used by imperial and papal bureaucracies, could be noted as well.[19]

An early calendrical problem was the finding of an 'era', or a beginning point from which to date all events. The ancient world had been remarkably careless on this point, calling years by the names of archons (Athens) or consuls (Rome), but not really developing any generally accepted starting date. Olympiads began in 776 BC, but were never widely used. The same was true of the date of the founding of Rome, 753 BC, introduced into historical writing by Livy, but never in common use. The eventual point chosen, the birth of Christ or the Incarnation, seems obvious enough to us – although the year of the Crucifixion was a serious competitor – but it was some five hundred years before Christians lit on this solution, and even then there was some disagreement as to the dating of this important event. This is still true. Eusebius, who composed an influential chronicle in the third century, which was translated into Latin by St Jerome, incorporated a bewildering variety of chronologies, including Hebrew patriarchs, Assyrian kings, Egyptian pharoahs, and the Ptolemies.[20] Other eras used in early Easter tables include the era of Diocletian (dating from 285 AD), the era of Constantinople (which dates from the creation of the world in 5509 BC), a variety of other *Anni Mundi*, and the Spanish era (dating from 38 BC). The latter was used in Spain from the fifth century into the late Middle Ages. Isidore thought the era dated from a census held by Augustus and made the connection between aes, aeris (bronze tablet) to the word era. Since Augustus held no census in 38 BC, a more convincing modern theory is that the date originated in a fifth-century Easter table, by tracing the 84-year cycles of Cyril back to a starting date before the birth of Christ.[21]

THE ILLUSTRATED COMPUTUS

The basic Paschal table seldom appeared alone. The earliest computus manuscripts added letters, real or invented, advocating one's own method of Easter reckoning and denouncing all others. Charles Jones lists over a dozen computus documents which were circulating through Europe before Bede's work became available.[22]

One of the most influential, the seventh-century Irish *De ratione conputandi*, was, like its title, practical and exhortatory: '*sciendum nobis*' begins each section – 'we must know' – and the student is led step by step through the intricate mechanics of calendar calculation. This document was one of those certainly available to Bede and subsequent computists, although it now survives in only two manuscripts.[23]

Among the diagrams that came to be associated with computus manuscripts are world maps. Unlike a regional map, a world map had a cosmic meaning which enabled it to fit in with other diagrams of universal scope. Such maps appear in some of the very earliest computus manuscripts which survive.

In an eighth-century Italian manuscript in the Vatican an Easter table and a chronicle are followed by a wind diagram. It is hardly a map – the round centre is labelled simply *kosmos/mundus* – but the cardinal directions and corresponding winds are shown. Immediately above the diagram is a listing of the eight different times of the night and below is a short text that seems to be a list of the 'Egyptian' or ill-omened days. A text on the next page discusses sailing, tempests, and the months when it is safe to travel by sea.[24] The wind diagram had classical origins and was arguably the oldest of the diagrams which came to form an integral part of the medieval computus manuscript.

A more impressive map precedes a small collection of pre-Carolingian computus material in another Vatican manuscript. This is the famous 'Isidore' map in the Vatican Library, MS lat. 6018.[25] Long attributed to Isidore, thanks to a librarian's misidentification, the manuscript is one of those compilations which are the despair of cataloguers and researchers.[26] It begins with a fifty-page glossary known as the '*abstrusa-abolita*' glossary, named for the first and last words of its first column. The rest of its pages – there are 131 folios in all – is made up of one- and two-page excerpts from a variety of sources, not all yet identified. If any theme ties them together, it seems to be biblical exegesis. Perhaps it was a preacher's or a teacher's handbook of useful information. The map spreads across two pages near the centre (fols 63ᵛ–64), following part of 'De nominibus hebreis' of Eucherius (fols 60ᵛ–62ᵛ).[27] Immediately preceding the map, on the verso of its first page, is an erased floral diagram, similar to the Annus-Mundus-Homo diagram of Isidore's De natura rerum. The pages that follow the map (fols 64ᵛ–71) are computus material: a rota of 'Egyptian' or ill-omened days (fol. 64ᵛ),[28] an horologium (fol. 65), a nineteen-year cycle showing the lunar epact for the Kalends of each month (fols 65ᵛ–66), another nineteen-year cycle with the date of Lent and Easter plus an explanation of the Roman calendar (fol. 66ᵛ), a twenty-eight-year table (fol. 67), a group of explanatory texts (fols 67ᵛ–68), a series of indiction (fifteen-year) tables from the year 771 until 1000 (fols 68ᵛ–71). There is no specifically geographical material here, nor any explanation of the map's presence. In short, it is a 'computus map' merely by association, but an association that we will see again, particularly in computus manuscripts illustrated with other diagrams.

The map spreads across two pages. It is bound in the book with south at the top, but the writing is every which way, so does not privilege any particular orientation. The ecumene is shown as a circle, enclosed within an oval of ocean. In the north-east and south-west corners appear lunar symbols. These may indicate the map's origin as part of the computus, where the earth was frequently shown flanked by heavenly bodies.[29]

The largest of the islands in the outer ocean is 'Laperbana' (Taprobane = Ceylon) in the east. It is divided into inhabited and 'bestial' sections with a note on its size and number of cities. In the usual location of Britain and Ireland in the north-west are two shapes labelled 'mare mortun . . . oceanus' and 'oceanus occiduus'. These may not be islands at all, but merely labels for the western ocean, the world-encircling ocean, and perhaps the mythical western land of the dead. The Dead Sea, located in its proper place in Palestine, is 'mare mortuum'. Glorie, who tries hard to think of rational explanations for everything on the map, suggests that 'mare mortun' in the west is meant to be 'mare nostrum', for the Mediterranean, but, even so, it is in the wrong place.[30]

Also in the encircling ocean, to the south, is another shape labelled 'insola incognita ori sl iiii partes mundi'. This mysterious message has been variously deciphered and interpreted. It comes temptingly close to Isidore's comment about the fourth part of the world, unknown to us on account of the heat of the sun: [ard]ori s[o]l[is]. Here, perhaps, the limitations of the page have transformed this hypothetical continent into a mere island.[31] However, an additional problem is that the term

4.2. One of the oldest detailed world maps we possess is this one. Placed with a group of computus materials in a manuscript of numerous short selections and highly varied content, it shows the inhabited continents as a circle surrounded by the ocean. To the south-west of Africa is the island which has been interpreted as a vestigial fourth continent. Paradise is represented by a rosette in the far east. The two apparent islands in the north-west are both labelled with the names of seas: 'mare mortun' and 'oceanus occiduus' (dead sea, or sea of the dead, and western ocean). Shown here with south on top. From a manuscript of the late eighth century, originated in southern France (?). MS Vat.lat.6018, fols 63ᵛ–64ʳ. Courtesy of the Vatican Library.

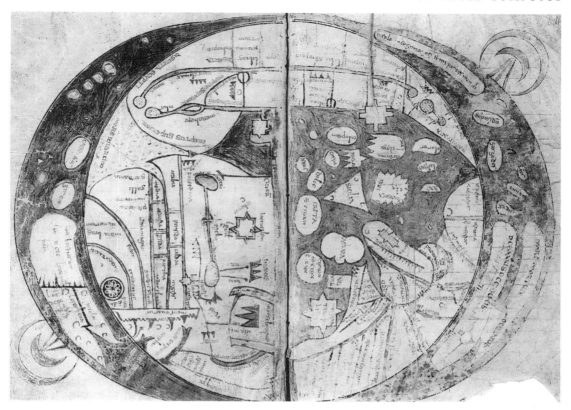

'*mundus*' was seldom used for the earth (*terra*) but only for the universe as a whole. It is this consideration which led Uhden to conclude that the inscription had reference to the '*partes mundi*', which were fire, air, water, and earth.[32] Such a connection would move this map closer to a computus diagram and away from a geographical/realistic depiction of the earth.

A very large Mediterranean takes up about a third of the inhabited world. It contains a dozen islands, including a triangular Sicily, Constantinople, and Achaia. Special city symbols highlight Jerusalem, Rome, Carthage, perhaps Alexandria, Constantinople, and Babylon. Elsewhere 'c' for '*civitas*' stands to represent unnamed cities. There are eight c's in Italy and eight in Ceylon. In the east a rosette is labelled '*Paradisus. Terra Eden*', and nearby five rivers flow from the mount Taurus range: the Crisacoras,[33] Gandis (Ganges), Indus, Tigris, and Euphrates. The Nile is shown flowing from the east, around the island of Merohen (Meroe). It is also shown as a separate body stretching the width of Africa from East to West with lakes at either end. Spiky mountains and squared off provinces complete the picture. Nearly all the 130 names on the map can be found in either Orosius or Isidore, or alternatively, were part of the general geographical vocabulary of eighth-century Europe.[34]

With its depiction of Paradise and the rivers, Bethlehem, Mount Sinai, the river Jordan and the Dead Sea, the map has clearly incorporated Christian content into the classical model. There is even a small (unlabelled) gap in the Red Sea to show the crossing of the children of Israel. No other map is quite like it, and it represents an early alternative to the Beatus maps, which also incorporated Christian theology. The original of the Beatus maps is almost its exact contemporary. As an item in a preacher's handbook, the Vatican map provided material much in line with the glossaries and questions on the Bible, found elsewhere in the manuscript. As part of the computus, it presented the world as one of several diagrams – the rest of the manuscript is unillustrated.

The mistaken connection of this very early manuscript with Isidore's *Etymologies* has resulted in confusion, leading scholars to imagine that the geographical book of this work was originally accompanied by a detailed map. The only other elaborate map to be found in an early *Etymologies* is in an eleventh-century French manuscript, now in Munich.[35] In contrast, over a hundred manuscripts have the T–O icon. These findings lead us to re-evaluate the connection between Isidore and world maps. Perhaps the very voluminousness of Isidore's text discouraged the would-be map-maker. Or, as Gautier Dalché and others have suggested, perhaps the written word was valued above the picture: if you had a verbal description, you did not need a map.

COMPUTUS AFTER BEDE

The sketchy computus in the Vatican Library, MS lat. 6018 shows no sign of the work of Bede, but soon after Bede's *De ratione temporum* appeared it became the centre of all computus documents. In his latest edition of the work Charles Jones lists 245 manuscripts,[36] but points out that there were probably many more, since Bede's works were used so frequently that they wore out and had to be replaced. Still the old material did not disappear. Bede's earlier *De temporibus* and *De natura rerum* were frequently copied along with *De ratione temporum*. Isidore's *De natura rerum* continued to be valued, probably for its greater detail on astronomical phenomena, its allegorical interpretations, and its diagrams.

Bede's work was originally accompanied by a calendar, a 19-year cycle and a 532-year table, as indicated by references in the text.[37] In the computus manuscripts which included his work, the calendar often appeared at the beginning, with a page allotted to each month and the saints' days noted, as well as regular astronomical phenomena. These pages were sometimes embellished with verses, characterizing each month, and sometimes with illustrations, showing the labour appropriate to the season.[38] The 532-year table covered the years from 532 to 1063, with columns for indictions, epacts, concurrents, the Golden Numbers, the Easter full moon, the date of Easter and the moon's age on that day, as well as a space at the end of each line for notes, which became the annals of medieval monasteries. (See Plate V.)

In the Carolingian period, probably shortly after Charlemagne's computus conference of 809, a weighty anthology of computus material appeared. A number of copies were made, some of which still survive.[39] This volume pulled together Bede's works, a calendar, a 532-year table, and excerpts from various writers including Isidore, Hyginus, Pliny, Macrobius, Aratus, Martianus Capella, and other anonymous labourers in the computus vineyard. Astronomical information covered eclipses, solstices and equinoxes, lunar movements, the orbits and nature of the planets, the signs of the zodiac (illustrated), and the relative sizes of the earth, moon, and sun. Under the subject of time were descriptions of the various divisions of time (from atoms to eons), an account of the six ages of world history, calculations of the number of years since the Creation and the Incarnation. There was also an arithmetic section with problems, the *loquela digitorum* (which explained how to count and calculate with your fingers), and a discussion of weights and measures. Specific to the computus were explanations of leap years, the *saltus lunae* ('the moon's leap,' a lunar day omitted once in nineteen years to bring solar and lunar calendars into closer conformity), epacts and concurrents, accompanied by the story of St Pachomius and the angel, as well as the mnemonic verses which were revealed to him. Of the surviving manuscripts the two representatives of the three-book version contain maps (Munich, Bayerische Staatsbibliothek, MS Clm. 210, fol. 132[v], and Vienna, Osterreichische Nationalbibliothek, MS 387, fol. 134), while only one of the seven-book editions (Paris, B.N., n.a. lat. 456, fol. 170) does.[40] It was a veritable encyclopedia whose popularity was instantaneous, but this did not prevent it from being constantly re-ordered, re-edited, and plundered. One small section of about five pages, which Faith Wallis calls a 'cosmological anthology',[41] included edited texts from Macrobius's commentary on the dream of Scipio from Cicero's *De Republica*, and Martianus Capella, *De nuptiis Philologiae et Mercurii* (Book VIII), which covered subjects omitted by Bede: the size of the sun and moon and their distance from the earth, and the size of the earth. This small group of texts travelled as a package for centuries and appears in numerous computus manuscripts. Another popular set of excerpts, known as the 'York excerpts', was from Pliny's *Natural History* (Book II), and was already in circulation by the eighth century. The texts selected had for their subject the positions and orbits of the planets.[42]

Supplementary tables, showing other time-linked phenomenon, such as the periods of the planets' rotation or the movements of the sun and the moon through the zodiac, were added. The number and variety of these was limited only by the energy and resources of the scribe. Already by the ninth century computus manuscripts could run to several hundred folios.

DIAGRAMS

Bede himself seems to have had a low opinion of diagrams and tables.[43] In ch. XIX of *De temporum ratione*, which contains directions for constructing a table of the moon's course through the zodiac, he says patronizingly, 'If someone unable to count is still curious about the course of the moon, we will accommodate our discussion to his ability, so that he who seeks may find.' His successors, more visually oriented perhaps, found tables and diagrams indispensable for negotiating the complex rules of the computus. Scribes were particularly fond of Isidore's *De natura rerum*, and copied the diagrams with or without the text, putting relevant ones in the middle of Bede's originally unillustrated text or placing them as a group elsewhere in the manuscript.

Also from Isidore, but this time from his *Etymologies* (IX.6.28) came a consanguinity diagram, which took several forms: as a tree or a circle, or superimposed on the body of a human being. It accompanied a section entitled '*De affinitatibus et gradibus*', or 'Of relationships and degrees', the aim being to show family connections through six generations, to aid in complying with ecclesiastical prohibitions on marriage. What such a diagram has to do with computus is not immediately clear, other than the general delight in graphing and calculating, but it can be seen as an expression of time in human form. Isidore's link with time is quite specific and may account for the inclusion of the diagram and passage in computus manuscripts. He writes,

> This consanguinity chart is divided into the ranks of descendants down to the last degree, at which point one ceases to be related; going back, the law forbids marriage and chastises the one who ignores this. Consanguinity

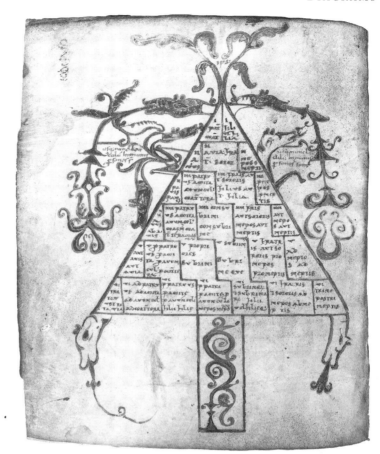

4.3. Consanguinity diagram, based on Isidore, *Etymologies*, Book IX.6. Father/mother (pater/mater) and son/daughter (filius/filia) are at the peak of the tree, with the self [ipse] assumed to stand just above them. Each of the bands below represents a degree of relationship. For example the second band includes brother, sister, grandparents, nieces, and nephews. From a ninth-century computus manuscript from Fleury, France. BL MS Harl. 3017, fol. 57ᵛ.

Courtesy of the British Library Board.

has been established as far as the sixth degree of relationship and is like the six ages of the world – when the existence of man is ended, then there will be no consanguinity in any of its degrees. (*Etym.*, IX.vi.29)

Macrobius was another good source of pictures, as noted above. His zonal map with its abstract presentation of the earth fit in well with the other scientific diagrams chosen to illustrate the computus. Occasionally the zonal format became the foundation for a more complex map, as in the encyclopedia of Lambert of St Omer and in the Ripoll manuscript of 1056, discussed below.

Another source of diagrams was Chalcidius's commentary on Plato's *Timaeus*. His work dated from the early fourth century, although the section on astronomy was older, being copied largely from the Pseudo-Aristotle.[44] The original seems to have been copiously illustrated.[45] His diagrams tend to be quite technical and only a few migrate to other texts. His depictions of the eclipses and the problematic orbits of

Mercury and Venus occasionally appear without him, but these may have a common, older source.[46] Chalcidius does not include a map, but his elaborate diagram of the heavenly zones could be adapted for earthly purposes.[47] In a Spanish manuscript from 1056 Chalcidius is carefully edited and excerpted, diagrams included, as the fourth book of an elaborate computus work.[48]

Pliny's great grab-bag of natural history, so much admired by Bede, was mined by many scribes. The selections from his work on the planets were illustrated with one or more of three diagrams, which may have classical origins. One is the great circle of planetary orbits which appears in the Leiden *Aratea* (fol. 93[v]). The positions of the planets reveal that the diagram represents the sky on 18 March 816, giving us a date for at least one version of this diagram.[49] Another illustration of Pliny is a curious rectangular graph which looks like a particularly exciting day on the stock market, but actually is meant to show the latitudes or courses of the planets in relation to the zodiac. These diagrams have been studied by Bruce Eastwood and Eva-Maria Engelen,[50] and Eastwood surmises that they were composed in the Carolingian period at the time the excerpts were chosen. In one manuscript from Boulogne, the scribe has surrounded the large planetary design with four small *rotae*, some of which are old friends from Isidore's *De natura rerum*: a five-petal zone diagram; a twelve-wind *rota* with a T–O centre, the cardinal directions and the characteristics of each wind; a circle of concentric planetary orbits which contradicts the larger picture (which has eccentric orbits), but gives the orbital periods; and a circular diagram (not from Isidore), which shows the visibility of the sun above the horizon during the summer and winter solstices and at the equinoxes. Eastwood says this latter diagram is from Martianus Capella.[51] Certainly it shows up in a number of Carolingian and later computi.

New diagrams, which may have originated in the Carolingian period, were drawn to illustrate the computus anthology. An example is a diagram of the tides created to accompany Bede's text on the subject. Although labelled '*ut Beda docet*' (as Bede teaches), it was not made by Bede but was probably created in the early ninth century at the Abbey of St-Benoît-sur-Loire, Fleury.[52] Bede lived on the east coast of Britain, a land of dramatic tides, unlike the Mediterranean. The monastery of Lindisfarne on that coast was transformed from a peninsula to an island at high tide – clearly local visitors had to pay close attention to this marine phenomenon. Bede's account of the relationship between the tides and the moon (ch. xxix, '*De concordia maris et lunae*') was partly based on Pliny's account in the *Natural History*,[53] but

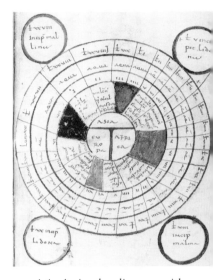

4.4. A circular diagram with a T–O map in the centre, illustrating the movement of the tides in the course of a month. The next ring shows the winds, with twelve spaces provided, but four blocked out. The next ring shows four cycles of seven or eight days each, surrounded by a ring labelled 'aqua, aqua' 29 times. The moon's age through the month appears in the outermost ring. The four circles give the days of the two highest (malina) and lowest (ledona) tides of the month. From a ninth-century manuscript from Fleury. BL MS Harl. 3017, fol. 135[r]. Courtesy of the British Library Board.

included his own observations. The diagram which became the standard illustration shows a monthly rather than a daily cycle of the tides. It has a T–O centre with Asia on top, surrounded by the winds, for Bede had mentioned the influence of the winds in augmenting or delaying tidal movement. The next round shows the alternating seven- and eight-day periods of the month which coincide with changes in the tides, while the outermost ring gives the days of a single lunar month. According to Bede, maximum high tides occurred at the full and new moons, while the lowest tides were at the quarter and three-quarter moons. The row between is labelled '*aqua*', probably to reinforce the watery subject of the diagram. In the four corners of the page are circles (moons?) with the lunar days of *malina* (greatest) and *ledona* (least) tides. An oddity of a number of these diagrams is that only eight winds are filled in, though twelve spaces are provided, demonstrating an admirable fidelity to the defects of the original diagram. In one manuscript the eight-wind tidal *rota* is followed only a few pages further on by a wind *rota* with all twelve winds.[54]

The Macrobian zonal map sometimes appears, for Bede has included in his text a brief reference to Macrobius's clashing tides which cause a difference in the timing of high and low tides from north to south. His use of this information was based not on slavish copying but on his own observation of the variable times of tides in different ports. These variations are due to topography, but Bede thought perhaps they were because of the sweep of ocean currents from the equator to the poles and back again. An example is the zonal map in the British Library, Cotton MS Tiberius B.V., part I, fol. 29. (See fig. 5.2.)

Another diagram, which probably has Roman origins, is the *horologium viatorum*, the portable or traveller's sundial. The months are grouped by pairs (January/December, February/November, etc.) in which the shadow of a man or a sundial's gnomon will be the same length at various hours of the day. For example, in January and December, at the first and eleventh hours, the shadow will measure 29 feet, while at the sixth hour (noon) the shadow will be eleven feet.[55] By contrast, in June and July the shadow at the first and eleventh hours will be 19 feet long, and a mere two feet at the sixth hour (noon). Of course, these figures should vary with the latitude, but manuscripts were frequently copied and dispersed without correcting these figures, so their practical use was limited.[56] What the *horologium* did show was a consciousness of the motion of the heavenly bodies (here the sun) and the determination of time.

Other diagrams include:

A rota of solstices and equinoxes, showing the position of

4.5. Horologium. Sometimes called the 'horologium viatorum', or travellers' sundial, this diagram pairs the months in which the positions of the sun are more or less the same. For example, in February and November the sun will cast a shadow of 27 feet at the first and eleventh hours, and so on. These calculations are presumed to be based on the height of the average traveller. The diagram can be found in various configurations and appears in nearly all computus manuscripts. This is from a ninth-century manuscript from Fleury, where it follows Isidore's chapter, 'De concordia mensuum', *De natura rerum* v, which is not usually illustrated. BL MS Harl 3017, fol. 88ʳ.
Courtesy of the British Library Board.

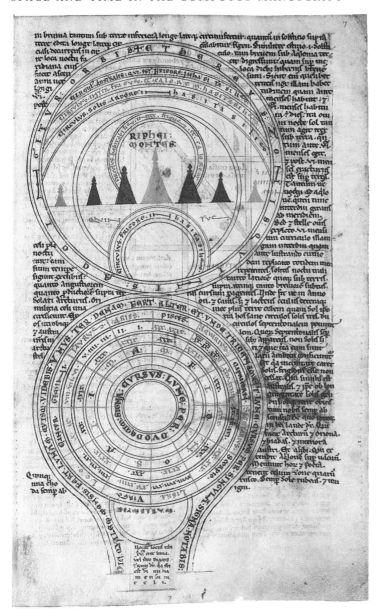

4.6. Zone map. This highly abstract and artistic zone map shows the earth as seen from the North Pole. The border between the arctic zone and the northern temperate zone is marked by the Riphaean mountains. The lower diagram shows the course of the moon through the zodiac. The surrounding text is from Bede, *De temporum ratione*, ch. XXXIV, 'De quinque circulis mundi'. From a late-twelfth-century English manuscript. Walters MS 73, fol. 7ʳ.

the sun, dates, and seasons.

Sphere of Pythagoras, or Petrosiris, or Apuleius, a conjuring diagram used to predict the outcome of an illness. The numerical value of the letters of the person's name was added to the day of the month on which he fell ill and the total divided by thirty. The resulting figure found on this *rota* signified either life or death.

Rota with seven phases of the moon and the relative positions of the sun and earth. This is a more complex diagram than the simple line drawing shown by Isidore.

This group of diagrams migrates from manuscript to manuscript with remarkable uniformity for several centuries. In some later manuscripts the group is broken up and the diagrams are distributed through the text at appropriate points. Some explanations are inserted by the scribe, as the pictures do not always speak for themselves. A set of excellent explanations by a later scribe are inserted in a manuscript now in Paris. Of one diagram the scribe writes, 'This figure, as it seems to me, is rather a cause of trouble than an invention to facilitate understanding.' And at the end, he notes, 'But all these things can be better explained orally than in writing.'[57]

The maps found in these computus manuscripts are sometimes no more than a simple T–O placed in the middle of a nest of planetary orbits or a wind diagram. Examples of these appear in works like the Walters computus manuscript in Baltimore. Brilliantly analysed by Harry Bober,[58] this compact late-twelfth-century English manuscript of nine folios contains 20 diagrams and 30 excerpts from Bede, Isidore, Pliny, and Abbo of Fleury. Both the written material and the illustrations are carefully chosen to illuminate aspects of cosmography which would have been necessary for students in a monastic school. Geography is strictly subordinated to cosmology, and, as one would expect, the maps are schematic. They include two T–O centres of tidal and wind *rotae* and two zone maps, as well as a copy of Isidore's five-petal zone diagram.

In more extended computus manuscripts there was more room to spread out. The eighth-century Vatican manuscript discussed above included a map, but no text to explain why it was there. Later, and possibly better preserved, manuscripts do more. In the next chapter we will examine three large computus manuscripts from the eleventh and twelfth centuries which contain especially interesting maps, along with other diagrams.

<table>
<tr><td>CHAPTER
5</td><td>Three Maps in Computus
Manuscripts</td></tr>
</table>

CHAPTER 5

Three Maps in Computus Manuscripts

Some of the most interesting maps which appear in codices of the eleventh and twelfth centuries are in computus manuscripts. In each case the compilers have gone beyond a limited concept of computus to include a wide spectrum of materials on related themes. These manuscripts reveal the broad implications of the computus for medieval science and learning in general, which had reordered the categories of its heritage from ancient science to serve its own world view. Seeking harmony between divine creation and human understanding of the world, the calculations which determined the Christian festival cycle reached out into many branches of knowledge, tying together the disparate and discrete phenomena of nature and human history to form a pattern of profound religious meaning.

Much of the scientific inheritance from the past came filtered through the Hellenistic period, when the ancient religious tradition had lost much of its power and science entered a period of free-wheeling scepticism. Medieval thinkers felt the need to re-attach science to religion, and it is not surprising that the mystical approach of the sixth-century BC philosopher Pythagoras found favour among them – in so far as he was understood. His musical intervals for planetary orbits show up in numerous medieval manuscripts, showing the harmonious nature of the universe. On another level, a divining circle, used to predict whether a sick person would live or die, had Pythagoras's name attached to it. Augustine and other early Christian thinkers urged their readers to regard the ancient heritage as a treasure from which they could take what they needed and discard the rest. This process was called 'despoiling the Egyptians,' from the story of Passover, when the departing Hebrews were instructed by God to borrow gold and silver from their Egyptian neighbours and then flee with their plunder (Exodus 11.1–3, 12.35–6).

Where the ancients left no guidance, medieval thinkers needed to create their own science. The correspondence of lunar and solar cycles was one such area. With the calendar reform of Julius Caesar, the west had essentially abandoned the lunar calendar and gone completely solar, but the legacy of the Jewish lunar reckoning could not be treated so lightly by Christians. The debate over the computus in the early

Christian centuries shows some of the best minds of the day tackling a knotty calendrical problem. 'We know well,' wrote Byrhtferth, an English monk of the eleventh century, 'that there was present neither invention nor composition of Virgil, nor investigation of the revered Plato, nor conjecture of Socrates his master' to explain the mysteries of the Paschal cycle.[1] Instead, he goes on to say, this knowledge came by the revelation of an angel to St Pachomius of Egypt.

The goal was not only to celebrate Easter correctly this year, but to project into the future an accurate cycle of Easters, based on the vernal equinox, the full moon, and the seven-day week. The plundered treasure of classical learning was reorganized around these new requirements. In her extensive analysis of the twelfth-century computus now at St John's College, Oxford, Faith E. Wallis classifies computus manuscripts into three types.[2] First is the 'classic computus manuscript' which contains calendars, tables and *argumenta*, or supporting explanations, mostly astronomical and doctrinal justifications for specific calculations. Second is the 'centrifugal computus manuscript', which adds to the computus base other materials used for teaching subjects, such as grammar. This approach emphasizes the computus as an organizing principle in clerical education. The third form is the 'centripetal computus manuscript', which contains a variety of related subjects, each of which has a specific tie to time and/or measurement. An example would be medical texts and recipes, as medical practice was closely linked to the seasons and the movements of the heavenly bodies. In the manuscript studied by Wallis there is what she terms a 'double-ring structure', with a central group of explanatory texts related directly to the calendar, consisting of astronomical information and the necessary mathematics, surrounded by two rings. One ring is composed of derivative materials, such as medicine, history, genealogy, and prognostication, all sharing a basis in time. The other is analogical, such as prosody, weights and measures, and music. These phenomena are like the computus in that they are subject to measurement, whether by the length of a syllable, a foot, or a note. All three types of computus manuscripts can be found from the Carolingian Renaissance forward.

Many computus manuscripts were lavish productions with numerous illustrations. Wallis surmises that, in the case of the St John's manuscript, it was less for use than for show, more like the gorgeously decorated missal carried in procession or the modern coffee-table book.[3] Her conjecture fits in well with Jones's observation that the text of Bede in the book is quite corrupt and carelessly copied, contrasting with the great care which was taken with the layout and the coloured illustrations. By the twelfth century the computus problem was more or less solved, and attention seems to have shifted from its core to its attractive penumbra of scientific learning and intricate illustrations. It continued to have symbolic significance, however, and Wallis links its production with the dedication of the new church at Thorney Abbey, the house of God compared to the architectural structuring of time found in the computus.[4]

Geography fits into Wallis's first ring, that of derivative materials, and also into the second ring, which concerns measurement. Computus manuscripts contain various geographical texts, such as the Marvels of the East, or selections from Isidore or Pliny on the size of the earth. Maps, where they appear, may accompany these writings or stand in another context, or even stand in splendid isolation, leaving the reader (or the teacher) to imagine the connection.

In this chapter I am going to consider three computus manuscripts of the eleventh and twelfth centuries which contain maps of unusual interest and detail. They are the British Library's Cotton MS, Tiberius B.V.1, the Ripoll manuscript now in the Vatican Library, MS reg. lat. 123, and St John's College, Oxford, MS 17. The first two are almost exact contemporaries (1050 and 1056), while the latter is half a century later (1110). Each contains several maps, one of which is a large world map. These maps have received scholarly attention in the past, but, in general, little attention has been paid to their place in the manuscript as a whole or to their immediate context.

THE COTTON TIBERIUS MANUSCRIPT

The richly illuminated eleventh-century manuscript in the Cotton collection of the British Library contains one of our oldest and most excellent world maps. (See fig 1.5.) Called the 'Anglo-Saxon' map, it dates from 1050, just before the Norman Conquest. The manuscript is bilingual with writings in Latin and Anglo-Saxon, and its English provenance is reinforced by the use of an Anglo-Saxon letter in the term Suð bryttas (Brittany) on the map. The detail and accuracy shown in its depiction of the British Isles have led some map scholars, such as P. D. A. Harvey, to conclude that it must be a copy of a Roman original.[5] The manuscript was compiled at Christ Church, Canterbury, but by 1100 it was housed at Battle Abbey. The book includes three picture cycles: a calendar with the Labours of the Months, the Marvels of the East with its griffins and dog-headed people, and the constellations, beautifully rendered in a classical style. The contents have been analysed under the direction of Patrick McGurk in a fine facsimile edition.[6]

The first nineteen folios are devoted to the computus and begin with a page of three *rotae* – a phases-of-the-moon diagram unsuccessfully mated with a twelve-month *rota*, an unfinished set of concentric planetary orbits, and the solstice-equinox *rota* (fol.2). This page is followed by one of explanatory tables and texts and then the illustrated calendar (fols 3–8ᵛ). Fols 9–19 contain a set of computus tables, followed by excerpts from Bede and others. McGurk observes that some of the computus passages are carelessly copied. Perhaps our scribe was more an artist than a scientist.

Continuing with the theme of time are documents of human chronology: lists of abbots and bishops of England, Alexandria, Antioch, Jerusalem, and Rome, as well as kings of the Anglo-Saxon kingdoms and their genealogies, with some historical notes. This section is followed by a brief account of Archbishop Sigeric's journey to Rome in 990, the places he visited there and on his route homeward.[7] Next comes *De temporibus anni*, a tenth-century Anglo-Saxon treatise on chronology by Aelfric, incorporating material from Bede and Isidore (fols 24–8ᵛ). Aelfric's titles (in Latin) include the first day of Creation or the vernal equinox, essays on night, the year, the universe, leap year, the *saltus lunae*, the twelve winds, rain, hail, snow, and thunder. There is also a set of annals from Battle Abbey, running from the year 6 to 1206 (now bound with Cotton MS Nero.D.I).

Another computus section runs from fols 49ᵛ to 54ᵛ and includes the common excerpts from Pliny, Macrobius, and Martianus Capella. Pliny's text on the *apsides* or extreme orbital positions of the planets is headed by a decorative *rota* of concentric circles which looks more like a dinner-plate than a scientific diagram (fol.53). Other than that, this part is unillustrated and looks rather heavy after the glorious constellations in the previous section.

The manuscript at one time contained three maps: the world map mentioned above, a celestial map now lost, and a Macrobian-style zonal map. In considering the role the maps play in the overall manuscript plan, one must tread cautiously, as the book has been rebound and there is uncertainty about the exact placement of all of its parts.[8] The Anglo-Saxon map was intended to accompany Priscian's geographical poem, a translation of the 'Periegesis' of Dionysius. Above the poem are the lines: 'Here begins the book, "Periegesis", by Priscian, grammarian of the city of Rome, professor of Caesarea (Africa), that is about the situation of the earth, gathered by him from the writings on ancient world maps; and to this work of three parts, that is to say, Asia, Africa, and Europe, there is painted a suitable (*aptam*) map in which the location of nations, mountains, rivers, islands, and also wonders are accurately arranged.'

Patrick McGurk, the editor of the facsimile of the manuscript, has followed Konrad Miller in dissociating the map from the poem, saying, 'Like nearly all world maps of its kind, it is not found attached to a particular text.'[10] Miller went so far as to construct a map which he felt would be a better illustration for Priscian's work.[11] The poem itself, like Dionysius's Greek original, has many references to visual elements – the shapes of geographical features, for example. It is Christian Jacob's view that Dionysius's poem is essentially the explanation of a map.[12] He argues that it would be impossible to construct a map from the text, but, considered as a mnemonic device, the poem would be useful for students, and it was, in fact, used in the schools for centuries afterwards. It was doubtless with education in mind that Priscian translated the poem into Latin.

In considering whether a map is a genuine illustration for a written work, the first problem is the limitation of the codex page. Cotton Tiberius B.V.1 is not a very large manuscript: the world map measures only 21 × 17 cm, compared to, for example, the Hereford Cathedral map which is nearly 60 times that size, l.58 × 1.33 metres. Priscian's poem, running for 34 pages, has many more names than the map could hold. Another problem is that Priscian, a sixth-century Christian grammarian, is here translating into verse (and editing) a second-century Greek account of the world. Inevitably, the poem is vague on parts of northern Europe, better known to our Anglo-Saxon scribe, and on places of Christian significance.[13] So it is difficult to imagine what sort of fidelity of illustration one can expect. McGurk asserts that the map was originally bound several pages later than the poem. He also says, however, that the map and the poem are in the same hand. Therefore, it seems that we ought not to ignore the inscription above the poem, referring us to the 'apt map'. While the map was probably not specifically made to illustrate the poem, a map was chosen as an illustration for it, because both the poem and the map are descriptions of the world, one verbal and one pictorial.

The map is justly famous for its interesting detail, as well as for its early date.[14] The vision of the world spread before us looks surprisingly like a map, compared to the dry little T–O icons seen in many computus manuscripts. The coastlines are wavy, the rivers meander, the seas are sprinkled with islands, and the shape of Great Britain is quite recognizable to a modern map reader. Several places appear for the first time on any known map, including six in the British Isles, though the

5.1. Zonal map. In this map geographical detail is subordinated to structure. The five climatic zones are shown ('articus, aestivus, aequinoctialis, hiemalis, antarticus') with a sketchy but plausible rendition of the inhabited world in the northern temperate zone. This sketch shows the Mediterranean with its islands, the Black Sea, and the Pillars of Hercules, and bears the legends, Aequitania, Asia Major and Minor, and Africa. The two towered buildings probably represent Constantinople and Jerusalem. The inscription in the centre describes how the globe is divided into four great islands with the ocean between, while that around the edge (beginning at the left, 'Hinc refluit oceanus ad septentrionem') explains Macrobius's theory of tides, which was also accepted by Bede. Diameter of map 275 mm. BL Cotton MS Tiberius B.V. 1, fol. 29^r.

Courtesy of the British Library Board.

newest of these is already centuries old – hardly current events. Compared to the Vatican map discussed above, the Anglo-Saxon map has a substantial biblical content, including Noah's ark, nine of the twelve tribes of Israel, the Hebrews' passage through the Red Sea, the lands of the Philistines, Amonites and Moabites, Mount Pisgah (here Fasga), Galilee, Bethlehem, and Jerusalem. Paradise is not shown. Major cities are represented by drawings of fortifications. One of these is London, and another in Ireland is thought to be Armagh. Mountains are coloured green, the Red Sea and the Nile are painted red, and there is a frisky-looking lion in the far north-east. In addition, there are a number of unlabelled provinces, rivers, and islands, leading one to surmise that this map was copied from a larger and more detailed wall map.

The marvels promised by the inscription above the poem are represented on the map by the Cinocephales (dog-heads), *gens Griphorum* (a conflation of griffins and people), Gog and Magog, the burning mountain, and the mountain of gold, the two last located in remote corners of Asia. The lions, monsters from the British point of view, ought perhaps to be included as well.

The zonal map in Cotton Tiberius B.V.1 was originally paired with a celestial map, which was followed by material on the constellations, mostly Cicero's translation of the *Aratea*, with pictures. The preceding text is Aelfric's *De temporibus anni*, which includes some meteorological material, but nothing one could call geographical. The five zones are labelled, and in the northern temperate zone appear two (unnamed) pictures of buildings, clearly meant to indicate cities, and two bulbous columns of Hercules. A rough topography is sketched out with bodies of water and islands. The only names are Africa, Aequitania, and Asia Minor and Major. In the centre band, or equinoctial zone, is a text which rather breathlessly condenses information from Macrobius, Book II.vi.2. 'Here the equinoctial zone begins which is almost entirely washed, both above and below, by the sea, which flows through the middle of the earth as if the whole earth were divided into four islands, being inhabited above in the [summer] solstitial zone and below in the *hiemalis* [winter solstice] zone. Thus it is that the sea runs through the middle and around the edge of the earth and is impassable due to either heat or cold, and the circuit of the entire earth is 252,000 stades.' Around the rim is inscribed a note on the course of the tides from the equator to the poles and back again, each journey being one of 63,000 stades. Elsewhere in the manuscript (fols 51, 54) are several selections from Macrobius on other subjects.

This manuscript, due to its diverse contents, is described in the sub-title of the modern facsimile edition as 'an eleventh-century Anglo-Saxon miscellany'. However, Geoffrey Harlow, the editor of the series, observes, 'To call it a miscellany hardly reflects the deliberately restricted range of interests that it represents: geography, science, history and ecclesiastical materials rub shoulders in its pages.'[15] A number of important connections can be made among the various documents it contains. The two schematic maps, celestial and terrestial, have particular relevance to the computus, as well as to the illustrated catalogue of the constellations. Geography is represented by Priscian's version of 'Periegesis', an extended description of the earth, its places, peoples, and resources. Priscian had not simply translated Dionysius's work, but had edited it, eliminating some of the more obvious references to the pagan gods (such as the invocation to the Muses), and adding colourful extracts from Solinus's *Collecteanea*. These contributed additional monsters, such as the Blemmye (headless folk with eyes in their chests), the Lotus-eaters, and the Amazons. Priscian was also interested in the precious stones to be found in outlying regions – dazzling emeralds, rich amber, crystals which shine like the sun.

The Marvels of the East are also geographical. The text, which originated in accounts of Alexander's eastern journey, is structured as an itinerary, and vestigial details of locations are given. It should be noted that not all the monsters are monstrous, for both Priscian and the author of Marvels include the

5.2. Marvels of the East. Speculations about the strange beasts and humans living in remote parts of the world circulated in many forms in the Middle Ages, most of the information dating back to antiquity. This text was an alleged letter from Pharasmanes to the emperor Hadrian and is put in the context of the journeys of Alexander the Great. The text, in both English and Latin, reads, on the left, 'The donestre live on an island in the Red Sea. They are partly human. They can speak various tongues and can entice men whom they eat up, save for the head, over which they mourn.' And, on the right, 'Men fifteen feet tall and ten feet broad, with big heads, fan-like ears, and bodies as white as milk. On seeing men, they take up their ears and then flee so quickly that they appear to fly.' BL Cotton MS Tiberius B.V. 1, fol. 83ᵛ.

Courtesy of the British Library Board.

Ethiopians, famous for their black skin and their remoteness on the southern edge of the inhabited world. The Ethiopians also appear five times on the map, spaced out along the southern edge. Other Marvels on the map, which are also in this version of the text, are the Cinocephales, the griffins (here all animal), the burning mountain, and the mountain of gold. In this manuscript the Marvels are immediately followed by a frightening picture of the magician Jannes in Hell, being questioned by his brother Mambres.[16] These two were the Egyptian magicians who defied Moses and Aaron in the Book of Exodus and kept producing plagues, but only up to a point: their powers extended so far as frogs but not so far as gnats (Exodus 8.18). They are not named in the Bible, and their story was elaborated in the early Middle Ages. A possible link between them and the Marvels is the great hairy devil stretching out his claws toward the still-living magician. Perhaps the devil is the ultimate monster.[17] At one time this page was followed by Hraban Maur's *De laude crucis*, an attempt to balance hell with heaven.[18]

Sigeric's itinerary from Rome is another geographical feature. As Archbishop of Canterbury, his journey may have been included out of local pride. Several of the Italian cities on his itinerary are pictured, but none of his many stops in France.

Looking at the work as a whole, the maps fit into a group of picture cycles that include the celestial (the constellations), the exotic (the marvels of the East), and the mundane (the labours of the months). In fact, the maps form a kind of bridge between these. In terms of the texts, the maps help illustrate the computus, particularly those on the measurement of the earth, and Priscian's poem. The calendar, with its human labours on the earth, sowing, reaping, hunting, threshing, provides a temporal dimension, as do the successive lists of archbishops, popes and kings. The earth, the subject of the map, is the space in which all this activity takes place.

THE RIPOLL MANUSCRIPT

At the Benedictine monastery of Ripoll in Catalonia the abbot Oliva put together, or ordered to be put together, a large computus book, which was finished in 1056.[19] In the centre of the book are two 532-year cycles of Easter with annals written in, covering the years from AD 532 to 1063 and from 1064 to 1596. The materials surrounding this lengthy chronology are divided into four books: *De sole, De luna, De natura rerum*, and *De astronomia* (about the sun, the moon, the nature of things, and astronomy). The work ends with a calendar and a martyrology, part of which is now missing.[20]

The writer has compiled a great pastiche of the writings of various authors on these subjects. Books I–III consist primarily of skilfully interwoven texts from the two chief works of Isidore and Bede's three works on time and nature, with occasional passages from other authors. Charles Jones notes that the compiler includes fourteen separate selections on leap year and thirteen on the *saltus lunae*, both knotty topics.[21] Sources are identified both in the body of the work and in the tables of contents for each section. Book IV, *De Astronomia*, begins with Bede and Isidore, but then turns to Hyginus for descriptions of the planets and constellations. The last section of this book is from Chalcidius's fourth-century commentary on Plato's *Timaeus*. The materials needed for Paschal calculations are most concentrated in Book II, on the moon, whose cycles demanded the most attention, but computus materials appear throughout, organized under the four topics. It is clear that careful planning went into this highly rational anthology. The vision is of an orderly universe, classified and described to reveal the divine plan.

Like many medieval works, this one purports to be, and largely is, made up of the writings of established authorities. 'Authorship' consisted of selecting and editing the passages, inserting an occasional transitional phrase or clarifying sentence. Only rarely does the author appear self-consciously, as on fol.131ᵛ. where he adds a line to introduce the wind diagram, following a selection from Isidore.[22]

The work is illustrated with scientific diagrams and with paintings of the personified constellations and planets, accompanying descriptive passages from Isidore, Hyginus, Fulgentius, and Aratus, interspersed with more analytic selections from Macrobius. The editor has copied the drawings and their classical style from the *Aratea*,[23] but has chosen other texts to go with them. The scientific diagrams are taken from an extensive library, including those of Isidore, Macrobius, Bede (the drawings in *De locis sanctis*), the Carolingian computus, and Chalcidius. With the exception of Chalcidius, the diagrams do not necessarily appear next to the passage for which they were originally made. The author feels quite free to move them around and adapt them to suit other texts. One drawing which may be unique to this manuscript is a *rota* showing the Saracen months (fol.22), and their correspondence with Hebrew, Greek, Roman, Egyptian, and English months.

Among the illustrations are two maps, one a full-page pictorial representation of the heavens (fol.205) in the section *De astronomia* and the other a double-page world map. The celestial map is labelled '*Macrobii Ambrosii de circulis signiferis*' (On the circle of the zodiac by Macrobius Ambrosius) and shows the constellations of the zodiac and other constellations lightly sketched. The planets are represented by five eccentric orbits. The drawing is similar to the Leiden planetary configuration studied by Bruce Eastwood, but it usually accompanies an excerpt from Pliny, II, 63–4. Indeed Macrobius describes the planetary orbits as being concentric.[24]

The world map, which occupies a single bifolium, is of the zonal type. It appears in Book III, *De natura rerum*, following a series of texts which carefully build up to it. Book III begins with the creation of the world and its elements, excluding fire, which is reserved for Book IV, *De astronomia*. Air is discussed first, including clouds, winds, thunder, and rainbows. The scribe moves on to water: the nature of water, the seas, the ocean, why sea water is bitter, the Red Sea, and the Nile. The description of earth begins on fol.141: the position of the earth, its global shape, the caverns within it which cause earthquakes. Leading up to the map, the selections concern the divisions of the earth, and the first passage is from Isidore's last chapter of *De natura rerum*, which describes the three continents and their borders, and gives the estimated size of the earth. Bede's chapter 51 from his *De natura rerum*, covering the same topics, follows. Both these passages are often followed by maps in other manuscripts. The next selection is from Pliny's *Natural History* (II.247–8) and is entitled by our scribe, *De armonica mundi ratione* (the explanation for the harmony of the universe), but the text actually present concerns the size of the earth and its relation to the size of the universe as a whole. The 'harmony' passage in Pliny, relating the distances between the planetary orbits to musical intervals, appears elsewhere in his second book: chapter 84.

The map is next and forms a chapter to itself, labelled *Mappamundi iuxta quorundam discriptione* (World map according to the description of various authors). This is the first use of the term *mappa mundi* to refer to a world map in a codex.[25] A short geographical text surrounds the map and is untitled, but Patrick Gautier Dalché has discovered another manuscript where the same text appears under the heading *Divisio orbis terrarum Theodosiana* (Division of the circle of lands according to Theodosius).[26] The Theodosius in question is the emperor Theodosius II, who ruled from Constantinople, 408–450. A poem which appears in several manuscripts describes him giving an order to have a map made in the year 435.[27] The text in the Ripoll manuscript makes no reference to Theodosius, but plunges right into the text: 'The part of the earth which we call the ecumene is divided into three parts, in that Europe is termed one part, the next Asia, and Libya the third.' What makes this work unique among late antique geographical works – Gautier Dalché dates it to the fifth or sixth century – is that it gives the measure of the circumference of each province. Other works from the ancient world give dimensions, length by breadth, with the exception of islands, which are often described by their circumference, perhaps because they could be sailed around. Where did these figures come from? One theory is that they might have come from a large map, drawn more or less to scale, and the author measured these distances directly on the map. The obvious candidate is the Agrippa map in Rome, because of its fame, its large scale, and its public location. Such a conjecture must remain in doubt due to our ignorance of the form and appearance of the Agrippa map.

The map in the Ripoll manuscript does not repeat the information in the surrounding text, but is not incompatible with it either. Oriented toward the east, the left-hand page contains the inhabited world, while the right-hand page has a number of inscriptions. The circle in which the map is inscribed is thirty cm in diameter and surrounded by red tongues of fire, which perhaps represent the celestial sphere of fire. The outer

5.3. Ripoll map. Compared to most maps in the zonal format, the Ripoll map incorporates a lot of geographical information. Oriented with east at the top, the map shows the northern temperate zone at the left with the three continents, the Mediterranean, Black and Caspian Seas, provincial borders and numerous city symbols, the largest of which is Constantinople. The right side of the map is taken up with inscriptions surrounding a figure of 'Tera'. The surrounding text describes the borders and dimensions of the countries of the world. The four elements of creation are shown: fire in the outside ring, then air in the form of the twelve winds, the ocean, and finally the earth itself. Size of map: 338 mm. in diameter. Vat. Bib. Apos. MS reg. lat. 123, fols 143ᵛ–144ʳ, 1055, or 1056, Spain. Courtesy of the Vatican Library.

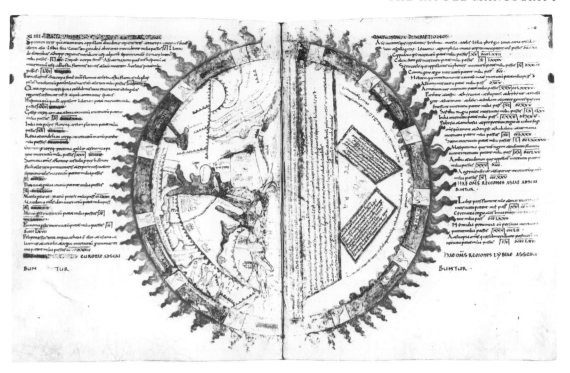

ring is the encircling Ocean (*Oceanus Meridianus*, the element
of water) which is punctuated by winged figures representing
the twelve winds (air). Their names are now almost completely
obliterated. The disc of earth fills the remaining space with its
wavy edges suggestive of shoreline. Thus the drawing of the
map recapitulates the four elements as described in the opening sections of Book III.

The zonal format which the mapmaker has chosen is
explained in a cartouche in the other half of the map in words
taken from Bede in the ninth chapter of *De natura rerum*. It is
supplemented by the Greek names of the zones, which were
probably garnered from Isidore[28], following the pattern of the
rest of the work which continually weaves together the work
of these two men. To the north of the *ecumene* an inscription
explains that this is the northern uninhabitable zone which the
Greeks called the Arctic. The equator is also given an explanatory label: the sun is so close to this region that it burns
Ethiopia with a violent heat and prevents residents of the
northern temperate zone from traveling to the southern temperate zone.

Ninety places are named, including the three continents,
and a selection of provinces, rivers, seas, cities, and mountains. Of all parts of the world Judea is given the most detail

with five cities, the only cities in Asia. In addition, the map shows the Lebanon mountain range, Mount Sinai, the Dead Sea, the Sea of Galilee, the river Jordan, and the route of the Israelites from Egypt.[29] Paradise is not on the map, but the rivers of Paradise are present (the Tigris, Euphrates, Indus, Ganges/Fison) as well as the Crisagoras (Chrysorrhoas), flowing from an unlabelled mountain range, probably Mount Taurus. The southern part of the *ecumene* is damaged, being in the binding of the volume, but the delta of the Nile can be seen in the south-eastern Mediterranean.

Cities, not all of which are named, are represented by sketches of towered buildings. The most imposing is Constantinople, which fact, along with other indications, such as the reference to Theodosius, leads Patrick Gautier Dalché to postulate a Greek source. The cities in Europe, in addition to Constantinople, are the French city of Sens, and in Italy, Ravenna, Benevento, and Rome. Africa contains Alexandria and Carthage.

Mountains, represented by uniform strips of triangles, can be identified with actual mountain ranges – at least Vidier strives to locate them all.[30] Only a few (Lebanon, Mount Caucasus, Mount Sinai) are labelled by the scribe. Other than the rivers mentioned above, the map names five rivers in Europe – the Danube, Seine, Loire, Yonne (the river at Sens), and Po. A number of other rivers are shown but are unlabelled. The Mediterranean/Black Sea complex dominates the centre of the map. The Mediterranean contains six large islands (Sicily, Corsica, Sardinia, Cyprus, Crete, and the Cyclades, shown as one island), plus two cartouches with inscriptions '*Africum pelagus*' (African shore) and '*ad portum Cartaginis stadia II*' (two [thousand?] stades to the port of Carthage). The Adriatic and the Gulf of Corinth are shown as major gulfs. The Caspian Sea is a gulf of the surrounding Ocean.

Provinces are squared off into regular shapes and include fifteen names in Europe, sixteen in Asia, and six in Africa. Descriptive phrases include '*ubi elefanti [nas?]cuntur*' (where elephants come from) in Asia and '*arenosas solitudines que discriminant Etiopiam a Mauritaniis*' (sandy deserts which separate Ethiopia from the Mauritanias).

The Ripoll map, while not exactly like any other map we know, is firmly within the medieval mapping tradition. The zonal type was well-known, and, though usually not so detailed, maps of this style frequently appear, especially in computus manuscripts. Both the Tiberius B.V.1 and the Oxford St John's College manuscript have zonal maps as well as world maps in a different format. What is unusual about the Ripoll map is that its role in the manuscript is so clearly defined. In Book III it is the culmination of the description of the three sublunar elements (air, water, earth), and it is followed by a description of the holy places (fols 145–150ᵛ), places on earth which are sanctified by the presence of God.

The right-hand page, which represents the unknown half of the world, carries a number of inscriptions. In the centre is a small human figure, labelled '*Tera*', holding a serpent in one hand and a cornucopia in the other. The imagery is ancient, but to a Christian it would signify the two aspects of earth, productivity and sin, good and evil. *Tera* is flanked by two boxes, each of which contains eight lines of verse, based on works by Theodulph, bishop of Orléans during the reign of Charlemagne.[31] Theodulph says that he had a representation of the world painted, so that 'you may understand a great thing in a small body' (*rem magnam in parvo corpore*). He refers to the ocean swallowing up the rivers, and earth and water as 'brother enemies', each staying in its proper place. The last two lines of the first poem list the five zones and are taken from another poem by Theodulph, in which he describes the globe held by Geometry, one of the seven liberal arts. In the second poem Theodulph says he has made a table which serves two purposes. One, the table itself, is for the nourishment of the flesh, and the other, the image of the world painted on it, is for the nourishment of the spirit. Contemplating this image, which seems to be a sort of educational place-mat, is a higher form of human activity than mere eating.

It is this verse, with its first-person reference, which led Vidier to attribute the Ripoll map to Theodulph. Although his palace was looted and destroyed by the Normans in the mid-ninth century, not long after his death, Vidier imagines that either a preliminary sketch or a copy of the painted map survived in a manuscript, and was eventually transmitted to Ripoll, a monastery in frequent communication with the houses of western France. However, the lines from Theodulph have been edited by our scribe, with the order and some wording being changed, so that one may conclude that the compiler of the Ripoll manuscript used this text for his own purposes as he did all others in the book. The bow to Theodulph as a son of Spain (he was born in Zaragoza) and as an authority enriches the map. There is no indication that the map comes from any production of his, other than the verse, in a manuscript which takes great pains to identify its sources. The map is specifically titled as based on the works of 'various authors', implying that it is a composite assembled by the writer of the manuscript.

The map is followed by the text of *De locis sanctis*, a brief work on places primarily in the Holy Land, adapted by Bede from the work of Adamnan. A description of the Basilica on Mount Sion is supplemented by a diagram showing the column where Christ was tied for the flagellation, the site of the Last Supper, and the place where the Holy Spirit descended on the disciples.[32] This work brings Book III to an end. Having begun with the Creation of the universe, examined its various parts, and descended from the air through the waters down to the earth, it concludes with those earthly places which were sanctified by a divine presence. The next book (*De astronomia*) moves on to the celestial spheres. The map fits into the total work, both as a graphic depiction of earth, one of the four elements, and as a body subject to measurement, as is time, the main focus of the computus. With its Biblical content and the following work by Bede, it is a witness to the sanctification of even the lowliest element by divine grace.

OXFORD, ST JOHN'S COLLEGE, MS 17

At the Benedictine monastery of Thorney in the fenlands of East Anglia, a large and elegant computus book was finished in 1110, designed to be an ornament of the newly completed church. As with other computus manuscripts, some individual features had attracted scholarly attention in the past, but it did not receive its definitive study as a whole work until Faith Wallis undertook to analyse it in 1985. She proposes that, far from being a random collection or miscellany, it is a rational and highly structured work on the computus and its related areas of knowledge. She calls its organization 'centripetal'; that is, the editors have grouped a number of texts around its computus centre. In her opinion the book was planned as a whole and its execution was a single operation. The pages are still in their original order.[33] The core texts (fol.58ᵛ–156ᵛ) are the three works of Bede (*De natura rerum*,[34] *De temporibus*, and *De temporum ratione*), Helperic's *De computo* from about the year 900, and tracts by Dionysius Exiguus with the Paschal tables. Fore and aft one may find a calendar and martyrology, a cosmographical anthology, works on mathematics and grammar, a set of annals (now moved to British Library Cotton MS Nero C.VII), and materials on medicine. It is the medical material which first attracted scholars.[35] The whole is illustrated by instructive diagrams, including five world maps: two T–O centres of *rotae*, two zonal maps, and one larger, more detailed map. There is also a very interesting and elaborate diagram of the *Annus-Mundus-Homo* variety, known as Byrhtferth's Diagram.

The two T–O maps and the world map appear in the opening section of the manuscript, which Wallis calls 'Miscellany of Computus-Related Materials', fols 3–7ᵛ, followed by 'Computus Texts and Tables', fols 8–15ᵛ.[36] This section contains a number of diagrams and short selections, not explicitly tied together. Here the scholar's imagination is most taxed to discover the editors' purposes. An acrostic poem to St Dunstan by Abbo of Fleury opens this part of the manuscript, followed by riddles, rhymes, horoscopes, alphabets, tables and passages on the degrees of affinity by Isidore, and a parody of Biblical exegesis called Scaena (here Coena) Cypriani or Adso's Nightmare.

Among the diagrams is a T–O centre of a rota showing the times of sunrise and sunset throughout the year (fol.5ᵛ) – the longest day is at the feast of John the Baptist in midsummer, while the shortest is at Christmas, with the equinoxes falling in between. It is the lowest of four *rotae* in a vertical row, the others showing the Easter limits (the earliest and latest dates for Easter) according to the systems of Dionysius, Victorius, and the Irish.[37] The rest of the page is occupied by a table of alphabets, including runic symbols. And, since the monks of Thorney abhorred a vacuum, a riddle is tucked into the remaining corner of the page. This may also be the reason why a T–O is put into the middle of the sunrise/sunset rota. The centres of the other three rotae above it are labelled according to the system being explicated. Wallis suggests that the T–O may be related to the larger world map on the facing page.[38]

The other T–O, a few pages further on (fol.8), is the centre of a tidal rota, of the type developed in the ninth century to illustrate Bede's chapter on the tides. It is neatly balanced at the top of the page by a 'life and death' rota, in Greek, also known as the sphere of Petosiris. Two rectangular tables below are a weekday table for the first of each month and a table showing the moon's position in the zodiac throughout the year. All these items frequently appear in computus manuscripts. None are presented here with accompanying text or even with a title. Either they were purely decorative, or the reader would depend on an oral explanation from a computus adept.

The detailed world map lies between these two on fol.6. Again, there is no introductory or accompanying text and no title. The page is composed with the map above and a weekday table arranged under arches below. It looks like nothing so much as a cathedral rose window with a row of lancets beneath. In this manuscript the artistry of layout seems almost to have subsumed meaning. Around the circle of the map the cardinal directions are (ostentatiously) given in Greek and glossed in Latin: for example, '*Anathole vel oriens vel eoi*', in the east. A note to one side says, '*Maior habet in oriente alexandriam pamphiliam*', a reference to Asia Major at the top

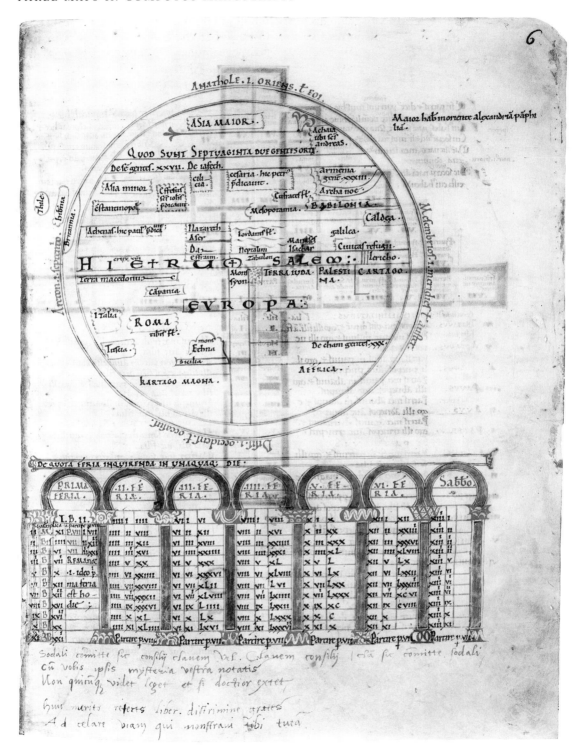

5.4. World map. A highly abstract presentation of a world map, this drawing from a massive computus manuscript is a hybrid between a chart and a diagram. East is at the top and Asia in the top half of the circle, with Europe in the centre and Africa in the lower-right-hand corner. The central diameter is labelled 'Hierusalem', and the centre of the world marked with a cross. Note Britannia, Hibernia and Thule floating in the left margin. Diameter of map 170 mm. MS 17, fol. 6ʳ, 1110, Abbey of Thorney, England.

Courtesy of St John's College Library, Oxford.

of the map.[40] The whole is laid out with impressive regularity. It looks like a T–O map, but the continents are not in their usual places and the centre bar, usually occupied by the Nile/Black Sea axis, is labelled 'Hierusalem' in large letters with a cross in the centre and an explanatory note *crux xpi* or cross of Christ. Below the cross is Mons Syon. The vertical bar, usually the Mediterranean, is also unlabelled. In fact, the only bodies of water to be named on this map are the rivers Jordan, Euphrates, and Tiber.

The continents are arranged with Asia at the top, Europe apparently in the centre and Africa in the south-west corner. Most puzzling is that the label for Europe crosses what would normally be the Mediterranean. Another oddity is that Achaia, 'where St Andrew [preached]' is in south-east Asia, far from Athens, the preaching site of Paul. Of the sons of Noah, Shem is found in Asia and Ham in Africa, as usual, but Japheth stands next to Shem in Asia, instead of in Europe. This placement could reflect the scribe's loyalty to the Biblical text, 'May God make space for Japhet, and let him live in the tents of Shem.' (Genesis 9.7)

The numbers of people in the world are announced as seventy-two ('*Quod sunt septuaginta due gentes orte*') but the total adds up to ninety: Shem, twenty-seven; Ham, thirty; and Armenia, thirty-three. The peoples descending from Japheth are not named. These are the usual numbers for the descendants of Shem and Ham, but the source of the numbers for Armenia and why this country is singled out are not clear.[41]

The map is dedicated almost entirely to places of significance in the Bible. The division of the earth among the sons of Noah, Noah's ark, seven of the twelve tribal territories of the land of Israel, Jericho, and the city of refuge (Joshua 20)[42] for those guilty of involuntary manslaughter under Hebrew law, all come from Jewish history. Paradise is not shown. The life of Christ is illustrated by the river Jordan, Galilee, Nazareth, and Jerusalem. Athens, Ephesus, Achaia, and Caesarea are mentioned specifically as sites where the apostles preached. The only places without a biblical link of some kind are in Italy (Sicily, Mount Etna, Tuscany, Campania), Constantinople, and Britain, Ireland, and Thule. These islands, the only ones represented, break the frame of the map, perhaps as a burst of patriotism on the part of the scribes. They are in the north, but so far east as to be immediately above Constantinople. 'Kartago Magna', which could be Cartagena in Spain as 'Cartago' appears elsewhere on the map, is another non-biblical site.

The peculiar format of the St John's College map may reflect the tables and other diagrams in the computus manuscript, where an artificial order is imposed on time as well as space. Wallis calls it 'a diagram containing a list of places'.[43] Unlike pure 'list maps', such as the verso of the Psalter map, there is some attempt at relative location and geographic verisimilitude in the sketching of Mount Etna, the Jordan river, and the British Isles, but as in the page layout, these qualities have, in general, been sacrificed to order.

A few pages beyond the map in the St John's College manuscript (fol.7[v]) appears a complex and fascinating diagram which is not a map in the usual sense, but reveals much about medieval ideas on the harmonious nature of the universe. It is known as Byrhtferth's diagram, due to the label above it '*Hanc figuram edidit bryhtferð* [sic] *monachus ramesiensis cenobii de concordia mensium aut elementorum*' (Byrhtferth, a monk of the house of Ramsey, produced this drawing of the harmony of the months and the elements). Byrhtferth, who lived about a hundred years earlier at the monastery of Ramsey, not far from Thorney, was a pupil of the computist Abbo of Fleury during his sojourn in England, 985–7. He is best known for his computus manual or *Enchiridion*, which he based largely on Bede and composed partly in Anglo-Saxon.[44] The handbook is chatty and hortatory, as he calls on 'noble clerks' to shake off 'all sloth from their mind and intellect in order that they might be able more excellently to give an account of the epacts in the presence of the reverend bishops'.[45] It sounds rather like a doctoral oral exam. Some mystifying aspects of the handbook have been clarified by Peter Baker's thesis that it was never meant to stand alone, but was the companion volume to a computus manuscript like the St John's College book. Byrhtferth had put into writing what the teacher would normally say in speaking to his students.[46]

The manual contains a number of interesting coloured diagrams showing the correspondence of things. For example, one shows the four Ember fasts, solstices, equinoxes, and the twelve months supported by the four cardinal virtues.[47] The diagram which should correspond to one in the St John's College manuscript is described on fol.12, but the following page on which it originally appeared ('sequens figura'), is mostly torn away.[48]

The St John's College diagram, which is thought by both Wallis and the Singers to be a copy of it, is an unusual shape, a sort of mandorla in a figure-eight, with two diamonds inside. Nearly all other diagrams of the *annus-mundus-homo* type were rotae, though Byrhtferth's original seems to have been rectangular. Wallis calls it a '*majestas Domini*', which it certainly resembles, emphasizing its religious implications.[49] Her interpretation of the form is that the artist has taken a religious rather than a scientific or pedagogical form and filled it with computus content.[50] The diagram is anchored by the four

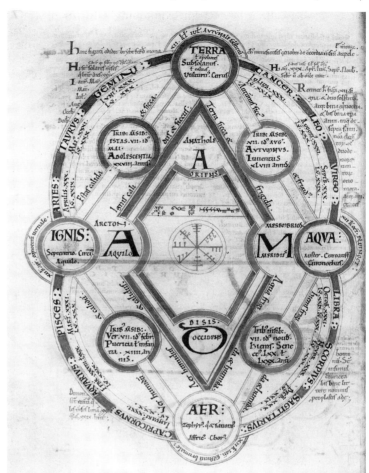

5.5. Byrhtferth's diagram. This diagram shows the harmony of the temporal and spatial elements of the universe, arranged by fours. The diamond in the centre shows the four cardinal directions, with east at the top. Their initial letters in Greek spell out the name of Adam, the first human being. The signs of the zodiac are arranged around the edge and the four elements appear in the large circles, accompanied by the names of the winds. The seasons and ages of man appear in the intermediate circles. MS 17, fol. 7ᵛ, 1110, Abbey of Thorney, England.

Courtesy of St John's College Library, Oxford.

elements (air, fire, earth, and water) and the cardinal directions given in Greek with Latin translations. The Greek names (Anathole, Disis, Arcton, Mesembrios), when recited in this order, as if making the sign of a cross, form an acrostic of the name of 'Adam', the original microcosm of the universe. Around the rim are the signs of the zodiac. Below each sign is the corresponding month and the number of days it has in the solar and lunar calendars. The dates of the equinoxes and solstices appear next to the four elements, each of whose circles also include three of the twelve winds. The lines between describe the qualities of the seasons and the elements, and a medallion in the centre of each line includes the starting date of the season and the appropriate stage in the life of a human being. In the centre are some interesting cryptic symbols, which, as far as I know, have not been satisfactorily deciphered. The letters '*xps et e f st*' have been tentatively translated by the Singers as '*Chr[ist]us et e[cclesia] f[uit] st[abilitas]*' (Christ and the church endure).[51] Like the symbols noted above, this may have had some private meaning for the scribe. Inscriptions around the outside of the drawing explain the phenomena within.

Aside from the stunning overall effect of this diagram, one must note some oddities or possible mistakes in its composition. North is properly linked with the winter solstice, but the element fire which appears here is not the usual association. The zodiac signs on either side are Pisces and Aries, and above Ignis the scribe has written the characteristics of summer and fire as being the same, linking them with the adolescent phase of human development. Indeed in Byrhtferth's own manual he connected winter with old age and the element of water, being cold and moist.[52] One of his surviving diagrams, which includes the zodiac, months, solstices, equinoxes, ages, and cardinal directions, is more logically arranged.[53] Again, the diagram in St John's College looks great, but is weak on meaning. Byrhtferth, had he still been alive, might have complained about having his name associated with it.

Map and diagram together give us some good insights into medieval ideas about time and space. Basically the two elements were congruent, even interchangeable. The winds and the cardinal directions from which they came were transmuted by the perceptive mind into the seasons of the year and even the ages of mankind. The diagram and the map have the cardinal directions in common. In fact the map might be considered a continuation or detail of the more cosmic diagram. It could have taken its place quite logically in the centre, though, given the space available, it would have sacrificed much detail. Thus the places of the earth, with their human historical associations, are part of the master scheme of time and space.

A similarly ordered map, though by no means identical, is found at the end of the almost contemporary Arnstein Bible.[54] Above the map is a chart of the taxonomy of knowledge, all classified under philosophy and divided into four branches: theoretical, practical, logical and mechanical. The world map below, which is untitled and has no accompanying text, shows the inhabited world of the northern temperate zone occupying an unduly large fraction of the sphere on which the other four zones are shown. Place names are divided up by continents, a little more accurately than in the St John's manuscript. The cross-bar of the T has 'Thanais' (Don) and 'Nilus' in it, as well as Tyre-by-the-sea, while in the vertical bar are Gades and Africum mare. Some places are moved out of line to suggest location: the British Isles (Anglia, Scotia, Hybernia, *and* Britannia), Hyspania, and the Athlas and Calpes mountains

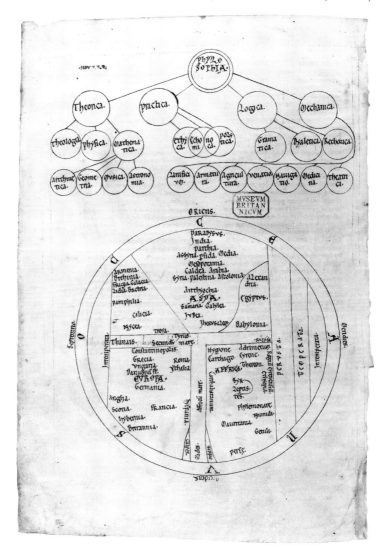

5.6. Arnstein Bible map. Similar to the St John's College map, the map in this German Bible is arranged in an abstract fashion, but it is more geographically accurate and is superimposed on a zonal format. East and Asia are at the top, with Europe to the left and Africa to the right. 'Occeanus' is written in the outer rim. Above the map is a diagram of the structure of knowledge or philosophy, divided into the theoretical, practical, logical and mechanical branches. Diameter of map 270 mm. BL MS Harl. 2799, fol. 241ᵛ, twelfth century, Germany.

Courtesy of the British Library Board.

facing each other across the strait. The most graphic representation is the two Sirtes shown surrounding the city of Leptis, though not on the coast. The names in Africa reveal acquaintance with a Sallust map – Catabathmon, the altars of Philemon, and most tellingly 'Perse', the wandering Persians of Hercules's Spanish army.

Despite its location in a Bible, the Arnstein map is not as religious in its content as is the St John's College map. Except for 'Paradysus' in the far east, most of the other names with biblical or Christian links (Samaria, Galilee, Nicea, Hippo) could be on any map. A nod to modernity is 'Francia' instead of the more archaic Gallia, and Babylonia in Egypt (now Cairo) which loomed so large in the crusading medieval imagination.

The Arnstein map is one of a group of interesting black-and-white drawings bound at the back of vol. II of this large and richly illustrated Bible. The page with the map comes first, followed by a page with (1) a zone map, showing the three continents in the northern temperate zone surrounded by the planetary orbits and the signs of the zodiac, (2) an *annus-mundus-homo* diagram including the four elements, seasons, humours and age of man, and (3) a diagram with the positions of the sun in winter and summer. This leaf is bound in the book upside-down. The next page (fol.242^v) has another zone map labelled '*Ortus ventorum sunt conisi phylosophorum*' (the place where the winds are produced according to the philosophers) and four drawings showing the progress of lunar and solar eclipses. On the last page (fol.243) is an array of seventeen of the monstrous races, including two pygmies doing battle, a Sciopod (here Scinopedes), a Cyclops, a dog-head, and others.[55] Brief tag-lines seem to be severe abridgements of Marvels of the East. The attentive reader will have recognized all these items as familiar denizens of computus manuscripts. This connection is reinforced by the fact that a set of annals was once part of volume one, and by a 'hand of Bede', which appears on the opening folio of vol. two.[56] The derivation of this wonderful device was Bede's chapter on finger reckoning which opens *De temporum ratione*. The joints of the fingers were labelled with various dates, and the adept should be able to calculate the times of Easter and related holidays through a series of manual gymnastics. Needless to say, Bede did not draw such a hand, but because of his chapter it became firmly associated with his name.

How these diagrams found a home in the Arnstein Bible is not known. Certainly their presence is unusual. Perhaps they were drawn for some other work, a computus book, which was never finished. It is interesting that they were thought to be religious enough to be bound with a Bible.

The zonal maps in the St John's College manuscript remain to be described. They are almost identical, showing a view from the North Pole looking south. The five zones are identified in terms of their climate and habilitability. The only geographical feature is the mythical Riphean mountains. The first zonal map appears on fol.40 accompanying chapter XXXIV, '*De Quinque Circulis Mundi*', from Bede's *De temporum ratione*. Here Bede specifically links space and time, saying, 'In order to talk reasonably about time, we must frequently remember the circles or zones, whether equinoctial, summer solstitial or winter solstitial.' This section of Bede is not from the complete copy of the work which appears later in the manuscript, but is excerpted as part of a short section Wallis terms the cosmographical anthology. In addition to Bede, Pliny and Isidore are represented here. The diagram appears again on fol.87^v, accompanying the same chapter of Bede in the complete text of *De temporum ratione*. Its double appearance shows the tendency of diagrams to stick to their texts in their peregrinations.

The St John's College manuscript contains, then, world maps in three formats: T–O, zonal, and a highly structured version with many place-names and religious references. This variety shows that the world could be viewed differently according to one's purpose. The T–O was simply a shorthand way of indicating the earth as the centre of lunar, solar, or other celestial phenomena. The zonal map illustrated a global world view with its reflection of the heavenly zones and the observation of the movements of the sun. The more detailed version here is a historical/religious picture of the inhabited or known world, presenting the history and divisions of the human race in a cosmic context.

CONCLUSION

The maps which appear in these three highly developed computus manuscripts show an interesting variety. The contents of the manuscripts themselves are not the same. Each editor/scribe chose different aspects of the computus to surround the core Easter tables and calendar. Astronomy, medicine, grammar, law, sacred history, geography, and genealogy radiate around some of the central computus texts, such as the works of Bede and Isidore. The use of diagrams in computus manuscripts seems to lead naturally to other pictorial representations, and our editors chose from a variety of sources, assembling great picture albums of natural phenomena. Some of the works which normally made up computus manuscripts carried their diagrams with them, and the copyists had a number from which to choose. Sometimes these went with the texts in question, but sometimes an intelligent editor, such as the scribe of Ripoll, carefully selected his diagrams and established his own context for them.

In the more narrow context of the writings immediately surrounding each map, we see sharp differences. The Ripoll manuscript frames the map with a geographical text which emphasizes numbers and measurement, following a series of texts on the same theme from Bede, Isidore, and Pliny. The Cotton Tiberius manuscript chooses one map to illustrate Priscian's geographical poem, while the other, zonal, map is paired with a celestial map, which leads immediately into the work on the constellations, the *Aratea*. The St John's College map is untitled and unexplained in a section of assorted diagrams whose relation to the computus required an oral explanation, almost like a set of transparencies that come with a textbook. We are left to infer the connection by examining other diagrams and written works in the collection.

And what is the connection? Time and space are inseparable coordinates of our world. They were created together and will end together at the Last Judgement. For the present they form the controlling limits of human life: the sky above, the earth beneath our feet, the birth and death of a single human being, the beginning and end of human history. The computus attempted to depict as a whole the marvellous, meaningful handiwork of an intelligent and beneficent God.

Maps in Medieval Histories

The study of history had no formal place in the medieval school curriculum and existed not as a separate discipline, but only as a branch of rhetoric. As a result, historical accounts tend to appear in surprising places, such as works of biblical exegesis, computus, encyclopedias, and treatises on the 'nature of things', as well as in separate books designated as histories. In these diverse works the historical accounts played a supporting role, reinforcing medieval ideas about the design of the universe and God's moral purposes.

Chronology was an obsession of the medieval historian, perhaps because it was so difficult to determine. The classical historians who had gone before were relatively indifferent to the problem – certainly a common dating system had never been worked out for the ancient world. The great Thucydides is reduced to statements like this, 'In the fifteenth year [of the truce], the forty-eighth year of the priestess-ship of Chrysis at Argos, the year when Aenesias was ephor at Sparta, and two months before the end of the archonship of Pythodorus at Athens, six months after the battle of Potidaea, just at the beginning of the spring. . . .' The event he is trying to date is the outbreak of the war which is his main subject.[1] Even today major questions of dating revolve around important events of antiquity. Eusebius in his *Chronological Tables* made a heroic effort to pull the chronology of various ancient civilizations together, and his work, translated into Latin by St Jerome in 380, formed a groundwork for medieval history.[2] The establishment of an era in the eighth century by Bede, who dated all events before and after the birth of Christ, was a key development, and within this structure we see medieval chroniclers making noble efforts to get the numbers right.[3]

One type of medieval history, the annal, evolved out of calendar-keeping and the computus. In its simplest form it was part of an Easter table, which had columns for the year, the indiction, the epact, the concurrent, the lunar cycle, the Easter limit and the moon's age on Easter. The scribe, writing in a separate column, in the margin or between the lines, recorded significant deaths, dedications of churches, translations of relics, unusual meteorological and astronomical events, wars, and invasions.[4] Since the great Paschal cycle extended for 532 years, historical notes had to be garnered from earlier sources and their collection extended over generations. It is not unusual to find a manuscript like Vatican Library, MS reg.lat.123 (the Ripoll manuscript), which was compiled in 1055, containing notes up through the year 1542.[5] The connection between Easter reckoning and historical record-keeping was further reinforced by Bede, in *De temporum ratione*, his great work on the computus, which ended with a description of the six ages, including an expanded chronicle from the Creation to his own time, and concluding with speculations on the last age and the end of the world. Scribes copying his work were often moved to extend the record to their own day and add details of local events.

The annals were used as source material for a more ambitious form, the chronicle. This work might still use the year-by-year format, but expand the information into paragraphs and pages for each year, instead of being confined to a column in a table. It is useful to distinguish the shorthand (the annal) from the longer form (the chronicle). The former is generally the raw material for the latter, though occasionally a wordy chronicle might be condensed into the shorter form. The great Anglo-Saxon chronicles betray their annalistic origin in their retention of the organization by years.[6]

Monks were the usual chroniclers, as they were the calendar keepers. In fact Galbraith suggests that we think of 'history in the Middle Ages as an occasional by-product of monasticism, written by men striving against the oblivion of time to preserve kinship and continuity with the great, almost mythical days of imperial Rome and the Caesars'.[7] Not all monasteries kept chronicles, but it was considered a normal thing to do, and some monasteries, such as St Alban's, became particularly famous for their lengthy and interesting histories. These chronicles were passed around, copied, and edited, creating a confusing tangle for scholars who try to trace them to their origins.

Another type of history, the philosophical history, took a larger view. Beginning with the Creation and ending with the Last Judgement, an author like Otto of Freising (d. 1158), a German bishop with royal connections, put the events of world history into a sweeping theological context. This type of history was more rarely written, but, as the more ambitious chronicles went back to Adam, the two types could become almost indistinguishable from one another.

Several frameworks were available for the medieval historian to give meaning to the miscellaneous events of history. The most authoritative was the six ages of history, popularized by Augustine and Bede. The ages were divided as follows:

First age: Adam to Noah
Second: Noah to Abraham
Third: Abraham to David
Fourth: David to the Babylonian captivity
Fifth: Babylonian captivity to the birth of Christ
Sixth: From the birth of Christ to the present[8]

In each of these stages Bede compares the development of the people of God to the growth of a human being. The first age, infancy, is the pre-history of the human race, for 'who can recall his babyhood?' In the second age (childhood), man learns to speak, and the Hebrew language develops. In the third age (adolescence) the human being matures enough to produce children. This is the age of Abraham, father of the generations given in the Book of Matthew. The fourth age (adulthood) is the age of kings, and the period in which a person would take on the adult responsibilities of governance. In the fifth age (old age), as the body begins to be weary with age, the Hebrew people are broken apart by a succession of evils. The last or present age (decrepitude) is consumed with the death of the whole world.

There was general agreement on the framework of the six ages, though they were sometimes divided slightly differently. In some versions the third age extended from Abraham to Moses, instead of to David's rule. The number of years in each varied according to the translation of the Bible one was using, as they were derived from the number of generations that had elapsed in each period. Eusebius had estimated that the creation of Adam took place 5198 years before the birth of Christ, in contrast to an estimate of 5500 years made by Sextus Julius Africanus (*c.* 220 AD). When Bede came along, he recalculated the period, arriving at 3952 years.[9] While this introduced some confusion, the question was relatively academic, as the beginning point for modern dates was the incarnation rather than the Annus Mundi.

An account of the six ages of history appears in many computus manuscripts, along with other documents on the measuring of time. The biggest problem with this format was that the sixth age was getting longer and longer and cried out for subdivision. Each author seems to have been convinced that he was living at the very end of the sixth age, judging by the numerous signs of the corruption and wickedness of humanity. Clearly the human race could not last much longer in this age of decrepitude. But like a tiresome old wealthy invalid with all his greedy relations hovering around his deathbed, he lingered, and there was a lot of ground to cover from the birth of Christ to the ever-advancing present.

Another way of organizing history was the progression of

Age	Metal	Age of Man	Body part	History	Hour of day
first	gold	infancy	head	Adam to Noah	first
second	silver	childhood	chest	to Abraham	third
third	bronze	adoles-cence	belly	to David	sixth
fourth	iron	youth	thighs	to Baby-lonian captivity	ninth
fifth	lead	old Age	lower legs	to birth of Christ	tenth
sixth	clay	decrepi-tude	feet	to Last Judgement	eleventh

Table 2. The Ages of the World

the four empires, suggested in the book of Daniel. Daniel's account was prophetic and necessarily vague, but a common interpretation was that the empires intended were, first, the Babylonian; second, the Median/Persian; third, the Greek/Macedonian; and fourth, the Roman. The succession of empires was modified from time to time to accommodate historical developments. In the early medieval period the big question was whether the empire of Charlemagne and his successors could be considered a continuation of the Roman Empire, which was supposed to endure until the Last Day. When things were going well, as under Charlemagne and Otto the Great, the continuation theory re-appeared. When matters were in chaos, chroniclers tended to despair.

In the twelfth century Lambert of St Omer tried to combine these two systems, by using the metallic symbols from the empires, in a glorious symphony of analogies, as shown in Table 2. Lambert represented all this with the aid of an *arbor allegorica*, a dreaming Nebuchanezzar, and the crowned statue cutting down the tree.[10] For Lambert, Asia was the home of history up until the birth of Christ, when the action moved to Rome and eventually to the kingdom of the Franks. Landmarks of the six ages are frequently featured on medieval maps, including Paradise, Mount Ararat in Armenia (where Noah landed), the tower of Babel, Chaldea (homeland of Abraham), Jerusalem, and Babylon.

The importance of geography to history had been established in the classical era. Sallust, who was much admired in the Middle Ages, had written a history firmly based in a geographical setting. Orosius had begun his history with a lengthy chapter describing the entire world. Some later historians, such as Ranulf Higden, copied this approach, but others, like

Otto of Freising, after a brief description of the three continents, suggested that the reader consult Orosius if he or she wished to know more.[11] Other historians might emphasize the influence of geography, especially climate, on historical events.[12]

An interest in geography did not necessarily produce a map. In fact a thoroughgoing geographical introduction might lead an author to believe that he might dispense with a map entirely. Anna-Dorothee von den Brincken, in her seminal article on maps and world histories, thought that the general philosophical histories were more likely to be accompanied by maps,[13] a reflection of the philosophical quality of the medieval world map. However, the examples below show that maps appeared in a variety of types of historical accounts. Due to either the accidents of survival or the failure to produce a map in the first place, maps are rare in medieval histories, even the most geographically inclined.

I have chosen several historical works accompanied by maps to show how maps were used. As a criterion for selection, I have chosen only those works in which the map appears in the autograph version (if it still exists), or was specified by the author, or in which more than one copy of the work contains a map. The works chosen include an epic poem (Gautier de Châtillon, *Alexandreis*), two encyclopedias (Lambert of St Omer and Honorius Augustodunensis), a historical and geographical miscellany (Guido of Pisa), a chronicle (Matthew Paris), and a universal history (Ranulf Higden) as samples of the kinds of works for which maps were thought to be appropriate illustrations. Much more research needs to be done in this area to flesh out our understanding. In particular, it would be useful if historians paid more attention to illustrations. Many admirable studies of manuscripts do not mention the maps they can be found to contain, much less study them. On the other hand, map historians tend to look at the map alone and spend little time on the pages fore and aft. Maps in books seldom stand alone, but need their accompanying material to explain their content. The reverse is also true.

Medieval maps in books are often divorced from their context by scholars who deny that this particular map is a genuine illustration for the text it accompanies. Certainly one may have an ideal of what an illustration should be, but this view may not have been shared by the compiler of the book.[14] The implication is that maps wander into manuscripts virtually on their own, or are selected by some later (mindless) bookbinder. To be sure, this can happen, but when a map is called for by the text and one appears in the manuscript, one can assume that an illustration was intended. The problem is usually that the nomenclature of the map, and sometimes even the

form, are not identical to that of the text. At what point –
50 per cent of the names, 80 per cent – does a map cease to
be a map-in-general and become a map-as-illustration? In
the works discussed below, the connection between work
and map is close, i.e., these are geographical/historical texts
whose need for a map seems justified. The correspondence
between form and content of map and text will be considered
for each work.

GAUTIER DE CHÂTILLON

> Above [the tomb of Darius] was erected . . . a concave
> dome, finely balanced, more transparent than glass,
> clearer than a still stream, similar to crystal or to the
> revolving sky.
>
> Upon it was beautifully traced the outline of the tri-
> partite world. Here Asia's domain extended over a wide
> area, there the twin sisters squatted with their smaller
> space. Here, marked by unmistakable signs, were places,
> rivers, peoples, cities, forests, regions, towns, mountains,
> and every island that is bounded by the fitful sea. Shown
> too were things a country lacked or possessed in abun-
> dance. Libya was fruitful; Ammon, close to the Syrtes,
> begged for rain; the Nile enriched Egypt, and ivory
> enriched India, whose shores were clothed in gems;
> Africa showed forth mighty Carthage's citadel, Greece
> divine Athens of immortal fame; Pallas' house prided
> itself on the growing Rome, Spain on Herculean Cadiz;
> the Sabaeans took pride in their frankincense, France in
> its soldiers, Campania in its celebrated wine, the Britons
> in their Arthur, and Normandy in its usual haughtiness;
> England flattered, love of gain consumed the Ligurians,
> and the Germans retained their customary fury.
>
> The glassy ocean encircled the outer edges of this
> large dome, and the sea, acting as a barrier in the middle,
> divided Asia from the territory of the other two conti-
> nents – the sea, to which all meandering rivers with their
> twisting banks descend and, following its lead, turn in
> winding curves and slip into the mighty ocean. And
> because Daniel's meaning did not escape Apelles, he
> engraved on the gilded marble the following inscription:
> 'Here is placed the figurative ram, whose two horns
> Alexander, the whole world's hammer, crushed.' In addi-
> tion, following the Jews and their writings and retracing
> the course of history, Apelles marked thereon the years
> of the human race from its creation right up to the war-
> like times of the triumphant Alexander. In all, one could

read four thousand, eight hundred and sixty-eight years.[15]

This elegant twelfth-century description of a world map is an imaginative reconstruction of the tomb of Darius, the Persian king defeated by Alexander, a tomb which would seem more appropriate for the world conqueror himself. All the elements of medieval cartography are present: the three continents, the surrounding ocean, the rivers leading to the seas, the mountains and other geographical features ('marked by unmistakable signs'), as well as the special characteristics of each land – ivory and gems for India, frankincense for Arabia. Prophecy and history are also included, a passage from Daniel being inscribed on the rim or on the map itself, while Carthage, Athens, Cadiz, Rome represent great events of the past. 'The years of the human race from its creation' are also mentioned, though exactly how they are represented our poet does not specify. A narrative relief carving of the entire chronology of the Old Testament had already been made to ornament the tomb of Darius's queen in Book IV. The king's tomb is the ideal medieval map, uniting time and space, history and prophecy, people and places in a glorious, awe-inspiring artistic whole.

The author is Gautier (or Walter) de Châtillon, born in Lille in the second quarter of the twelfth century. A student at Reims, Paris, and Bologna, he became a teacher himself, and eventually found a patron, William, archbishop of Reims (1176–1202) to whom his book, *The Alexandreis*, is dedicated. The work is an epic poem on the conquering career of Alexander the Great, the popular subject of many works of varying quality throughout both the classical period and the Middle Ages. Because of his far-ranging travels (to Jerusalem, to Ethiopia, to the ends of the earth), Alexander left his mark on every medieval map and is inextricably entangled with every work of geography.

Alexander's genuine travels and his conquests, forming one of the four empires predicted in the book of Daniel, were significant enough, but even before he was in his early grave other adventures had become attached to his name, such as his ride in a submarine and his flight through the air. These were retailed in numerous supposed letters, abbreviated accounts, tales, and even comic-book versions for the delectation of medieval junk readers.[16] Monastery libraries nearly all possessed one or more of these Alexander books, and one pictures the monks breathlessly scanning them in stolen moments – was this the kind of reading St Benedict had in mind for them?[17]

The poem is rich in geographical description. In Book I

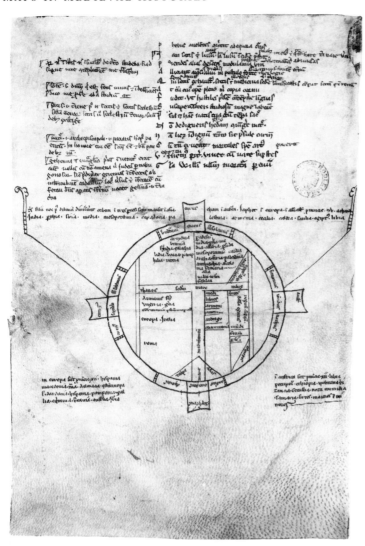

6.1. Gautier de Châtillon world map. The text which surrounds this tiny but detailed T–O map refers to the division of the earth among the sons of Noah, revealing its origin from another work, as Gautier does not mention this event. The 'Medes, Armenians, and Persians' appear in Africa, following Sallust's history. The map is located at the end of the poem and contains 59 geographical names, in addition to the cardinal directions and the twelve winds. Oriented to the east, the areas marked off in the north and south may be the remnant of a zonal map. In short, this is a composite world map, drawn from a variety of sources and here included as relevant to the tale of Alexander, who conquered the world. Diameter of map 70 mm. MS Bod.527, fol. 189ᵛ, English, thirteenth century.

Courtesy of the Bodleian Library, Oxford.

there is an extended account of places in Asia, for which Alexander is embarking. In Book II, in response to the insulting gift from King Darius of a child's ball, perhaps the original of Shakespeare's story in *Henry V*, Alexander fumes, 'The ball's round form well denotes the spherical appearance of the round world which I shall subject to myself' (II, lines 34–44). Elsewhere are described the Sahara desert (Book III), Scythia (Book VIII), and India (Book IX). In the final book the gods take fright that Alexander will explore all the secret places of the earth, including the source of the Nile, the Ocean, and the Antipodes, and even besiege Paradise (X, lines, 82–107).

Death snatches him away just in time.

After the poet's sonorous geographical descriptions, one is disappointed by the maps actually included in the manuscripts of *The Alexandreis*. Destombes lists nine, out of several hundred surviving manuscripts, and most of them are simple T–O constructions with only a few names.[18] One exception is in a manuscript now in Paris. In format it combines the T–O with the zonal model, is oriented with north at the top (though the writing is oriented to the east), and has 50 names and legends. In Africa are found some quotations from a Sallust map: the telltale Medes, Armenians, and Persians, the remnants of Hercules's army. Destombes, who reproduces this map, suggests that the more plentiful names in Asia are drawn from its description in Book I of Gautier's epic. It is probable that a closer search of these manuscripts might find others, but the work itself has value for its excellent description of the supreme medieval map with all its qualities.

LIBER FLORIDUS OF LAMBERT OF ST-OMER

Lambert, a canon of St Omer in Flanders, compiled his *Liber Floridus* over a period of years in the early twelfth century (1112–21), pillaging the chapter library for ancient and medieval texts to copy. His title, 'Flowery Book', refers to his gathering of the best of almost 200 authors, what we might call a 'treasury'.[19] An artist as well as a scribe, Lambert illustrated his book with numerous drawings and diagrams, among them a complete picture cycle of the Book of Revelation, a set of personifications of the constellations, and a detailed world map. His autograph manuscript still survives, and has been described, with all its alterations, marginal notes, and pasted-on additions, as a 'first rough draft', which today 'would probably not be accepted for publication'.[20] Indeed, it was kept at the chapter library of St Omer to be used for making copies, a number of which survive. Six of them are illustrated, as was the original.

In 1906 Léopold Delisle described the work as a totally disorganized, even bizarre, compilation, based on whatever readings Lambert happened upon which struck his fancy, inducing him to copy out excerpts, short or long, and illustrations as well.[21] Subsequent scholars have struggled to find an order in the book, and one, Yves Lefèvre, has suggested that Lambert was striving for a systematic vision of the world, which he kept trying to wrestle into shape, constantly editing, revising, deleting and adding, as he found something new.[22] Clearly he needed a word-processor. His world vision was permeated by Christian theology, from the Creation to the imminence of the

Last Judgement. The wonders of God's creation called forth a bestiary, astronomy, as well as numerous accounts of miracles and marvels. Extracts from geographical works (the *Cosmographia* of Pseudo-Aethicus, Orosius's geographical chapter, many excerpts from Isidore) and a detailed world map provided a setting for these phenomena. Lambert put it all into a historical context, making use of genealogies, a history of popes (the *Liber Pontificalis*), lists of kings, and the annals of his own and near-by monasteries. Historians he liked were Josephus and Hegesippus on the Jewish past, Bede and Nennius for England, the ninth-century bishop Freculphus of Lisieux, Gregory of Tours, as well as Orosius. He also uses his contemporary, Fulcher of Chartres, for an account of the stirring events of the First Crusade and the Christian conquest of Jerusalem in 1099, a sign of the last day. His interest in the coming Judgement, which would occur only when every Jew was converted, led him to include several dialogues on the superiority of Christianity to Judaism, such as Gilbert Crispin's *Disputatio Iudaei et Christiani* (*c.* 1093). Lambert also puts in a calendar and a nineteen-year Easter table, as well as miscellaneous short tracts on various aspects of the computus.[23]

The most recent study of the *Liber Floridus* is by Danielle LeCoq, who centres her study around the world map itself, using it as a focal point for the entire work. Moving back and forth between picture and text, she shows how the two complement one another to bring forth a complete vision of the world, spatial and temporal, physical and spiritual.[24]

Lambert drew not just one world map to illustrate his book, but ten different cartographic representations, ranging from a T–O at the centre of a wind diagram to a fully developed world map.[25] His ten maps are as follows:

1. Spera triplicata gentium mundi. A list map in T–O format, giving the names of peoples of the three continents. Text from Pseudo-Aethicus, *Cosmography*.[26]

2. Ordo ventorum XII et natura ipsorum. Wind diagram with T–O centre.

3. Globus terrae. A zonal map, surrounded by the orbits of the seven planets and the zodiac. The inhabited world has more than a dozen names.[27]

4. Spera Macrobii. A zone diagram showing the ecliptic. No geographical names.[28]

5. Sfera geometrica. This is his big map, with 140 legends. It is presented in zonal format, with a greatly enlarged northern temperate zone.[29]

6. Octavianus Augustus. A painting of the emperor holding a sword in his right hand and a T–O globe in his left. The surrounding inscription refers to Augustus's survey and mapping of the world.

7. Rota, untitled, with the lunar phases surrounding a zonal map.

8. Circuli cursus orb. VII planetarum. T–O map surrounded by the seven planetary orbits.

9. Ordo VII planetarum et spera celi et terrrae secundum Macrobium. Christ in glory presiding over another rota of planetary orbits with a T–O centre. Some constellations in addition to the zodiac are graphically depicted. In the outermost rim are noted the presence of cherubim, archangels, and other celestial beings.[30] In some manuscripts this is immediately followed by another depiction of the seven planetary spheres with a zonal map in the centre.

10. Europa mundi pars quarta. Map of Europe shown as a quarter circle, as it would be on the larger world map. This appears only in the Ghent manuscript.[31]

In characterizing these maps, it is interesting to note how frequently the zonal format is used. We have already seen a peculiar tendency of maps used for biblical commentary to employ a zonal form (compare the Arnstein Bible, and Oxford, St John's College).

In addition to the cartographic diagrams, there are many other rotae and astronomical diagrams, most of which would not be out of place in a computus manuscript. Here one may find a sphere of Apuleius (the life and death divination rota, sometimes ascribed to Pythagoras or Petosiris), a circular diagram of the Labyrinth of Crete, rotae of the courses of the sun and moon, a rota of interlaced circles showing the twelve months in relation to the seasons, elements and qualities (heat, cold, etc.), and a sphere showing the six days of Creation and the ages of man. The Paris manuscript also contains a circular plan of the city of Jerusalem.[32]

It is difficult to talk about the specific context of each of Lambert's maps as they are placed differently in the different manuscripts, and the autograph edition was repeatedly reassembled during its period of composition. The large world map itself was apparently moved three times.[33] One must look at the manuscript as a whole, including the text. In general, one may say that Lambert places the world in both its cosmological and its historical context. The T–Os and the simpler zonal maps illustrate the earth within the cosmos, while the larger world map, the map of the world's peoples, and the map of Europe serve to illuminate the course of human history.

De Smet suggests that the guiding principle of Lambert's historical consciousness is the six ages of the human race, with its numerous connections and analogies.[34] The six days of Creation, seen as the key to the ensuing history of the world, tie these two together, and the book contains materials on

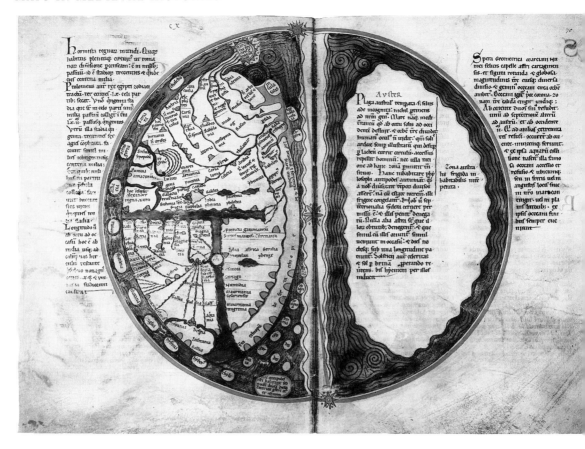

each of the created elements – the sun, moon, firmament, stars, and earth, with its people, plants, and animals. Lambert recurs to the six ages again and again, noting every historical event in terms of its appropriate age.[35] For example, in a miniature of King Solomon, he notes that he lived in the fourth age. De Smet notes also what Lambert does not include: unlike numerous other medieval encyclopedias or miscellanies, he has nothing on grammar, rhetoric or dialectic. His interests run to history, religious and secular, cosmology, and analogies.

The classical form and content of the most detailed world map in the *Liber Floridus* was noted by Konrad Miller,[36] who hypothesized that Lambert must have copied a map from some ancient source. This thesis was picked up by Richard Uhden, who studied the map in 1936, concluding that it was a copy of a map from the work of Martianus Capella,[37] which is exactly what Lambert says in the text on the right of the map: 'Spera geometrica marciani numei felicis capelle affri cartagi-

6.2. Lambert of St Omer, world map from the *Liber Floridus*. Lambert has drawn a detailed world map in a zonal format. East is at the top with Paradise a small sunburst to the left of top centre, with the rivers (Tigris, Euphrates, Nile, Ganges) flowing from it into Asia. The island just to the lower left of centre is the Antipodes. The two land masses shown are divided by the ocean crossed by the solar ecliptic. On the right a text describes the 'temperate southern continent, unknown to the sons of Adam'. Diameter of map 392 mm. Cod. Guelf.I.Gud.Lat., fols 69ᵛ–70ʳ, c.1180.

Courtesy of the Herzog August Bibliothek, Wolfenbüttel.

nensis et figura rotunda et globosa magnitudinis terrae eiusque diversa divisio et geminus occeani circa orbem ambitos. '[The geometric sphere of Martianus Felix Capella, of Carthage in Africa, and a round and global figure of the extent of the earth with its various divisions and the double band of the ocean which surrounds the world].[38] This fifth-century author had written a book on the seven liberal arts, *On the Marriage of Philology and Mercury*, which was widely distributed in the Middle Ages and in Book VI, on geometry, gave a complete description of the earth, with a wealth of geographical place names.[39]

Uhden's evidence for the antique paternity of the map, other than Lambert's attribution, included the use of the term 'sphaera' for the map, a term rarely used after late Antiquity. He noted also the zonal format, which came into the west from the Greek geographers and was less common as an organizing principle than the T-O. Looking at place names he observed that 82 per cent (105) were of antique origin, 57 per cent (73) being identical with names in Martianus' text, while only 17 (13 per cent) were later than the fifth century. No map has ever been found in any copy of Martianus's work, perhaps because he seems to be describing a three-dimensional globe, but Uhden was undaunted by this point. He observed that many ancient and medieval geographical works, which surely had maps in their original state, no longer have them.[40] Uhden noted also the preponderance of antique names, but this is the rule rather than the exception among medieval maps, particularly when their purpose is historical exposition.

While biblical names (as opposed to classical names) are few on the map, counting the names alone, as Uhden does (seven, or five per cent), is a little misleading, for other clearly scriptural conformations appear on the map without labels. For example, the four rivers are shown streaming from Paradise. They are not named on the map, but they are discussed elsewhere in the manuscript. The Jordan River, with its double source in the mountains of Lebanon, flowing through the Sea of Galilee to the Dead Sea, is also plainly visible. In addition there are biblical names (Judaea, Galilea, Philistea, Palestina, Ydumea) used by Martianus, who was not a Christian, but not in the context of the Bible.

The biblical names Lambert has chosen to use are significant ones. He shows Paradise as an island in the far East with Enoch and Elijah, both of whom were believed in the Middle Ages to have been translated to Paradise without the painful expedient of dying.[41] He also gives us 'Moab, Og, Basan' to the east of the Holy Land. The text from which these names come (Deut. 1.4–5) describes the position of the Israelites in the fortieth year of their wanderings, about to enter the

Promised Land. They had recently defeated King Og of Bashan, and were at the time in the land of Moab. This rather obscure Biblical reference represents an important transition in world history. Elsewhere, in the far northeast, are the thirty-two[42] savage nations confined to an enclosure, a detail of Alexander's history not found in Martianus's work. These are identified with Gog and Magog, mentioned by both Ezekiel and the Book of Revelation, and in the Middle Ages their confinement was attributed to Alexander the Great. Their eventual emergence, with attendant atrocities, would be one of the signs of the approaching end of the world. Throughout the work Lambert makes repeated references to this event. He believes that the success of the First Crusade in placing a Christian king on the throne of Jerusalem is a clear sign that the Day of Judgement cannot be far off.

The fourth or southern continent appears on the right-hand side of his map, covered with a lengthy descriptive text from Martianus Capella. In addition, Lambert puts a small island in the far west, which he calls the Antipodes, observing that the inhabitants here have night when we have day and vice versa.[43] Several suggestions have been made concerning this feature. Could it be an indication of the Norse discovery of Vinland? Returning to Martianus Capella from which he draws his abbreviated inscription, Lambert seems to be trying to indicate a body of land on the opposite side of the world. The problems of representing a sphere on a flat piece of paper has ever bedevilled mapmakers. Lambert's solution – to stick it in the margin of his map, like Alaska and Hawaii on a map of the USA – is as sensible as any. His reference to days and nights and seasons can refer only to a continent in the southern half of the western hemisphere.

The historical content of Lambert's map has been brilliantly analysed by Danielle LeCoq. Asia, she says, represents the past, the rich golden age of mankind, but also the future, as Enoch and Elijah are waiting in the earthly Paradise for the last day. Europe is the scene of present events, but signs of its past are included. In Lambert's own area, Flanders, the modern name is put alongside the 'Morini', the tribe which settled there in Roman times.[44] Italy is labelled as 'Magna Graecia' as well as Italia. The Island of 'Scanzia' or Scandia is shown as the origin of the Gothic peoples. Africa below the familiar northern coast is a land of deserts, 'full of dragons, serpents, and cruel beasts'. Its cursed inheritance from Ham is compounded by its current occupation by the children of Ishmael.[45]

Names on the main map are largely of provinces, with only a few mountains, rivers, or cities included, while peoples of the world are presented in the list map. The map of Europe follows the format of the world map, providing more detail and including the islands of the Mediterranean (only Sicily is on the world map). Altogether this map has 82 names in Europe as opposed to 48 on the larger map. The maps provide a framework for the numerous historical events described in the texts which make up the historical parts of the book. One of Lambert's favourite historical characters was Alexander the Great, whose short-lived empire was a precursor of Rome's more lasting achievement. He copies out a good part of Julius Valerius's *Epitome* of Alexander's history, as well as the supposed letter to Aristotle. Danielle LeCoq describes Alexander as a typological Christ figure for Lambert – a unifier of the physical world, compared to Christ's unification of the spiritual world.[46] Other parallel features are his godlike appearance, his father's addressing him as 'Lord of the whole world', his reputed visit to Jerusalem where he made a sacrifice in the temple, and his early death (aged thirty-two).[47] The map shows Macedonia, the savage tribes immured in the far north, and various places visited and sights seen by Alexander, including the oracle trees of the sun and moon located at the ends of the earth in Asia.[48]

The historical content of Lambert's maps is thus fully understood only when one looks at the written portions of the manuscript. Some expand on the subject of place, with lists and descriptions of places, while others fill in the historical narrative which gives meaning to the bare schema of the maps. Thus, while he may have copied the main outline of his map from Martianus, the context as well as his additions definitely Christianize his map. Hovering over all is the expectation of the Last Judgement with its attendant events. Looked at in conjunction with his astronomical diagrams, one can arrive at a rich and complex picture of the world, as the lowest body in the cosmos, but, as the home of change and decay, surely the most exciting.

THE IMAGO MUNDI OF HONORIUS AUGUSTODUNENSIS

An almost exact contemporary of Lambert, Honorius Augustodunensis (fl. 1098–1156), composed his *Imago Mundi* as a digest of knowledge, designed for isolated communities of monks without access to large libraries. His work, part of a prodigious literary output, also became popular among the increasingly numerous educated nobility of the twelfth century, and hundreds of manuscript copies survive.

The identity of Honorius is a mystery which has been energetically probed by scholars. 'Augustodunensis', originally

translated as 'of Autun', then as 'of Augsburg', is now completely uncertain. The most probable hypothesis is that
Honorius was a nobleman, either German or Irish, originally
named Henry, who abandoned a career as a secular cleric for
the Order of St Benedict, changing his name to Honorius. He
travelled in the course of his life to England, spending some
time in Canterbury, but is most associated with Regensburg
(Ratisbon, in Germany), where he died a *solitarius* or hermit
in 1156.[49]

Most of the manuscripts of *Imago Mundi* identify the
author as Honorius, but between the table of contents and the
text in the Cambridge manuscript (which contains the map
under study here) is a note: 'This Henry who compiled this
book was a canon of the church of St Mary of the city of
Mainz.' This note, which may refer to Honorius in his previous life before his conversion,[50] has led to the identification of
the map as being by 'Henry of Mainz'. As an added wrinkle,
several manuscripts contain a dedication 'from Henry to
Henry'. The identity of this additional Henry has been the
subject of much conjecture, Henries being rather thick on the
ground in those days. Flint surveys the various possibilities
and concludes that the strongest case can be made for Henry,
Archdeacon of Huntingdon, who wrote a history of his own,
the *Historia Anglorum*. Indeed Destombes's catalogue attrib-
utes two of Honorius's manuscripts with maps to him.[51]

Honorius introduces the *Imago Mundi* by saying 'This little
book has the title, image of the world, because one might see
in it the description of the whole world as if in a mirror.' He
goes on to say that his work is totally based on ancient
authorities, a guarantee of quality in the Middle Ages.[52] His
modern editor notes that the strongly conservative nature of
the book must have been reassuring in a time of change and
novel ideas, such as the twelfth century. Unlike Lambert,
Honorius does not assemble a huge scrapbook of snippets of
text, but welds the numerous sources he had consulted into a
continuous and coherent work of his own. Instead of a world
bursting at the seams with marvels, proverbs, stories and
poems, Honorius's world is strictly disciplined and subdued in
the service of a greater world order.[53]

Imago Mundi is basically a *De natura rerum*, divided into
three books. They are not titled, but their subject matter is, in
Book I, a description of the universe, beginning with the earth
and its waters, and ascending through the realms of air and
fire (a reversal of Isidore's order in *De natura rerum*); Book II,
on time, including the computus; Book III, on history, a concise narrative uniting biblical events with those of other civilizations, within the structure of the six ages. This section
contains also lists of Roman consuls and dictators, the ten per-

secutions of the Christians, the high priests of the Jews after Moses, and the emperors from Augustus to the German emperors of his own day. In the manuscript of the 1110 edition Honorius notes that he is completing his work on the occasion of the betrothal of the German emperor Henry V with Matilda, daughter of the king of England.

Book I begins with a detailed geography of the world. As the frontispiece of a late-twelfth-century or early-thirteenth-century manuscript now at Cambridge there appears a world map with more than 200 place names and legends.[54] The authorship of the map and its relation to the text is another puzzle. There is an important time gap. The text of the Cambridge manuscript is from Honorius' first edition of the work, 1110, while the manuscript may be as much as a century later. So, though a map might have accompanied the original work, this one is, at best, a copy.

As LeCoq observes, the title of the work, *Imago Mundi*, strongly suggests a visual element. The abbot Christianus, in a letter requesting Honorius to compose the work, asks that he might describe the situation of the world as if on a 'tabella', or painted tablet. Honorius replies, 'I have depicted for you the shape of the whole world so that you can refresh your bodily eye as well as the eye of the heart, browsing in the field of the universe.'[55] Although words like 'tabella' and 'formula' are notoriously vague, both parties to the exchange seem to imply that a visual aid, beyond mere words, has been given. Seven additional manuscripts also contain world maps, but these are mere sketches, unlike the detailed map under consideration here.[56]

P. D. A. Harvey, the most recent scholar to tackle the problem, maintains that it would be best to refer to the map henceforth as 'the Sawley map', after the Yorkshire abbey where it was housed not later than the early thirteenth century. 'To call it the "Henry of Mainz" map is a misnomer that can only mislead,' writes Harvey. 'Henry of Mainz had nothing to do with the map, if, indeed, he ever existed at all.'[57]

The map in question, like Honorius's text, is an impressive production. While the two are not identical, they are not contradictory either, and it is easy to see that they can be regarded as complementary. Like Lambert's world map, the Sawley map presents a world view, founded on classical antiquity but illuminated by Christian theology. The island of Paradise is at the top of the map in the far east, and the map is flanked by four angels, one of whom points an admonitory finger toward the 'gens imunda', the walled-up tribes of Gog and Magog who will emerge before the Last Day. The angels stand in place of the winds, which often surround medieval world maps, and perhaps are intended for the four angels of

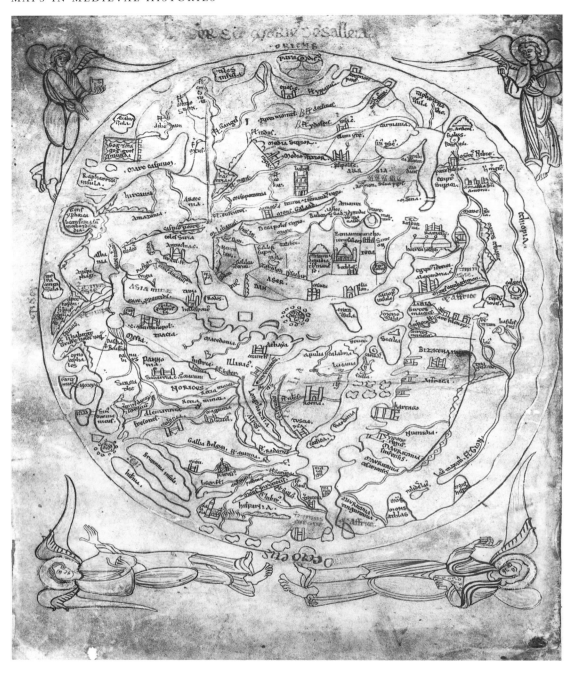

Revelation 7.1, who hold back the winds after the opening of the sixth seal. Much of the nomenclature is relentlessly classical, largely derived from Orosius, especially in Asia and Africa, but in Europe modern names and in Palestine biblical information supplement this basic picture.

The inhabited world is shaped as an oval. Otherwise, the overall configuration of the map with its sinuous coastlines and irregularly shaped bodies of water most recalls the Anglo-Saxon map. To call it a T–O seems a perversion of the term. The continents are not named, nor is there any reference to the sons of Noah. The Mediterranean occupies the centre, making a ninety-degree turn to the north as it passes the tip of Italy, while the Tanais flows from the Black Sea into the northern ocean. The Nile demonstrates several alternate theories about its course, appearing and disappearing in the desert sands in the south of Africa, but also flowing from a source near the Red Sea, labelled 'source of the Nile'. There is no fourth continent, nor indication of the zones, which Honorius describes in his text (I.6). The whole appears to be centred on the island of Delos, surrounded by the other islands of the Cyclades. Also in the Mediterranean at the tip of Italy is a barking dog's head to represent the perils of Scylla, while a spiral indicates Charybdis.

To read Honorius's map aright, one must consult not only Book I (geography) but also Book III (history). The six ages, which structure the latter, are represented by landmarks such as Armenia (where the Ark landed), Babel (from which the nations dispersed), the barns of Joseph and the passage of the Hebrews through the Red Sea, and Jerusalem. Honorius also outlines the succession of empires in this book, and the map shows Babylon (here identified with Babel), Persepolis, Macedonia, Carthage, and Rome, as well as Cologne and Mainz, centres of the contemporary German empire. The progression of history from east to west is marked not only by Paradise in the East, but also by two of the first cities founded, Cain's Enoch (Genesis 4.17) and Nisa (Nysa), established by Jupiter to shield Dionysius from the wrath of Hera.[58] In Spain there is an unlabelled drawing of a large church which can only be Santiago. The new church was under construction in Honorius' day and already a centre of pilgrimage, although it was not completed until 1211. Located at the ends of the earth, it served as a sign that civilization had reached its western limits and that the end was near.

The treatment of Syria, where Honorius gives an impressively accurate rendition of the Promised Land in purely biblical terms, is noteworthy. The eleven tribal divisions of land are indicated with a high degree of accuracy, marked off by straight lines, the only boundaries to be indicated in this way.

6.3. Honorius Augustodunensis, Sawley or 'Henry of Mainz' map, from *Imago Mundi*. This elegantly drawn world map is flanked by four angels instead of the usual winds. Paradise and its rivers occupy a circle at the top (east), while the entrance to the Mediterranean is slightly right of lower centre, labelled 'terminus europae et affricae'. At the upper left Gog and Magog are noted to be immured in a square fortress. Size of map: 295 × 205 mm. MS 66, p. 2, late twelfth century, England.
Courtesy of the Parker Library, Corpus Christi College, Cambridge.

Borders elsewhere are delineated by mountains and rivers. The mapmaker shows also the limits of the Holy Land as expounded in Numbers (chapter 34) and Joshua (chapter 13), with the Wadi of Arnon, the Dead Sea, the Jordan River, Gilead, the Sea of Galilee, and the Mountains of Lebanon and Tabor. Unusual Biblical sites include Midian, home of Jethro, the father-in-law of Moses, and Jaboc (Jabbok), the river where the angels appeared to Jacob on his way to a meeting with his brother Esau. Honorius's principal source here, other than the Bible itself, was Jerome's *De situ locorum Hebraicorum*, a glossary of biblical place-names.

Modern names in Europe include the mercantile city of Pisa, then at the apex of its wealth and glory, as well as Rouen, Mainz, Cologne, Paris, and the provinces of Poitou (Pictavos) and Anjou (Andagavis). Oddly enough, considering his English connections, the islands of Great Britain are featureless and he uses the Roman 'Britannia' instead of the more modern 'Anglia'.[59]

Around the edges of the map, where the forces of civilization, emanating from the centre, grew weaker, appear a scattering of monstrous races (Troglodites and cannibals) and beasts (griffins, basilisks, and dog-heads), drawn from Alexander's adventures, as well as fantastic islands, largely culled from Aethicus Ister's *Cosmography*. Here we find the sunless isle of Apterofon (Pteroferon), where it is always winter, and Terraconta, inhabited by descendants of Gog and Magog, who had teeth like crocodiles and bred dogs so ferocious that they could take on leopards, lions, and bears. The extremes of human organization were illustrated by Iceland, the home of patriarchy, contrasted with Amazonia, where women ruled. Even in these distant outposts, there was the hope of conversion. In Hungary the map shows Sabaria, the city of St Martin who converted the once-savage Huns. In the remote Egyptian desert is found the monastery of St Anthony, another place of great holiness. And one must not forget Christopher of the Cynocephales, who, though a mere dog-head, became a Christian saint.[60]

Honorius's vision of the world of space and time, caught up in the drama of creation, salvation, and eventual destruction, is aided by the combination of text and map in the Cambridge manuscript, one illuminating the other. While we cannot know that the map is his, it was well chosen to illustrate his book, sharing the quality of his writing in its clarity, accuracy, and meaning. Both Lambert and Honorius have used a geographical model of physical reality, which includes places of times past, to illustrate what is an essentially spiritual point of view. They see no conflict between the presentation of an other-worldly message and the world as it exists, presented as

Plate I Portolan map: Carte Pisane. Probably made in Genoa in the late thirteenth century, this is the oldest example of a portolan or nautical chart based on compass sightings. It shows the Mediterranean coasts with an impressive degree of accuracy, while sketchier on the Atlantic and northern coasts. The grids shown may indicate an alternate idea of mapping, but this is not clear. BN Rés. Ge. B 1118. Size 50 x 104 cm.

Courtesy of the Bibliothèque
Nationale, Paris.

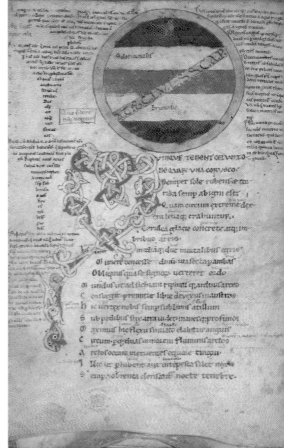

Plate II Monsters on the Psalter map. Exotic animals and the variations on the human form were a part of travel and geographic literature from earliest times. On this small map from an illustrated psalter they appear neatly arranged along the southern edge of the world. From east to west: four-eyed man, six-fingered man, person who imbibes food through a reed, ear-less man, nose-less man, flat-foot, big-lips, Blemmye (headless) – twice, Troglodyte (cave-dweller), person who walks on all fours, cannibal, Cynocephalus (dog-head). BL Add. MS 28681, fol. 9^r (detail), mid-thirteenth century, English, possibly London, c. 1265 Diameter of entire map, 114 mm.

Plate III Map from the Georgics of Virgil. A zonal map frequently accompanies Virgil's poetic description of the parts of the globe in his poem. In this highly decorated manuscript the five bands are labelled appropriately while on the diagonal strip appear the initial letters of each of the twelve signs of the zodiac. Surrounding the diagram is Servius' commentary. An ornamental Q adorns the relevant passage. BL MS Harl. 2533, fol. 18^v, diameter 80 mm.

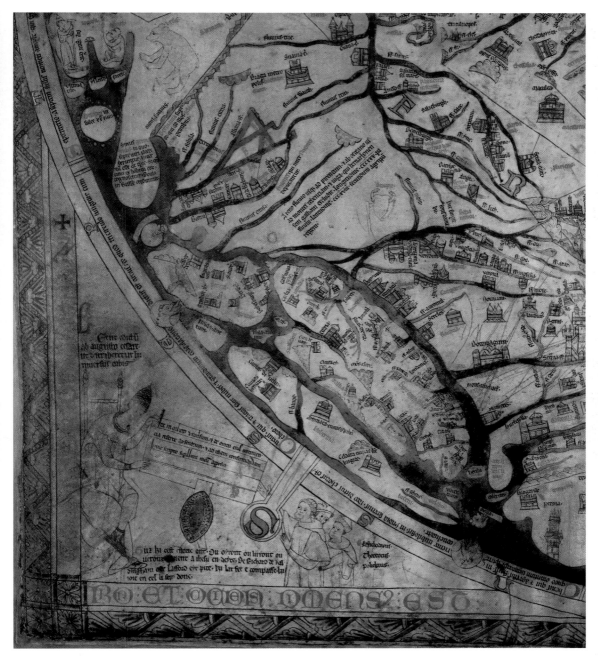

Plate IV Augustus and the geographers, from the mappa mundi of Hereford Cathedral, lower left corner. Augustus, wearing a papal-type crown, holds an impressive document of medieval appearance to which his seal is appended. He orders the three geographers before him to go forth into the wide world and to report to the senate on every continent within it ('Ite in orbem universum et de omni eius continencia referte ad senatum'). Above, another text refers to the decree from the gospel of Luke that the whole world be 'described'. Most modern interpreters believe this passage refers to a census, rather than a geographical survey. Around the rim of the map the measuring of the lands is attributed to the command of Julius Caesar. Thus the mapmaker has covered all possibilities.

Courtesy of Hereford Cathedral.

Plate V Illustrated calendar page. The month of February is here illustrated by a lively scene of workers pruning vines. This is the oldest calendrical cycle to be illustrated exclusively by scenes of rural activities, the famous 'labours of the months', soon to be so common in medieval art. Each day in the calendar below is given a line of verse to make a metrical calendar for the month. This calendar betrays its Irish origin by the number of Irish saints included. The month begins, for example, with St Brigid, 'Gloria Scottorum'. To the immediate left of the verse is the date in the Roman calendar (nones, ides, kalends). The letters and numbers in the columns on the left are keys to various computistical tables. The sign of Aquarius, in which the month begins, is represented by the medallion in the lower right corner. BL Cotton MS Tiberius B.V.1, fol. 3ᵛ, mid-eleventh century, Canterbury.

Courtesy of the British Library Board.

Plate VI Psalter world map. This map includes all the features of the great mappae mundi of the thirteenth century on a greatly reduced scale. Christ presides over the world, flanked by two angels and holding an even smaller orb in his left hand. East and Paradise are at the top, Jerusalem in the centre (marked with a bull's eye), and islands and winds are spaced out around the rim. Its presence in a psalter underscores the spriritual benefits of contemplating such a map. Size of map: 90 mm. in diameter. BL Add. MS 28681, fol. 9, English, possibly London, c. 1265.

Plate VII Richard of Haldingham or Sleaford, Hereford Cathedral map, entire. Size of parchment:
1.58 x 1.33 meters. Lincoln (England), c. 1285.
    Courtesy of Hereford Cathedral.

Plate VIII Hereford Cathedral map: Crossing of Red Sea. The map shows the Israelites leaving Egypt from the city of Ramesse on the day after the Passover. Nearby is the 'orrea ioseph,' or granary of Joseph, an identification of the pyramids in the Middle Ages. Their path leads them through the Red Sea, past Mt Sinai where Moses is shown receiving the tablets of the law from the hand of God. They pursue a torturous course through the wilderness until they cross the Wadi Arnon, the border of the Holy Land. They trek past Lot's wife in her saline form, cross the Jordan and wind up at Jericho.

Courtesy of Hereford Cathedral.

Plate IX. Hereford Cathedral map: Tower of Babel. The Tower of Babel is, suitably, the largest structure shown on the map. Though long since destroyed, it lives on here. The lengthy text nearby refers to the great city of Babylon, its founding, its construction, and its great size. The tower and the city are sometimes combined into one on medieval maps, and that may be the case here, as the Euphrates river is shown flowing through the tower.

Courtesy of Hereford Cathedral.

Plate X Hereford Cathedral map: Garden of Eden. At the top of the map, just below a rather demonic-looking wind figure, appears the walled garden of Paradise with its four rivers and its doors firmly closed. This part of the map is rubbed away, but one can still make out the figures of Adam and Eve. Below to the right an angel holding a flaming sword drives them away ('Expulsio Adae et Evae'). Above their heads is the 'arbor balsami id est arbor sicca,' which has also been expelled from Paradise and will experience the ignominy of supplying the wood for the cross of Christ.

Courtesy of Hereford Cathedral.

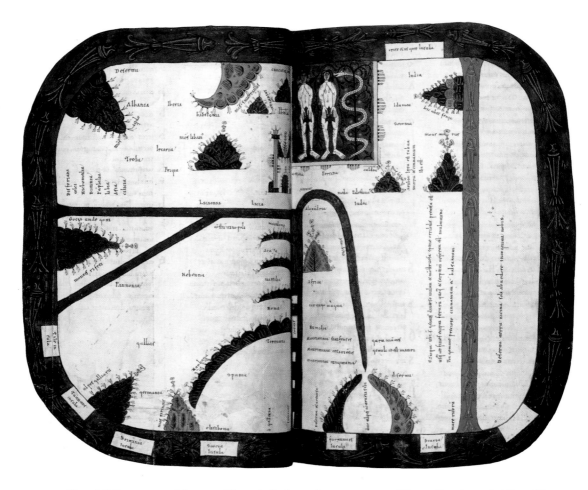

Plate XI Beatus, world map of Branch II, from the monastery of Santo Domingo de Silos. The map is oriented with east and Paradise at the top, and the Mediterranean a narrow strip in the lower centre. On the right a fourth continent is shown, separated from the ecumene by a line of the ocean coloured red. Jerusalem is marked by a shrine, the only city to receive a symbol. This map is descended from the map of Magius, described in the text. Size of map 320 x 430 mm. BL Add. MS 11695, fols 39ᵛ–40ʳ, late eleventh/early twelfth century, Spain.

accurately as they know how. Just as the human soul inhabits a body, a significant portion of human history takes place on the physical earth in real time and real space, and a map is an appropriate accompaniment to their writing.

GUIDO OF PISA

The *Liber Historiarum*, or book of histories, by Guido of Pisa dates from 1119, contemporary with Lambert and Honorius, and survives in six manuscripts, two of which contain world maps.[61] Guido, of whom nothing more is known, composed his work in six parts. The first three deal with geography, Book I focusing exclusively on Italy, and Books II and III on the rest of the world. His geographical sources are the Ravenna Cosmographer of the seventh century, the Antonine Itinerary of the Roman Empire (214–15 AD), and our old friend, Isidore of Seville. The last three books are concerned with history. Book IV is a chronicle 'from Jerome and Augustine', extending to the year 1108, and including an account of warfare between the Pisans and Genoese and the Saracens. Book V contains the adventures of Alexander the Great,[62] and Book VI, the tale of Troy with its ramifications for Italy, ending with excerpts from the eighth-century Italian history of Paul the Deacon.

6.4. Guido of Pisa, world map from *Liber Historiarum*. Guido presents the world on a map of simplified forms: an angular Mediterranean and thick curving lines for rivers. At the top (east), instead of Paradise, an inscription says 'Here are the three Indias'. Place-names are provinces, rivers, a few cities ('Irlm'=Jerusalem), and natural features ('Mons Caucasus'). Another map in the same manuscript shows Italy in more detail. Diameter of map 130 mm. MS 3897–3919, fol. 53ᵛ, 1119, Italy.

Courtesy of the Bibliothèque Royale, Brussels.

A simple T–O appears in both manuscripts, with a more detailed world map and a map of Italy in the Brussels manuscript alone, along with other illustrations. Guido's map is less detailed than those of Lambert and Honorius, with 54 legends on the world map and 21 on the map of Italy. The overlap between the two is eleven names. Both maps are simplified sketches. The world map has a sharply triangular Mediterranean, while the rivers are thickly painted. The Red Sea and Persian Gulf have become a single body. The map is oriented to the east, with no Paradise shown, and the four rivers of Genesis apparently flowing from the Caucasus mountain range. The names are mostly provinces and cities: Athens, Carthage, Jerusalem, Troy, Alexandria, and Constantinople. No islands are shown, not even the British Isles. The map of Italy with its surrounding coasts, seas, and islands, is dominated by a large drawing of a building, labelled 'Roma'. Miller thinks that Guido has copied a larger world map without really adapting it to his text.[63] Beneath the world map he gives a list of the names of 'philosophers' who have described the world, leading off with Castorius, the oft-cited source of the Ravenna geographer.

Despite his fidelity to his source, Guido does not repeat the Cosmographer's division of the earth's surface into 24 segments, corresponding to the sun's passage over it in the course of a day and providing a division by longitude rarely even attempted in the Middle Ages.

MATTHEW PARIS

With Matthew Paris we move from maps in encyclopedias, which include historical material, to a chronicle, a work of pure history. Matthew (c. 1200–59), a Benedictine monk, inherited the task of writing the great St Alban's chronicle when Roger of Wendover died in 1235. Editing and amending his predecessor's work, he continued it to cover current events until his own demise in 1259. He embellished his work with lively pictures of battles, expeditions, ceremonies, executions, and deathbed scenes.[64] Among these illustrations were his maps. Each copy of the Chronica Majora was originally accompanied by a mapped itinerary from London to Apulia in southern Italy, a map of Palestine, and one of England and Scotland.[65]

Matthew Paris experimented with a variety of forms, and his maps may be said to represent most of the possibilities of medieval cartography. There is the itinerary, a strip-map showing city by city a journey from London to Otranto in Apulia and, alternatively, to Sicily, either one an embarkation point for the Holy Land. He tried his hand at a *mappa mundi*, which he said was a copy of the ones by Robert Melkeley and at Waltham Abbey.[66] He also made a copy of the world map belonging to the royal palace at Westminster, but the book into which he copied it has not survived. It is usually assumed that the surviving *mappa mundi*, now bound with Corpus Christi College, Cambridge, MS 26, is similar to the royal map, possibly the 'magna historia' which Henry III ordered to be preserved in 1236.[67]

Matthew drew a succession of maps of Britain notable for their accuracy and progressive development. Yet he also drew a diagram in which the various kingdoms of Anglo-Saxon England are represented abstractly in a floral emblem, reminiscent of an Isidorian zone diagram.[68] Another map of Britain shows the four chief Roman roads intersecting (which they actually do not) in schematic fashion. The wind diagrams which he drew to accompany the two Cambridge copies of the *Chronica Majora* have been hailed for their division into sixteen winds, as was later to be the case of wind roses on maps, rather than the traditional twelve winds of antiquity.[69]

An idea of the range of Matthew's work can be best grasped by reviewing a list of his cartographic productions, no two of which are the same.[70]

1. Maps of England and Scotland (four 'geographical,' two schematic):

  a. London, British Library, Cotton MS Claudius D.VI, fol.12^v (now bound separately).

  b. Cambridge, Corpus Christi College, MS 16, fol. v, verso.

  c. BL, Cotton MS Julius D.VII, fols 50^v and 3^r (now bound with map 'a' above).

  d. BL, Royal MS 14.C.VII, fol. 5^v.

  e. *Scema Britanniae*, BL, Cotton MS Nero D.I, fol. 187^v, a sketch map of the four main Roman roads.

  f. *De partitionibus regnorum Angliae* (Of the divisions of the kingdoms of England), BL, Cotton MS Julius D.VII, fols 49^v–50.

2. Maps of Palestine (three pictorial, one with more names than pictures):

  a. BL, Royal MS 14.C.VII, fols 4^v–5.

  b. Cambridge, CCC, MS 16, fols ii verso – v.

  c. Cambridge, CCC, MS 26, fols iii verso – iv.

  d. Oxford, CCC, MS 2* (bound separately).

3. World maps:

  a. Cambridge, CCC, MS 26, p. 284.

  b. BL, Cotton MS Nero D.V., fol. 1^v, a later, not-quite-faithful copy of the above. Not in Matthew's hand.

4. Itineraries:

  a. BL, Royal MS 14.C.VII, fols 2–4.

  b. BL, Cotton MS Nero D.I, fols 182^v–183.

  c. Cambridge, CCC, MS 26, fols i–iii.

  d. Cambridge, CCC, MS 16, fol. ii (incomplete).

Another map which has recently been attributed to the influence of Matthew Paris is a world map, bound with the chronicle of John of Wallingford, a colleague at St Alban's.[71] John's chronicle is almost entirely derivative from Matthew, and the volume contains some works in his mentor's hand.[72] The world map appears separated from John's chronicle in the manuscript, but in his handwriting, and takes the unusual form of a climate map. A Greek invention, the division of the inhabited world into seven climates was well known in the Middle Ages, as it had been described by Pliny and repeated by Bede in *De temporum ratione* (chapter XXXIII), but maps were rarely made according to this description. One problem was that the northern regions were poorly described. Pliny's seventh, or most northern, climate, which he takes from the Greeks, goes only so far as Milan and Venice. Although he goes on to add three more northerly climates, he does so in a sketchy fashion.[73] For those living beyond the climatic pale, this could not be very useful when translated into pictorial form. John's map adds an eighth climate, with Anglia,

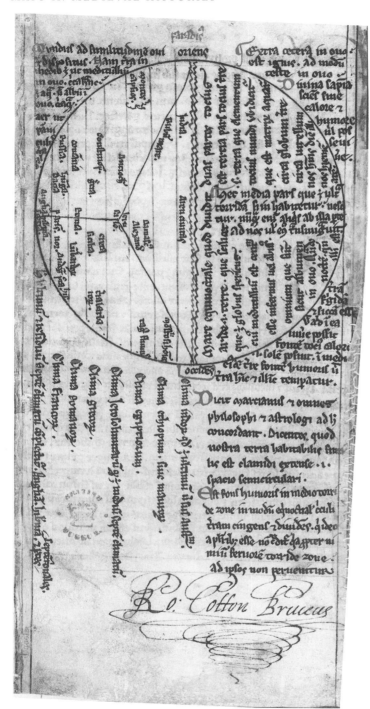

6.5. John of Wallingford, world map. This is a climate map, in which the inhabited world is divided into eight climates, seven of which come from Pliny. 'Aren civitas' in the far south shows the influence of an Arabic map. Jerusalem is at the juncture of three lines which roughly divide the continents. The text in the southern hemisphere describes the universe surrounding the earth 'like the white of an egg'. Other notes on cosmology, including a list of the climates, fill the page. Diameter of map 82 mm. BL Cotton MS Julius D.VII, fol. 46ʳ, c. 1250, England.
Courtesy of the British Library Board.

Hibernia, and Scotia practically at the North Pole. The earliest example of a climate map in the West is from a work of 1110 by Petrus Alfonsus, a converted Spanish Jew, who derived it from Arab sources, where this format was more commonly employed.[74] Although it is by no means certain that Matthew had a hand in John of Wallingford's map, it is tempting to link him with yet another cartographic innovation.

Matthew's chronicle shows his avid interest in all aspects of human activity, from village scandals, to international politics, to meteorological catastrophes. Far from being a stay-at-home monk, we know that he travelled to London and Norway, and conversed with many visitors to St Albans, including members of the royal family. His maps demonstrate the same restless curiosity as his writing. The most detailed are the ones of Britain and Palestine, both of which loom large as venues of his history. He revised and rearranged his British maps as he did the chronicle itself.[75] His practical orientation to map-making is also illustrated by a map of Palestine not attached to the chronicle but found in a Bible at Corpus Christi College, Oxford. This map, which is now attributed to him,[76] was probably made around 1240, either in preparation for or as a reflection of the crusade of Richard of Cornwall, and is packed with up-to-date information, 120 names, including fortifications, holy tourist sites, and lands controlled by the various sultanates. It also gives an indication of scale in days' journeys between the coastal cities. Notes at the side suggest corrections to the map (the river Jordan does *not* flow through Damascus) and give information about places outside its range (300 leagues from Cyprus to Acre).[77]

The other Palestine maps, which were bound with the various editions of the *Chronica Majora*, have many fewer names, more pictures, and a wildly varying scale in order to accommodate more detail in areas of interest, such as the fortifications of Acre, constructed by St Louis during his Crusade in the 1250s. While these maps have been adapted as illustrations – nearly all the names on them appear in the chronicle – the Oxford Palestine map seems to have functioned more as a source, notes in graphic form, which the historian could use in making sense of news reports from the ever volatile Holy Land.[78]

The itinerary maps, which stretch from London to south Italy and beyond to Sicily, including various points from which one might embark for the East, are a rare pictorial version of the kind of geographical information which usually comes down to us in written form. Matthew structures his map as a journey, with stations a day's travel apart, a vivid demonstration of the link between time and space. Alternative routes are also shown, and features important to the traveller

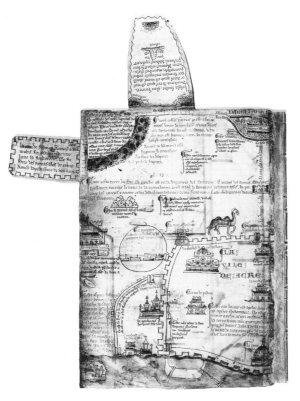

– high mountains, sea crossings, rivers, bridges – are clearly indicated. The sequence becomes less accurate as the distance from England increases. One can imagine Matthew's sources, which we might presume to be travellers, arguing heatedly over whether they had stopped at Pisa or Lucca first, and was that where they stayed in such a terrible inn?

An itinerary has also been suggested as the basic framework for Matthew's maps of Britain, which are the most detailed regional cartography to be found in the Europe of his day. A bee-line from Dover to Berwick dominates each of his British maps, despite the inaccuracies of placement that ensue. Another suggestion, made in a recent article by P. D. A. Harvey,[79] was that Matthew began with a general outline of the coasts of Britain taken from a *mappa mundi*. Harvey cites Matthew's use of the cardinal directions and the indication of neighbouring countries (this way lies Norway, etc.) to show how he thinks of Britain in a world context. Both theories could, of course, be true. We already know, by Matthew's own testimony, of his exposure to world maps, as well as his construction of an itinerary. He also used information from an itinerary in the making of his Oxford map of Palestine,

6.6. Matthew Paris, Palestine map. Matthew's map of Palestine is a visual aid, with boats, castles, churches, and a camel. Jerusalem is the square at the upper right, with a much larger Acre occupying the centre. The extension of its city walls to the left show the fortifications constructed by St Louis during his crusade in 1252–4. At the upper left is the enclosure in which Alexander confined Gog and Magog, but Matthew notes that they have now emerged in the form of Tartars, an ominous sign. Size: 350 × 450 mm. BL MS Royal 14.C.VII, fols 4ᵛ–5ʳ, after 1254.

Courtesy of the British Library Board.

which indicates the number of days' journey between various points.

The world maps of Matthew Paris are most important because of their relation to large wall maps, now lost. Many medieval world maps in codices have been thought to be copies of such maps, but Matthew is specific about it. It is a pity that the 'correct and complete' copy in his ordinal does not survive, as the one that does is rather sketchy. Europe occupies most of the space, with Africa reduced to a coastline, and it is not clear whether this format reflects the original – probably not. The Mediterranean curves to the north at the tip of Italy, like Guido's map, and has deeply indented gulfs on either side of Asia Minor. Matthew records the names of provinces, rivers, seas, and islands, giving only a handful of cities. The British Isles do not appear at all.[80] The most interesting text is that in the upper right, which tells of the map from which this one was copied. Other legends of note include 'Hierapolis, where Philip the apostle preached' in the east, 'Sitia [Scythia] where Peter preached' farther north, and 'Pontos, the island where Ovid was exiled' in the Black Sea. The Ebstorf map shows the apostle Philip buried in Hierapolis, but the other two notes do not appear on any other medieval map.[81] Most of the other places here are common currency among medieval maps.

The historical content of Matthew's maps is relatively slight compared to the many contemporary sites on them. Where he notes historical places, such as St Columba's Island (Iona) or the Hadrian and Antonine walls, these are places which are still important, though he does include some purely historical notes for their own sake, such as the descent of the Welsh from the Trojan, Brut. Sites in Palestine such as Rachel's tomb and the salt statue of Lot's wife were thirteenth-century tourist attractions, and, as such, of intense current interest, albeit signs of a religious-historical consciousness.

One purely historical diagram which he did construct, however, and in several versions, was the floral diagram of the Heptarchy, the seven Anglo-Saxon kingdoms of England, which looks rather like one of Isidore's floral zone maps. In the surrounding text he explains, 'By means of this circular diagram can be known the various kingdoms as they were formerly distinguished from one another by the English. Actually the form of England is oblong, as is shown in the following folios.'[82] He arranges the kingdoms as close as possible to the appropriate cardinal direction, indicating cities, bishoprics, and occasionally events. So here we see Matthew constructing a historical 'map', or diagram, and it is much more abstract than the maps he made for the chronicle.

A great number of the place-names on Matthew's various

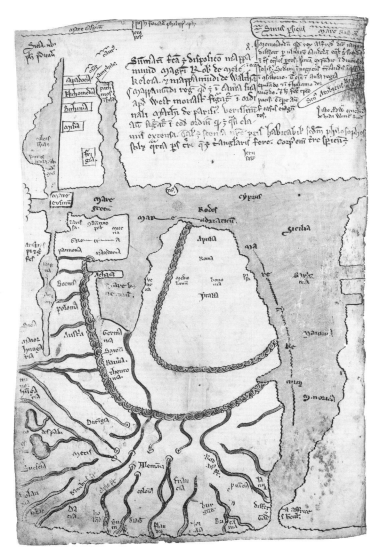

6.7. Matthew Paris, world map, from the *Chronica Majora*, c. 1250. The chief importance of this map is as a record of the mappa mundi of Westminster which Matthew says that he is sketching. Europe takes up most of the space with Africa reduced to a coastline and Asia to a scattering of names around the inscription, which mentions other full-scale mappae mundi, noting that the inhabited world is actually in the shape of a chlamys spread out and occupies only a quarter of the globe. At the top of the map is the Caspian Sea and the city of Hierapolis on the left, and the Persian Gulf and Red Sea on the right. Size of map: 354 × 232 mm. MS 26, p. 284.

Courtesy of the Parker Library, Cambridge, Corpus Christi College.

maps appear in the chronicle as well, though, as scholars have noted, there is not a perfect correspondence. For example, the names of natural features tend to appear on maps, while unmentioned in the text.[83] However, the purpose of the maps, which was to illustrate the chronicle, is made abundantly clear. Matthew simply cannot resist adding or guessing at new names, and sometimes he finds it impossible to fit everything in. In addition to his maps we have several sets of cartographic notes, some of which have obviously been collected from travellers, to guide him in his future productions.[84]

Matthew's chronicle, while a vivid picture of day-by-day

6.8. Matthew Paris, regions of England. The highly abstract floral design of this map shows that Matthew Paris tried every map format known in his day. The seven kingdoms of the heptarchy are shown, beginning with Essex at the right of top centre and progressing clockwise: Kent, Sussex, Wessex, Mercia, Northumbria, East Anglia. The map is oriented with east at the top and the kingdoms arranged more or less appropriately. In the text at the side Matthew notes that 'by this circular figure the various kingdoms which once were in England can be distinguished', but he adds, 'Actually the shape of England is oblong, as is shown in the following pages.' Diameter of map 125 mm. BL Cotton MS Julius D.VII. fols 49ᵛ–50ʳ.
Courtesy of the British Library Board.

events in the world, was haunted by omens of the approaching end of the world. Earthquakes, outstanding examples of human wickedness, the battle successes of the Moslems, were all seen as portents. Particularly ominous was the appearance from the north-east of the Tartars or Mongols around 1240. Descriptions of their appearance and behaviour fill pages of the chronicle, for Matthew is convinced that this new race is the offspring of Gog and Magog, about to wreak vengeance on humanity. He shows the enclosure from which they escaped on the pictorial maps of Palestine. His most lengthy apocalyptic statement comes in 1250, the year when he had intended to end his chronicle, but his account is peppered throughout with forebodings. After describing an earthquake in the neighbourhood of St Alban's, he writes: 'Thus, in this year, unusual and dreadful disturbances were experienced, both by land and sea, which imminently threatened the end of the world. As the gospel menaces, "There shall be earthquakes in divers places."'[85]

RANULF HIGDEN

The medieval historical tradition was continued into the fourteenth century in the *Polychronicon* or *Universal Chronicle*, of Ranulf Higden, a monk from St Werburgh's Abbey in Chester. Higden entered the Benedictine order in 1299 and died in March 1363, having spent 60 years in the service of religion. He produced his first version of the history in 1327, an intermediate version in 1340, and another in 1360 just before his death. The book was immediately popular, and numerous copies were made for other monastic houses and for the libraries of colleges at Oxford and Cambridge. It was probably Higden's prestige as a historian that caused him to be summoned to the court of Edward III in 1352.

The *Polychronicon* is based on Higden's extensive reading in classical and medieval sources. Only occasionally does he break into his own voice to express scepticism at someone else's outlandish tale, which he nevertheless repeats for his readers' delectation. Citing his authorities in the text, he refers to all the usual suspects: Josephus, Pliny, Sallust, Solinus, Isidore, Orosius. He also used some later works, such as John of Wales, *Compendiloquium*, and Bartholomeus Anglicus, *De proprietatibus rerum*.[86] His reading was wide and his touch sure as he mined the resources of the monastery's library for moral examples, shocking incidents, and ominous precedents. His historical account was arranged in seven books, like the seven days of Creation, he noted, thereby modestly comparing himself with God. He began, naturally, with Adam and Eve, and continued to his own time. The last two books were devoted exclusively to British history. His example inspired others, and some owners of his manuscript were moved to add the events of their own times. These continuations of Higden are important source material for the study of the succeeding century.

There are eight things which people need to know if they would understand all history, wrote Higden. First are descriptions of places where events occurred. The others are the state of the world (that is, before and after Christ), the three categories of time (before the law, under the law, and under grace), the succession of regimes or the four empires, the progression of law through time (from the state of nature through Jewish, Christian and Islamic law), the course of the (six) ages of the world, the seven qualities of human actions (active, contemplative, political, military, etc.) and how worthy actions are rewarded and evil actions punished, and the various methods of calculating time (Hebrew, Greek, Roman, Christian).[87] It is clear from this chapter that Higden sees the progression of historical events in a theological context, or a variety of theo-

6.9. Ranulf Higden, world map. The smaller of two world maps which appear in a manuscript of the *Polychronicon* produced at Ramsey Abbey, this map is closely related to other Higden maps. It appears to be unfinished, as the sketch of Paradise at the top is roughly done and now not entirely legible. It contains 150 names. Note the British Isles at the bottom (west) appear in schematic form. BL Roy. MS 14.C.IX, fol. 2ᵛ, fourteenth century.

Courtesy of the British Library Board.

logical contexts. The description of places is the only category in this list not defined in specifically religious terms, though, in the course of Book I, he will of course note events of spiritual history where relevant.

Since place came first in the list of eight things, it is understandable that Higden's first book was devoted to the geography of the world, which he called a *mappa mundi*, a term which could refer either to a description such as this was or to a graphic presentation. Higden's description of the world runs to several hundred pages, beginning with the size of the earth, its division into three continents, the Mediterranean Sea, the Ocean, and moving on to the 'provinces of the earth, of which the first is Paradise'. For each place Higden weighs the various authorities, describing, like a modern geographer, customs as well as physical characteristics. Occasionally in this section he

[127]

even makes excursions into history, such as the conquests of the Scythians, the foundation of Carthage, the early civilization of Athens, and the succession of French kings. The description of the city of Rome is particularly rich, giving a medieval view of its history and monuments. As he proceeds Higden is not averse to including miracles (the wonderful properties of the Colossus of Rhodes) as well as scandals (divorce laws in ancient Rome).

It was not until the second version in the 1340s that it occurred to the author that a map in graphic form would be a good addition to all these words. At the end of his prologue he announces that a map will be included.[88] World maps have been found in nineteen of the numerous surviving manuscripts, all belonging to the intermediate version. Several centuries later Henry VIII of England was to have a cheap unillustrated edition of Higden close to hand in his study, and an illustrated deluxe edition with a map with his 'fine' books.[89]

The manuscript which is housed today in the Huntington Library in California comes from St Werburgh's and is believed to have been Higden's own working copy.[90] Thus the map it contains is of particular interest. It is oval in form with east at the top, where Adam and Eve stand in the garden of Eden on either side of the snake, which is coiled around the tree. The three continents of the known world are surrounded by a blue band of ocean, punctuated with islands. In the upper right (south-east) appears the Red Sea/Persian Gulf, coloured red and containing several islands. There are 150 geographical names on this map. Like most larger-scale medieval world maps, Higden's artist has departed from the iconic T–O format to one of greater verisimilitude. The Nile follows a meandering course in the south, and the Mediterranean and Black Seas are given undulating coastlines. Jerusalem appears on the map, but is not in the centre.[91] Two large dog or monster heads in the upper corners may have been intended for winds.

Several other maps in Higden manuscripts are similar to the Huntington model with its oval shape, depiction of Paradise, and bulbous shapes of provinces.[92] The largest and most detailed of these appears as one of two maps in a manuscript from Ramsey Abbey, now in the British Library.[93] This map occupies two pages, has over two hundred geographical names, and includes explanatory inscriptions. Although it has no connection with St Werburgh's, Chester, or Higden, it displays an unusual fidelity to Higden's text. It looks as if the artist combed carefully through the *Polychronicon*, selecting places and condensing information for placement on the map.

The correspondences are many. For example, in Asia near the city of Babylon a note reveals that 'Babylonia is the name of the region, Babylon of the city, but Babel is the name of the tower', thereby clearing up a major source of confusion on most medieval maps.[94] These words on the map are taken directly from Higden's text, where he ascribes them to Petrus Comester's *Historia scholastica* (ch. XII, pp. 94–6 and map). Sardinia is free of serpents, but produces the herb *apium* which causes men to die laughing (ch. XXX, p. 304 and map). The Fortunate Islands are as fertile as Paradise and have trees 140 feet high (ch. XXXI, p. 320 and map). Iceland is inhabited by people who are prophets and has a king who is a priest (ch. XXX, p. 322 and map). Norway is broad, cold, and the people are pirates (ch. XXX, pp. 326–8 and map). This is not to say that the map does not occasionally give information not in the text. For example Scylla and Charybdis are described as monsters in the text (ch. XXX, p. 314), but as 'two springs opposed by nature' on the map. The people of Arabia are described on the map as being carefree, a point not made in the text (ch. XIII), but an item of common knowledge in the Middle Ages. The map also includes some places not mentioned in the geographical portion of the text at least. Examples are Arside (Achillea), Tyrno (?), Appolitana (Apollonia) in the Black Sea, and Abidos, Cestos (Sestos), and Propontides in the straits. This map also describes, but does not draw, over two dozen monsters, distributed among Asia, Africa, and the islands. Nearly all of these appear in the text, described in similar terms.

The depiction of Britain, which is treated summarily on other Higden maps, is quite detailed on the larger British Library map, with fourteen cities shown, and notes on Ireland, Scotland, and Wales. Pictorial elements on the map include twelve wind heads arranged in the ocean, a variety of city symbols, including an ornate oriental-looking canopy for Babylon, literal columns of Hercules, and Noah in the ark. The artist may have died or departed before he could finish, for at the top of the map there is a blank square where Paradise should be, awaiting his interpretation of the crucial scene.

The smaller map in the same manuscript follows on the verso of the larger one. It contains 150 names, fewer than the larger map, and no inscriptions. Adam, Eve, and a winged head (angel? snake?) are roughly sketched in the square at the top reserved for Paradise. Britain, instead of receiving the detailed presentation it does in the other map, is reduced to several rectangular islands in the ocean: Anglia, Wallia, Hibernia, Scocia, Man. The Nile follows a meandering course as it does in the Huntington manuscript, but here deposits its waters in the Red Sea instead of the Mediterranean, in defiance of Higden, who spends several paragraphs on this interesting river. Why does the manuscript have two maps, particularly when it appears that the finer one was drawn first and the second added as a kind of afterthought? Peter Barber suggests that the scribe might have seen, belatedly, a manuscript closer to the original model and copied the map from it.[95]

Another strain of Higden maps shows the world shaped as a mandorla, pointed at the east and west, and place-names written in without geographic configurations or boundaries.[96] Destombes lists six maps of this type.[97]

Leaving aside the large British Library map, which is a remarkably well adapted illustration, to what extent can the other Higden maps be regarded as illustrations for the *Polychronicon*? Certainly there is a high degree of correspondence between places on the map and places mentioned in the text, though the latter are far more numerous. The archaism of the maps, the extensive use of Roman provincial names, fits in well with a work of history. The Higden maps, while having some family characteristics, such as the oval shape and the square for Paradise at the top, have many similarities to other *mappae mundi* of the period. Probably the artist simply adapted one of these to the service of the *Polychronicon*, without combing the text to make sure that the two absolutely corresponded. It is interesting to note that the Higden maps show no influence of the portolan charts, which had appeared in the previous century. The representation of England is much less sophisticated than that of Matthew Paris a century earlier. It shows none of the scale and accuracy of the Gough map which was its near contemporary. Instead it is completely traditional in its presentation of the world, as is Higden's history itself.

A 'Higden map' which has been found outside the *Polychronicon* is the map commissioned for Evesham Abbey in Gloucestershire around 1390, now at the College of Arms in London.[98] Presented in a large format (940 × 460 mm), the Evesham map was designed to be hung on a wall rather than enclosed in a book. Its oval shape, square scene of the Garden of Eden, even the peculiar course of the Nile and the bulbous coastlines proclaim its kinship to the maps which appear in Higden's book. The map has some characteristics all its own. Here the Garden of Eden is given an elaborate frame similar to the back of the throne occupied by the abbot of Evesham. This symbol of divine rulership reinforces the idea that the world is God's and that human history serves his purposes. The island of Britain at the bottom (west) of the map is much more elaborate and contains many more names than is true of the Higden maps. It is the conclusion of Peter Barber, who recently studied the map, that while its maker may have seen a Higden map in one of the continuations of the *Polychronicon*, the map is really a generic world map, designed to give the viewer a general idea of the shape of the world, independent of any particular text.

Reviewing the maps which accompany historical works as presented in this chapter, we can see a tendency to use archaic names, which is clearly explained by their function. One would hardly ridicule a modern historical atlas for showing such things as the borders of Alexander's empire or the city of Troy on the grounds that they no longer exist. Matthew Paris, who makes the most modern maps, does so to illustrate events of his own time, which he was responsible for adding to the St Alban's chronicle. When driven to represent the past, he does so in a much more abstract manner. Even current events, though, such as the appearance of a new people, the Tartars, are quickly plugged into a historical framework – surely these are the descendants of Gog and Magog, walled up by Alexander and now escaped to punish a sinful world. The continuance of place-names from the Roman empire is a special case, for to many medieval thinkers the empire never really ceased to be.[99] The flux of modern history, and the appearance of jumped-up kingdoms were a tiresome and insignificant blip in the larger, eternal picture dominated by Rome. The Roman imperial background of the New Testament served to reinforce the authority of these names.

The most perfect vision of a map is Gautier's in his epic of Alexander, but it is imperfectly realized in manuscripts of his work. Lambert requires ten maps to present his view of the world, just as it took many bits and pieces of text to compose his book. Honorius's mapmaker, better organized, presents a single world map, pulling together biblical and classical history, as a framework for discourses on time and space. For Guido, too, history and geography are inseparable, and if his work is largely copied from others, we must remember that that was not considered a bad way to proceed in the Middle Ages. Higden, the most verbose of our authors, spreads out a detailed description of the world in the opening book of his seven-book *Polychronicon*, and does not think it too much to add a map as well. These maps show to us a medieval vision of the world, which was firmly rooted in past times, though not indifferent to contemporary happenings. Jewish history, the life and mission of Jesus, the journeys of the apostles through the peace of the Roman empire led one's historical consciousness to the commencement of the sixth age, the age of decrepitude. The Last Judgement, thought to be coming soon, would bring an end to history as well as to the physical world, all displayed on the map.

Histories Without Maps, Maps Without Histories

HISTORIES WITHOUT MAPS

Matthew Paris is unusual for his day in that he created and used maps as an adjunct to the writing of history. In the next century he was to have successors in Ranulf Higden and Paolino Minorita, both of whom wrote extensive geographical sections and included maps as an integral part of their histories.[1] Most other historians, even those who demonstrated a consciousness of the geographical setting of events, did not have the talents, the resources, or the interest to prepare relevant maps or even to include irrelevant ones. Some of the greatest historians of the Middle Ages, such as Otto of Freising, come to us usually unillustrated and always mapless. There are tantalizing references to maps in histories which do not now contain them. Such a remark in Gervase of Tilbury's *Otia Imperialia* ('Royal Leisure', 1211) led scholars to search for the map he says he drew and find it in the stunning Ebstorf world map, the largest to survive from the Middle Ages to modern times.[2] The map Gervase said he was making (or having made) was a purely classical production, based on the Roman administrative districts, which he called 'the natural order of the provinces'. Innovations, added on the initiative of the individual painter, could only distort the entire picture, and Gervase was severely critical of the 'lying pictures which the vulgar call mappae mundi'. However, he recognized the need of 'eager minds and thirsty ears' for visual evidence. Hence he was providing a reliable map.

The connection between Gervase and the Ebstorf map can only remain hypothetical, but it is possible that some historians assumed their readers would consult a free-standing map, one with much more space for detail than the cramped page of a codex. To what extent such independent maps were available we can only guess. Many a medieval library noted the presence of a now-lost *rotula*, *spera*, or *ymago mundi*, all of which could have been maps. We are hampered by the fact that there was no name used exclusively to mean a map as such throughout most of this period. Such a work as Gervase of Canterbury's 'Mappa Mundi' turns out to be a disappointing list of bishoprics and monasteries, most of them in Britain. So a *mappa mundi* could be no more than a list of places or, at best, a geographical description.[3]

A large map, recently discovered at the College of Arms in London, is an example of a map without a book. Originally made for one Nicholas of Herford, whose library inventory includes other works of geography and history, it was left to Evesham Abbey in Gloucestershire at his death in 1392. Highly pictorial, with large letters, it appears to have been designed to hang on the wall as an educational ornament, like the globes which adorn our libraries, rather than as an adjunct to any particular text.[4] Evesham Abbey is also noted as a centre of chronicle writing, having produced a history of the life and reign of Richard II, though the Evesham map is too general to be much help in following the tangled events of fourteenth-century English history. The map could serve instead as a general reference work, as well as a symbol of the intellectual activity that went on in the Abbey library.

Alternatively, historians might have expected their readers to call upon memory. The ability to commit enormous quantities of material to memory was a highly valued one in the Middle Ages, as it had been in classical antiquity. Such written works as Priscian's geographical poem had a mnemonic purpose, for it was much easier to memorize information put into poetic form. The function of the popular list map was also perhaps an aid to memory, as the orderly arrangement of geographical terms was more amenable to mental retention than the irregular shapes of the physical world. We find writers calling on their readers to visualize to an extent we would find onerous if not impossible today. Such expectations, however, only lead us back to the need for maps for teaching, for how else were students to furnish their memories?[5]

So many medieval maps have disappeared that the study of these now invisible artifacts is a lively area of scholarly activity. From the world map supposedly constructed or ordered by Marcus Agrippa during Augustus's reign to the fourteenth-century map of Ambrogio Lorenzetti in the Siena town hall, these maps continue to intrigue scholars, who try to derive their content from descriptions which are often infuriatingly vague.[6] Maps formed part of the ornamentation of some churches, for we have sermons delivered in front of them and even a mass composed on the theme of the *mappa mundi*.[7] They played a role in education, with the teacher engaged in the timeless activity of lecturing and pointing. They also furnished royal palaces, allowing their denizens to contemplate either the grandeur of what they controlled (and perhaps to exaggerate its extent), or the transience of worldly fortunes.

The maps which appear independently of books are often loaded with enough text to qualify as books themselves. 'Reading a map' in the Middle Ages could mean scanning great blocks of written matter, describing geographical, anthropological, and historical features. The Hereford map asks for the prayers of all those who 'see, read, hear or possess' it. Although this is the only great wall map of the thirteenth century to have survived intact, we have enough fragments of, as well as information about, maps now lost, to hypothesize a general world map of the era. The *mappa mundi* of Hereford Cathedral, the world map from the convent at Ebstorf (Germany), the map at the Cathedral library in Vercelli (north Italy), and a fragment of a world map now belonging to the archives of the Duchy of Cornwall are all products of the thirteenth century.

While the maps are not copies of one another, the overall structure is similar and indicate a community of agreement on what the world should look like. The principal organizing feature is the three continents and the bodies of water which separate them, although these larger, complex maps do not follow the simplified T–O form. Relatively accurate and often modernized in Europe and the Near East, the mapmakers become increasingly vague as they move to the south and east. Here, as had been traditional since classical times, pictures of exotic animals, peoples, and plants and explanatory paragraphs replace the dense array of city symbols in the better-known parts of the world. The explanatory material is often the same from map to map.[8] The outer ocean surrounds the three continents, pierced by the Caspian Sea (nearly always shown as a gulf) and the Red Sea and Persian Gulf. Islands in the ocean range from the easily verifiable Britain and Ireland to the more problematic Thule and Thanatos. The Nile is often shown twice, once flowing from a source near the Red Sea and once flowing from east to west across the southern part of Africa. Most of the variations are in the realms of the imagination: were the dog-heads in Scandinavia or Ethiopia? Was Paradise an island or simply a walled fortress in eastern Asia?[9] These variations demonstrate that maps are individual and that each mapmaker felt free to introduce improvements (or make mistakes), but I would argue that they are founded on a common visual image, something one cannot say of early medieval maps. The production at this time of such a number of lavish world maps – and they were expensive to produce – indicates a lively interest in the world and its peoples, such as stimulated the contemporary travels of the Polos and the Franciscan emissaries to the Tartar kingdom.[10]

[134]

The overwhelming interest behind these maps was, however, not geography alone, but geography in the context of history, particularly ancient history, both classical and biblical. David Woodward has described the typical world map of this period as 'a projection of history onto a geographical framework'.[11] The maps are crowded with text and surrounded by more writing and pictures, many devoted to the theme of the passage of time. In one fragment, the Duchy of Cornwall map, we find the last half of a series of the ages of man, beginning with maturity, passing to old age, and then to two post-terrestrial figures: a soul in purgatory holding a bowl of fire, and, finally, an angel. Each character delivers a moral message.[12] The story of Julius Caesar (or Augustus) and the three (or four) surveyors he commissioned to measure the world appears in the margin of the Hereford, Ebstorf, and Duchy of Cornwall maps. This story, which may have been a late antique invention, gave a solid thousand-year-old pedigree to the world map as well as the authenticity of a genuine survey. Such a project had been out of reach of European civilization, both administratively and technically, since the fall of the empire.

A significant number of these maps have English connections. For example, the Vercelli map is perhaps a souvenir brought home by Gualo Bicchiere, a papal legate who had been sent to the court of Henry III of England in 1216–18.[13] He also visited Paris and was closely associated with the Victorines there, who could have been another source of a cartographic model. While most of this map survives, it is in a sadly tattered and faded condition.[14] It is the smallest of the surviving maps (0.8 × 0.7 m, or 0.56 sq. m). The map was designed as a circle, but the surviving piece of parchment is rectangular and much of the northern and southern sections are gone. The map was never finished, and may have been a sketch for an unrealized project. One oddity is that the islands in the Mediterranean and Red Seas are so large that the water is reduced to thin trickles. The Vercelli map was originally mounted on a roll. Such a map, kept in the reference section of the library, could be taken down and unrolled for the reader of books with geographical content, such as histories.

We have lost the maps we know were painted in the royal palace at Westminster (1230s) and at Winchester (1239). Other *mappae mundi* once existed at Waltham Abbey, at Walsingham, and at Lincoln and Durham Cathedrals (1195). The Psalter map of the mid-thirteenth century, although a mere nine cm. in diameter, gives a feel for these grand productions, and may be a copy of one. (See Plate VI.)[15] This elegant little map shows Christ at the top holding a tripartite orb and flanked by two incense-swinging angels, while the world is

supported below by two picturesque wyverns, or two-legged, winged dragons. Jerusalem is the bull's-eye centre of the map, while puffing wind faces and islands surround the whole. As on the Hereford, Ebstorf, and Cornwall maps, the monstrosities are tidily lined up in the far south, and their order is identical to those on the Cornwall map, as well as on a recently discovered fragment from the fourteenth century, the Aslake map.[16] Since this order is quite arbitrary and the texts from which they are derived understandably vague, the agreement points towards a common graphic ancestor. Other features include a painted Red Sea, no Persian Gulf, a walled enclosure for Gog and Magog in the north-east, and a medallion in the far east with the faces of Adam and Eve and the four rivers pouring out below.

The verso of this page contains a world map in another format, this one being a list map, with the continents divided T–O style and the various provinces (and a few cities) of each named. Christ appears here, too, this time embracing the world, surrounded by four gesticulating angels, and trampling two dragons under foot. This Psalter map has generally been ignored in favour of the more geographical one, but it is significant that both were included. The persistence of the list map shows an alternate form of regarding the earth and its places which maintained its vitality in the face of what we might see as more logical arrangements.[17]

Psalters, which were guides for daily devotions throughout the Christian year, usually are organized around a calendar, and this one is no exception. After the opening pages, which bear heavily gilded illustrations of the life of Christ, comes the world map, followed by a detailed calendar listing saints' days. A picture of Christ on the page preceding the world map shows him enthroned, holding a T–O globe and surrounded by the symbols of the four evangelists. It is thought that these illustrations of the life of Christ were incorporated into the Psalter at a later date, while the map and the calendar were part of the original manuscript.[18]

The existence of a world map in a psalter is rare, and its presence here may indicate that a world map was an increasingly common image, now finding its way into books which would not ordinarily have one. However, the patient reader who has followed us so far will remember the connection between maps and calendars in medieval computus manuscripts.

The world map now in the archives of the Duchy of Cornwall was originally at the College of Bonhommes in Ashridge, Hertfordshire. It appears to have been given to the college as a gift at the time of its founding in 1283 by Edmund, Earl of Cornwall. Another gift, composed in the

7.1. Psalter map, verso. Diameter of map 90 mm. Here the earth is embraced by Christ, who tramples the two dragons underfoot. Instead of a pictorial representation of the world, a list of provinces, cities and islands is given, divided into the three continents. BL Add. MS 28681, fol. 9ᵛ, English, c. 1265. Courtesy of the British Library Board.

same handwriting as the map and donated at the same time, was an illustrated copy of the *Historia Scholastica*, or School History, of Peter Comestor.[19] Originally written in the late twelfth century, the *Historia* was a compendium of Biblical and pagan history which became a standard textbook. Designed to elucidate one another, the map and book were a natural pair. Together they would have made a useful addition to the educational resources of Ashridge. Only the lower-right-hand corner of this map survives, showing Africa, with the source of the Nile and various beasts and human monsters. In its original condition, it would have been slightly larger than the Hereford map, being 2.44 sq. m. (1.6 × 1.6 m.). Outside the frame of the map is a familiar text on the geographers of Julius Caesar and five circles showing the end of a sequence on the ages of man. On the rim the winds are depicted as horn-blowing heads, accompanied by abbreviated descriptive lines from Isidore. All of these appear in similar form on the Hereford Cathedral map.

The Ebstorf map was the largest of all.[20] Painted on 30 goatskins sewn together, it covered 13.56 sq. m. (3.6 × 3.6 m.). The head of Christ appears in a square frame at the top (east) of the map, while his hands protrude at north and south and his feet at the bottom (west). In the centre Jerusalem is represented as a square walled city in flattened perspective, with Christ rising from his tomb in the centre. Oddly enough, this scene is sidewise in relation to the map as a whole – Christ is made to face the north.

The map was discovered in a convent of nuns at Ebstorf in north Germany in the nineteenth century, and now it is thought that perhaps it was made there.[21] The date, some time in the thirteenth century, has been revised several times in the last few years as the map has come under intense scholarly scrutiny. The link with Gervase of Tilbury is tempting, but unprovable.

The text surrounding the map includes a bestiary, an account of the creation of the world, definitions of various geographical terms, and a sketch of a T–O with an explanation of the division of the continents. The content of the map itself is a history of the world, beginning with the book of Genesis, and incorporating pagan with biblical history. The human race sets out from Paradise, with Adam and Eve, the snake, and the fountain of the four rivers, in the far East. The tower of Babel, Noah's ark, the Dead Sea with its drowned cities, the oracle of the sun and the moon visited by Alexander, the holy places of Palestine, and some of the burial sites of the Apostles make up a rich tapestry of historical events. Relatively few recent events are pictured, though Europe contains a number of modern towns, and near Ebstorf is shown the graves of three martyrs, whose cult became important only in the thirteenth century.[22] Still the leading geographical sources are Pomponius Mela, Pliny, Solinus, Jerome, and Isidore.[23] The bombing of Hanover in 1943 destroyed the map, which must now be studied through a set of black-and-white photographs taken in 1891 or through several colour facsimiles made before its demise.

The map that Henry III had painted in his bedroom at Westminster, which may have influenced other thirteenth-century productions, was also a work of history. In fact, it may be the wall painting referred to as the 'magna historia', which Henry ordered to be preserved in 1237, implying that it had already existed for some time.[24] This may be the world map at Westminster of which Matthew Paris made a sketch. A fire in 1263 forced the redecoration of the palace, but in 1799 fragments of the wall paintings were revealed under paint and plaster, and sketched, before the building was completely gutted by fire in 1834. Our knowledge is vague, but it appears that other works of art in the room might have been history paintings, although not necessarily factual histories, as one of them showed the virtuous King of the Garamantes being rescued from his seditious subjects by his loyal dogs. There was also a wheel of fortune. The message for the king, surveying it all from his royal bed, was the importance of virtuous kingship. Looking from wheel to map, perhaps also in wheel-form, he could either reflect on the transience of earthly things in the form of vanished kingdoms or rejoice at his present, though temporary, position at the top of the wheel. In case the message was not thoroughly driven home by the pictures, Henry had the following text inscribed on the wall: 'Whoever does not give up what he possesses shall not receive what he desires.'

THE WORLD MAP AT HEREFORD

Of the great wall maps of the thirteenth century, only one survives entire, the famous possession of Hereford Cathedral. It was made on a single piece of parchment, 1.58 × 1.33 m. (2 sq. m.) in size, and is dated to the late thirteenth century some time after 1283, when Edward I built Caernafon castle in Wales, which is pictured on the map. 'A kind of encyclopedia, arranged geographically', is P. D. A. Harvey's descriptive phrase for the Hereford map, which helps us to focus on its many-sidedness.[25] The representation of space, the sole concern of most modern maps, is here just one of its multiple aspects. Time, too, 'the fortunes of the human race, and Paradise, as forming the starting point in the stream of time', was a major theme, as its creator attempted to present a historical narrative in a geographical space.[26] Historical time flowed down the map, from the expulsion from Paradise in the east, through the parade of empires, to the newest cities in the west. The author himself called his map an 'estorie', a history, asking for the prayers of those who might possess, read, see, or hear it. This inscription suggests the various functions of the map. The possessor might enjoy it as an accoutrement of power. The illiterate might see it and have the text read to him. The literate could read it, as well as see what was spread before him. (See Plate VII.)

The form of the inhabited world is immediately recognizable as belonging to the family of maps discussed in the previous chapter and in this one. There are particularly close correspondences with the map accompanying Honorius Augustodunensis's *Imago Mundi*.[27] The Hereford Cathedral map is oriented to the east, with an island-crammed Mediterranean in the lower centre, which makes an abrupt right-angle turn to form the Aegean, the Propontis, and the Black Sea. Jerusalem is the centre, marked by a drawing of crenellated battlements, seen in flattened perspective, but that looks rather like a cog-wheel, the gear on which the whole universe turns. The city is surmounted by a crucifixion scene. Paradise is a fortified island at the very top, the Red Sea and the Persian Gulf, painted red, are to the right, and the whole is surrounded by a thin ribbon of ocean, with its islands. To make room for the vitally interesting islands of Britain, the mapmaker has carved a piece out of northern France. The map does not follow the iconic T–O form, the shape of the Mediterranean and the Black Sea being too irregular and the Nile diverted to the east, coming from a source near the Red Sea. The most obvious error on the map is the reversal of the names for the continents of Europe and Africa. Various ingenious suggestions have been made to explain what happened here, but, unlike other maps which show these continents in mirror image, all the *places* for Europe and Africa are correctly arranged. It can only be a scribal error, and one can imagine the distress when he discovered what he had done – and in gold leaf, too.

The survival of the map is miraculous. During its long life it was stuffed in a closet, folded lengthwise, and had other objects, specifically, 'a quantity of glass lanthorns', piled next to it. In 1989, when its financially strapped cathedral home threatened to sell it at auction in order to raise money for the maintenance of the ancient structure, it was again threatened with disappearance into anonymous private hands and saved only by a patriotic fund-raising campaign.

The question of its original function in the cathedral is an interesting one. Its author helpfully (and unusually) signs his name on the map as Richard 'of Haldingham or Lafford', a village and a town in Lincolnshire, but his identity is still somewhat in doubt. Indeed, it is not clear whether he was one or two people. It does appear, from internal evidence on the map, that it was made in the vicinity of Lincoln and transferred to Hereford.[28] But what was it for? Richard Gough, an eighteenth-century British antiquarian, saw the map in 1770 and said that it had 'formerly served as an altarpiece to the high altar', until 1686 (actually 1666) when the new altar and organ were installed. As this was a full century before his visit, and Gough's reliability is impugned by his date being twenty years off, one may fairly consider this piece of information hearsay. A drawing by John Carter, commissioned by Gough, shows the map as the central scene in a triptych with the two wings depicting the angel and the Virgin of the Annunciation. As Marcia Kupfer points out in her examination of the map's original presentation, 'In the half millenium between the completion of the map and the execution of Carter's drawings, surely the presentation of the work could have been altered (even more than once).'[29] Kupfer goes on to suggest that maps were more likely to be found in an educational, rather than a devotional, context. When present in churches, as wall paintings for example, they are found not behind the altar, but on nave walls, next to the space occupied by the lay worshippers.[30] In Hereford the map is more likely to have been associated with the cathedral library or school than the high altar. In fact, the Lady Chapel at Hereford, in which Gough saw the map, was functioning at the time as a library.

All that we know of medieval spirituality makes it very unlikely that a representation of the terrestrial sphere was an object of worship, and the unabashed secularism of some of the images on the map reinforce this view. A separate building has now been built to house the famous map, where its enshrinement symbolizes a twentieth-century worship of the material world, either in the form of the map or of the tourist revenue.

The frame of the map has lent some credence to the altarpiece idea, for at the top is the scene of the Last Judgement, with sinners being scolded by an angel and led away by devils on Christ's left hand (our right), and on his right hand the just are rising from their graves and lining up in orderly fashion to enter Paradise. Below this scene, the Virgin Mary pleads the cause of her devotees by throwing open her gown to reveal her breasts, reminding her son of his fleshly past: 'See, dear Son, my bosom within which you became flesh and the breasts from which you sought the Virgin's milk. Have mercy, as you yourself have promised, on all those who have served me, who have made me their way to salvation.'[31] Four large letters are placed around the map to spell MORS, death, and emphasize that this world is the scene of human mortality. Also around the rim are the twelve winds, four represented by squatting, naked gargoyles and eight by spouting dragon heads, accompanied by Isidore's description of their qualities. In the lower-left-hand corner the emperor Augustus, wearing a papal-style crown, holds a large document with a formidable seal and instructs three surveyors to measure the world. (See Plate IV.) Above the emperor is his edict from St Luke's telling of the Christmas story, which in the Vulgate Bible called for the world to be 'described' (*ut describeretur universus orbis*) rather than 'taxed', as Luther would have it. The mapmaker does not seem bothered by the inconsistency that the inscription around the map rim identifies Julius Caesar as the fellow who commissioned this survey.[32]

In the right-hand corner a horseman is followed by a small figure carrying a bow and leading a pair of greyhounds. This personage, usually called 'the huntsman', says to the rider, 'Passe avaunt', or 'go ahead', and the rider raises his hand in acknowledgement.[33] The meaning of this scene has been disputed, but the horseman may simply be a traveller, following one of the many itineraries represented on the map.

After the necessary limitations of maps in books, the richness of the Hereford map is dizzying. There are over 500 pictures on the map: 420 towns, fifteen Biblical events, 33 plants and animals, 32 peoples of the earth, and five scenes from classical mythology.[34] The vision is of a world crammed with marvels and bursting with action. How can one organize what one sees? In 1966, G. R. Crone made a careful study of the places on the map and concluded that many of the names come from itineraries, some quite antique and some contemporary with the map itself.[35] The most ancient traveller is Odysseus, whose travels range from Troy, to the land of the Lotus-eaters (the island of Menix), to Calypso's Isle, to the Pillars of Hercules and back through the perils of Scylla and Charybdis, to Corcyra, where the prow of the boat can be seen turned to stone.[36] Another voyager of classical mythology, Jason, is represented by the figure of the Golden Fleece at the east end of the Black Sea. The next travellers are the children of Israel, and their wanderings from the parted waters of the Red Sea, past Mount Sinai where a horned Moses holds the tablets of the law, past the golden calf mounted on a pedestal, through the wilderness, are shown as an elaborately looped and curving line. (See Plate VIII.) The conquests and adventures of Alexander the Great are plentifully represented, including the oracle of Ammon at an oasis in the Libyan desert, and the 'sons of Cain', which he walled up in the north-east to wait for Judgement Day. The monsters, neatly arranged along the southern African coast, are largely derived from accounts of Alexander's travels, though he found most of them in Asia, not Africa. The journeys of Paul (marked by Tarsus, Philippi, Corinth, Gortyna in Crete, Pozzuoli, among others) and the other Apostles can be followed on the map, but their landmarks were the same as those of the Roman empire, so it is difficult to know if this is the intention of the mapmaker or a by-product of his dependence on Roman nomenclature, preserved by the New Testament. Crone also noted the use of the Antonine Itinerary, a third-century AD written plan for an imperial journey.

More unusual, and uncovered by Crone's detective work, are the contemporary pilgrimage and trade routes.[37] One consists of the main stations in France from a thirteenth-century guide to the wool trade, while another, the 'Voie Regordane', is an itinerary from the Mediterranean to the fairs of Champagne. Better known is the pilgrims' route to Compostela, with Paris at one end, the mountain passes of the Pyrenees in the middle, and the *Templum Sancti Jacobi* and the lighthouse of Brigantia at the terminus.

Certainly the Hereford map was an unwieldy guide to take on an actual journey, but Crone's observations lend support to the idea of the itinerary, or actual travel experience, being at the heart of later medieval map-making, pointing the way to a more practical and less theoretical sort of geography, which even at the moment of the Hereford map's completion was producing the portolan charts of seafarers.

The biblical content of the map is substantial, though somewhat dwarfed by the masses of material introduced from the rest of the world. The area of Palestine is enlarged beyond its proper proportion in order to fit in all the important place-names and possibly also to get Jerusalem into the centre of the map. Pictorial features include Lot's wife, looking regretfully back at the cities of Sodom and Gomorrah, now engulfed by the Dead Sea. Further afield are Noah's ark with the passengers' faces in the windows, looking exactly like tourists on a bus. The tower of Babel is the largest single structure on the map. (See Plate IX.) A lengthy text which runs alongside it describes the grandeur of the ancient city of Babylon. Adam and Eve are shown twice, first in the walled island of Paradise accompanied by the snake and the four rivers, but also below, being driven away by the angel with the flaming sword. (See Plate X.) Behind them the city of Enoch stands, while ahead are two jovial-looking dog-headed creatures whose size belies their label as 'giants'. Overhead the *arbor balsami* or dry tree has a complex history, being derived from the oracle trees visited by Alexander, but transmuting itself into the tree of the forbidden fruit, from which the cross was made, and which is preserved to play a role in the last great battle.[38] All in all an excellent example of the hijacking of ancient mythology by the Christians, and here serving as a symbol of classical past, Christian past, and the future.

In addition to the itineraries and the Bible, the sources for the Hereford map include all the usual suspects. Solinus gets his name on the map, Isidore is quoted, and Aethicus Ister provides some of the fantasies in northern Asia. In the lower-right-hand corner, just above the rider and the huntsman, the map's maker informs us that the map 'within' is a description by Orosius of the *ornesta* of the world, a redundancy in that the term *ornesta* is derived from a contraction of *Orosii mundi historia*, the history of the world by Orosius.[39] In the Middle Ages it became another name for a world map, and doubtless it is true that Orosius's widely-known and much-copied geography was the foundation stone.

The Hereford map shows plainly, and in much more luxuriant detail, the image of the world framed by the divine cycle of creation and judgement. As events unrolled down the map – the expulsion from the garden, the Flood, the wanderings of the Hebrews from Egypt to Canaan, the sacrifice and resurrection of Christ, the evangelical missions of the Apostles, the extension of civilization to Europe as far as the western coast of Spain and the building of St James's church – the Christian was instructed in the meaning of history. However, he could not help being distracted by the tabloid quality of some of the news from the world: two-headed monsters, cannibals, and people with other disgusting and fascinating habits. As the Hereford map was being finished, the Polos were setting out on their eastern journeys, not deterred at all by these phenomena, but rather hoping to see some of them. In the next century these money-minded Italians, the sea-savvy Portuguese and their Catalan Jewish mapmakers were to transform this world view, until its very base, the *ornesta mundi*, had to give way to something new. The present time began to seem more important than the historical sense fostered by the old *mappaemundi*, as places the Romans never knew were explored, named, conquered, and put on the map.

Spiritual Maps

The earth as the still centre and lowest, darkest point of the whirling spheres of light, the earth borne up by angels or held in the hands of God, the earth strictly defined by the words of the Bible with its four corners and four rivers: these visions took the form of maps with varying degrees of relationship to physical reality. In the medieval passion for analogies, mystical mapmakers conceived of the earth as the prototype of various divine structures, such as Noah's ark or the tabernacle described to Moses in excruciating detail in Exodus, chapters 25 to 31. The very literalness of these descriptions in cubits and material specifications added to their importance and demanded visual representation. From these drawings some sensitive thinkers derived the form of the earth. Was this what God was really telling us?

The purely visionary map is the stereotype of the medieval map in the popular mind, though they are actually rather rare. The maps we have looked at so far had their bases in physical reality, both temporal and spatial, though they might be pressed into the service of religion, as, for example, in biblical commentary. Even the diagrams and maps in this chapter, with the possible exception of that of Cosmas, are intended as an interpretation, not a copy, of physical reality. Few medieval thinkers, no matter how mystical, lost their grasp of the hard and intrusive facts of physical existence. While Hugh of St Victor describes the world imposed on the form of Noah's ark, he also gives a detailed and factual description of another, less mystical map. Both have their uses.

THE WORLD IS A TENT

The earliest and most doctrinaire of these inspired mapmakers was an Alexandrian Greek, whose name we do not know. He called himself an 'anonymous Christian'. His nickname 'Cosmas Indicopleustes' became attached to his works centuries later and means, more or less, 'Mr World Sails-to-India'.[1] He tells us that he was a merchant who had travelled widely, perhaps as far as India, as his sobriquet suggests, although India was an extremely vague term in those days, as any glance at a medieval map will attest. He retired to a

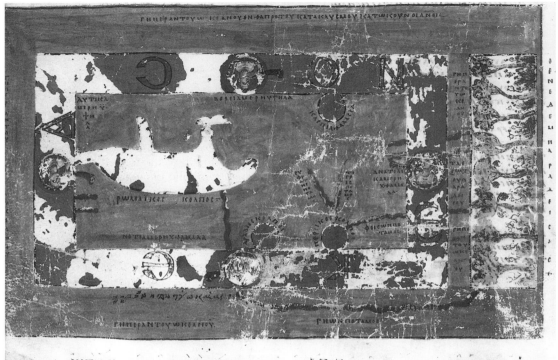

monastery at the end of his business career, and perhaps took vows, though this is not certain. His book was written in the welter of theological controversy preceding the Council of Constantinople in 553 AD at which a variant of Nestorian Christianity was denounced, and his polemical tone seems to be part of the general fray.

Self-taught and fiercely dogmatic, Cosmas believed that his business success gave him authority in other fields as well: Americans in the 1990s will recognize the voice of Ross Perot. He attacked the theory that the earth was a sphere, both on the grounds of its pagan origin and common sense, and he was particularly anxious to discredit the existence of the Antipodes. How could rain fall up in the southern hemisphere? How could people hang upside down by their toes? Beazley notes that 'he carried the popular tradition to the furthest extreme'.[2] His vituperation against Greek science is a sign of its continuing vitality in Alexandria on the eve of the Arab invasion.

Cosmas constructed a world which united physical and

8.1. Cosmas Indicopleustes, world map. Cosmas, a sixth-century Alexandrian businessman turned monk, maintained that the earth was flat and depicted it here in a rectangular format. North is at the top, and Paradise in the east. Here the human race dwelt until the Flood, when they were transported across the now-impassable Ocean. We cannot get back to Paradise, but the four rivers regularly flow from that world to this by means of submarine passages. Size of map 233 × 315 mm. Vat. MS gr.699, fol. 40[v], ninth century.
Courtesy of the Vatican Library.

spiritual reality, based on scattered clues from the Bible. His jumping-off point was a reference by St Paul in II Corinthians, chapter 5, to our terrestrial home as a tabernacle, or tent, contrasting it with the eternal habitation made for us by God in the heavens. In the letter to the Hebrews, chapter 9, Paul expounds further on the symbolic significance of this construction. The first tent, made during the wandering of the Israelites in the wilderness, is 'a symbol of the present time,' with its material sacrifices and regulations imposed upon the body (Hebrews 9.9). Cosmas, establishing the tabernacle as his primary structure of the physical earth, goes on to analyze all its appurtenances as symbolic of worldly space and time. For example, the four corners of the table are the four tropics (solstices and equinoxes) of the year, while the seven lamps represent the seven days of the week, and the twelve loaves of shewbread are the twelve months (II, 36; V, 33–4). Placed on the table in groups of three, each group of loaves stands for one of the four seasons.

Cosmas's structure is of a flat, immobile earth with the sky draped over it like a tent with four poles at the corners. The inhabited world is a rectangle in the centre, pierced by the four great gulfs: the Red Sea (or Arabian Gulf), the Persian Gulf, the Caspian Sea, and the Mediterranean. The ocean surrounds the earth and beyond, to the east, is another strip of land where the earthly Paradise may be found. The human race lived there until the time of Noah, when the ark made its voyage from that world to this (II, 24, 25). The ocean is not navigable by human beings, who are restricted to sailing in the four gulfs. The four rivers of Paradise cleave a passage through or under the ocean to appear on our earth in the form of the Nile, Tigris, Euphrates, and Ganges (or Indus) rivers (II, 81). Cosmas's uncertainty on the last river reinforces the idea that he never travelled to India. The sons of Noah divided the earth into the three known continents, but Cosmas sticks to his theme of fours by citing the four peoples who inhabit the extremes of the four cardinal directions. These are the Celtic people in the west, the Scythians in the north, the Ethiopians in the south, and the Indians in the east. He reproduces a map at this point in the manuscript, saying it is copy of the map of the Greek historian Ephorus (405–330 BC). Other fours include the four elements, symbolized by the four colours of the veil of the tabernacle, and the four empires from the book of Daniel.

Cosmas has religious explanations for meteorological phenomena, too. Earthquakes and rains are the work of angels under the command of God. Night occurs when the sun goes behind an enormous mountain in the north in its circular course above the earth. The northern part of the earth is elevated higher than the south, which explains why the course of the Tigris, flowing from the north, is rapid, while the Nile, flowing from the south, is sluggish.

Cosmas proves the temporary existence of the human race by the progress he sees in the arts and sciences, for if the earth were eternal, he argues, history would be mere repetition. One example of an art perfected by human intelligence is the calculation of Easter so that it is predicted many years in advance and celebrated simultaneously throughout the whole world (III, 67–8). He asserts that 'any old woman or peasant in the field' knows more about natural phenomena than Plato or Aristotle did, not to mention the all-important knowledge of the resurrection of the dead and the heavenly kingdom. Above the earthly tent is another, spiritual home of the human race, inhabited now by God and the angels. While this tabernacle below will be destroyed, the latter will last forever.

Despite his travels, Cosmas does not give much geographical detail in his book, though he says he wrote another book about his journeys which does not survive. His primary interest is the construction of his fantastic world scheme to support his individual interpretation of Christianity, and what geographical details he includes are purely in support of his theory.

The original manuscript, now lost, was illustrated. Cosmas announces in the prologue that the book will have pictures and urges his readers to examine them with care. Again in his exposition he tells us that the illustrations are provided for people 'who wish to teach themselves visually'.[3] Altogether he provides 22 cosmological and geographical diagrams, including the maps, in addition to the other illustrations. The map of the inhabited earth and the diagram of the structure of the universe both appear in Book IV in all three manuscripts of his work which survive.[4] The one shows the flat, rectangular earth with its gulfs and rivers, the surrounding ocean, and Paradise in the east. The cardinal directions are indicated and the four winds appear, personified, blowing through horns. The Mediterranean is configured to show the Adriatic and the Aegean, but they are not labelled. The diagram of the universe has the observer looking in from the side, with the ocean in the foreground and the world mountain behind. Overall is draped the tent or tabernacle of the heavens.

Throughout his writing Cosmas interweaves time and space. History for him is simply prophecy fulfilled, and he tracks back and forth between past and future with ease. He gives a history of the march of power through the four empires, and repeats an account of biblical history. He also speculates on dating systems and the calendar and weighs in with a theory on the month of creation, which should be the

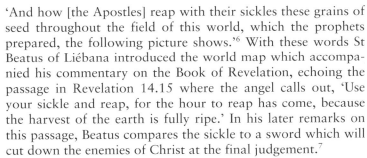

same as the month of Passover and of the Resurrection. None of this, however, appears on his maps.

Cosmas fascinates us by his weirdness, although it is probably true, as he asserts, that he copied most of his ideas from others. His influence on subsequent generations of mapmakers was negligible. What he represents is a kind of know-nothing approach to science, which exists in every period of history and seems ominous here because of what was to follow. While ignored in the Middle Ages, he became a favourite example of medieval obscurantism in the minds of nineteenth-century writers, wishing to demonstrate the superiority of modern scientific thinking.[5]

THE WORLD IS A FIELD

8.2. St Beatus, as he is portrayed on the church door of his monastery, now Santo Toribio in Liébana in northern Spain.

'And how [the Apostles] reap with their sickles these grains of seed throughout the field of this world, which the prophets prepared, the following picture shows.'[6] With these words St Beatus of Liébana introduced the world map which accompanied his commentary on the Book of Revelation, echoing the passage in Revelation 14.15 where the angel calls out, 'Use your sickle and reap, for the hour to reap has come, because the harvest of the earth is fully ripe.' In his later remarks on this passage, Beatus compares the sickle to a sword which will cut down the enemies of Christ at the final judgement.[7]

A Benedictine monk, Beatus lived at the monastery of St Martin, now Santo Toribio,[8] in a narrow valley in Asturias among the precipitous mountains of northern Spain. His lifetime (about 711–800) coincided with the Arab invasion of Spain and the retreat of the Christians to a small stronghold in the northern mountains. However, far from being isolated, Beatus, employed as a tutor to members of the royal family, had access to both royal and monastic libraries. He was also deeply involved in international church politics. In 794 he probably attended a church conference in Frankfurt, called by Charlemagne to deal with the heresy of Adoptionism, the theory that Christ was God's 'adopted' son.[9] Beatus had already written a pamphlet denouncing this heresy, which he seems to have found a greater threat to Christianity than the Moslem invaders.

His commentary on the Apocalypse, originally composed in 776, was revised several times by him during his lifetime.[10] Beatus includes the entire text of the Book of Revelation in his work, with each quotation followed by an explanation. Far from being original, the commentary was a collection of excerpts from the church fathers. 'The things put into this little book are not by me,' he says in his introduction, 'but by the holy fathers, whose interpretations I have found in books signed by these authorities, that is to say, Jerome, Augustine, Ambrose, Fulgentius, Gregory, Tyconius, Irenaeus, Apringius, and Isidore.'[11] What is most unusual about the work, and what has made it famous, is the illustrations, which are called for in the text and were apparently part of the first edition. Plainly Beatus regards visual enlightenment as important as reading. In the original text there were 68 illustrations of scenes taken from the words of the Apocalypse, as well as seven illustrations based on the Commentary. Some manuscripts contain well over 100 illustrations in all, many full-page and some, of which the map is one, spreading over two pages.

Beatus manuscripts are the treasures of the libraries fortunate enough to own them.[12] Dating mostly from the tenth to the thirteenth centuries, there are a total of 34 manuscripts, of which twenty are complete, or almost complete, and 26 contain illustrations.[13] The pictures, in many cases the work of superlative artists, blaze with colour and translate with extreme literalness the terrifying visions of St John, in contrast with the allegorical interpretations urged by Beatus's text.[14] From the initial revelation to John, to the opening of the seven seals, to the plagues brought on by the blowing of the seven trumpets, to the scary seven-headed beast and the ecstatic adoration of the lamb, the book bursts with marvellous imagery and brilliant realizations of John's words. One student of the work has called it the 'Book of Fire', both for its luminous colours and for its passionate emphasis on the terrors of the coming judgement.[15]

The stemma of the Beatus manuscripts has been exhaustively studied and the latest (may we hope, final?) version can be found in John Williams's comprehensive new work on the illustrations.[16] There are two main editions, both of which appear to date from Beatus's own lifetime. By the early tenth century, if not earlier, the book included Jerome's commentary on the Book of Daniel (also illustrated) and a genealogical table of the ancestors of Christ, with historical notes. Other, shorter works added to the collection are Gregory of Elvira's treatise on Noah's ark as an allegory of the Church, tables on the numerology of the Antichrist, and two short selections from Isidore's *Etymologies*: Book VI, 13–14, on books, and Book IX, 9, 'De adfinitatibus et gradibus', on family relationships.

Fourteen Beatus manuscripts retain their maps today. A map does not seem a very obvious illustration for such an other-worldly book as a commentary on the Apocalypse, and indeed no other Apocalypse picture cycle contains such an illustration.[17] In Beatus's work it follows his long prologue to

Book II, which covers the organization and personnel of the Church and is largely lifted from Isidore's *Etymologies*, Books VII and VIII. It introduces the commentary on Revelation 2, the messages to the seven churches in Asia. After following Isidore through his section on the apostles, Beatus goes to another source, the *De Ortu and Orbitu Patrum* (Of the location and burial of the fathers) to list the Apostles' mission fields. His assignments are: Peter, Rome; Andrew, Achaia; Thomas, India; James, Spain; John, Asia (Minor); Matthew, Macedonia; Philip, Gaul; Bartholomew, Lycaonia (south-central Asia Minor); Simon Zelotes, Egypt; James, the brother of Jesus, Jerusalem. Paul's assignment is the entire world of the Gentiles.[18] The map follows, and in some cases a group portrait of the apostles is included.

The Beatus maps, like the text of the manuscripts, fall into two groups. The largest and oldest group, in terms of surviving manuscripts, are those of Branch II. The first of these, now at the Pierpont Morgan Library in New York, was originally drawn by the scribe Magius for the monastery of San Miguel de Escalada, near Leon. It is dated 964 of the Spanish era (926 for the rest of the world), but its principal scholar John Williams thinks this date an impossibility for such a sophisticated product,[19] and suggests the dates 940–945 instead. The manuscripts of the group to which this one belongs represent a revival of the Beatus tradition in the tenth century, and it is thought that the illustrations were substantially revised at that time. Thus we cannot assume that the map we see is an exact replica of Beatus's eighth-century production.

The map Magius made is a large rectangle, occupying two pages. The ocean, painted gold and scattered with decorative blue fish and a few square islands, surrounds it like a frame. East is at the top, and off centre to the right appears the Garden of Eden with Adam and Eve clutching their fig leaves while the snake looks on from a nearby tree. The Mediterranean occupies the centre with square islands arranged like stepping-stones. The Nile flows into it from the west, while the Black Sea/Don River complex, unlabelled and painted blue, flows straight north to the ocean. Only one other river is shown, and it appears to be the Danube, though it also is unlabelled. Decorative mountains topped with token vegetation are placed around the map, some with names (Caucasus, the two Lebanons, Riphaean, and *mons aquilo*), others without. The only city symbol is the one for Jerusalem. (See Plate IX.)

The most unusual feature of this map, and this is a characteristic of all Beatus maps, is the existence of a southern continent, separated from Africa by a band of water, here labelled as the Red Sea. The inscription on this map reads *Deserta terra vicina soli ab ardore incognita nobis* (wilderness land

8.3. Beatus, world map, from Burgo de Osma. Paradise is at the top (east), marked by the four rivers. The apostles appear in their assigned mission fields. Saint James is shown (lower left) enshrined in his new cathedral at Compostela. The one-legged man on the right probably represents some confusion between the Antipodes and the Sciopods. He is protecting himself from excessive solar radiation with his large foot. Size of map: 300 × 380 mm. Cathedral of Burgo de Osma, Cod.1, fols 34ᵛ–35, Spanish, possibly Navarre, 1086.
Courtesy of the Cathedral of Burgo de Osma.

near the sun unknown to us because of the heat).[20] Longer inscriptions appear on other versions of the map, and their variety reveals the confusion about the location of this fourth continent. The conventional interpretation is that it indicates the presence of a continent in the southern hemisphere, as was shown on zonal maps. The confusion is heightened by reference to the Antipodes, which properly speaking should be located in the western hemisphere, not in the eastern. The presence of a fourth continent has earned Beatus maps a special category in medieval-map classification as 'quadripartite' maps. (See Plate XI.)[21]

The vague description on Magius's map makes this region sound like Ethiopia, but on the Magius manuscript Ethiopia is labelled separately across the band of water in Africa. 'Ethiopia,' writes the mapmaker, 'where there are people with strange faces and monsters of horrible kinds. It lies beyond the border of Egypt. It is also full of serpents and wild beasts. Here there are precious stones, cinnamon, and balsam.' These 'facts', taken from Isidore's *Etymologies*, xiv, 5, are the standard characteristics of marginal lands, with their exotic qualities, both attractive (precious stones) and repellent (monsters).

As for the Red Sea (Mare Rubrum) it seems to be a generic name covering the Indian Ocean, the Red Sea, and the Persian Gulf, which, as parts of a single body of water, are occasionally conflated in medieval maps. Witness, for example, the numerous maps which show only a single gulf for both Red Sea and the Persian Gulf. In classical times the entire complex was called the Erythraean Sea. In the Isidoran inscription used on some other Beatus maps this fourth part of the world is referred to as being across the 'interior ocean'. It is Williams's suggestion that the mapmakers have tried to draw the body of water accordingly. It is an interesting reflection that, according to Ptolemy's sophisticated cartography, the Indian Ocean was, in fact, an 'interior sea'. He applied the term *Mare Rubrum* to the part which lay south of Arabia.[22]

While Magius's manuscript is the oldest of the commentaries to survive, it was copied almost two centuries after the original. Scholars also regard it as a sample of the second edition of the text, though it should be recalled that both editions date from Beatus's lifetime. A member of Branch I, the first edition, may be found today at the Cathedral of Burgo de Osma, and it is tempting to see this map as Beatus's original version because of its design. While Beatus gives no specifications at all for his map, other than that it will show the apostles' mission fields, the Osma map has small portrait heads of the Apostles placed on the map. The same is true of the map fragment surviving in the commentary in Lisbon, and recently another map with heads was discovered in Milan, though not now attached to a work by Beatus.[23] Still another map showing the dispersion of the Apostles and containing their portraits has been uncovered on the wall of the rock-hewn church of San Pedro de Rocas in Galicia.[24] Although the map is supposed to show the apostles on assignment, the portrait heads on the Osma map definitely suggest reliquaries, and thus, in addition to representing the spread of Christianity, the map could be seen as a travel map for pilgrims in quest of holy bones.

Unlike most of the maps in the commentaries of Branch II, the Osma map is circular. Paradise lacks the pictures of the sinful first parents, and is shown as a square with the four rivers, a more maplike configuration. Aside from the heads of the Apostles, pictorial elements include lighthouses in Alexandria and Brigantia (Spain), a fortification in Carthage, and city symbols for Toledo, Tyre, Troy, Constantinople, and Antioch. Peter is shown enclosed in a towered church in Rome, with Paul nearby, while James gets an even larger church in Spain. The date of the manuscript coincides with the Christian conquest of Toledo (1085) and the rebuilding of the church at Santiago de Compostela, which was given cathedral status a decade later, in 1095. The ocean, with an even spacing of rectangular islands and fish, surrounds the map, and there is a decorative border around the outside.

The fourth continent on the Osma map is cut off from Africa (here, Libia) by water and has a red sun-disk on it to illustrate its torrid climate. The most unusual feature is the presence of a Sciopod, a one-legged man, shielding himself from the sun with his single enormous foot. The inscription tells us that 'This region remains uninhabitable and unknown to us on account of the heat of the sun. It is said that the Scopodes live there, who have single legs and [travel] with amazing speed. The Greeks call them Sciopodas, because, lying supine on the ground during the summer, they are shaded by the great size of their feet.'[25] A Sciopod appears on one other Beatus map, now in Paris, but without any text, and a text combining Sciopods and the Antipodes is also on the Lorvâo manuscript in Lisbon.[26] This confusion between Sciopods and Antipodes seems natural enough, given the remoteness and/or unlikelihood of both. The monsters, whose whereabouts was always vague, eventually found a home on the southern edge of Africa in thirteenth-century maps. The Sciopods, thanks to their built-in beach umbrellas, were always associated with the south and its superabundant sunshine. Two tenth-century Isidore maps have a *terra de pedes latos* (*sic*, land of the broad feet) in west Africa, cut off from the rest of the continent by a band of water, and this map tradition may be the source of Beatus's Sciopods.[27]

The Church was understandably uneasy about the existence of human beings in an inaccessible part of the world. Were they descended from Adam and Eve? How was the Christian message to reach them? Isidore in his account of the inhabitants of the fourth continent, part of which is quoted on most Beatus maps, carefully uses the world 'fabled'.[28] Even in the brief text on the Osma map, one notes the ambivalence of an uninhabitable land, which is nevertheless inhabited, even if it is by monsters.

The inclusion of a fourth continent on nearly all Beatus maps makes a peculiar combination with the theme of the missionary Apostles. As John Williams observes, 'For a Beatus map to present lands impossible to know because of an uncrossable ocean would be counter to its purpose. . . .'[29] Possibly the model was a zonal map, taken from a computus manuscript and adapted by Beatus to his theological purposes. The result, like his conflicting quotations from his sources, was puzzling, for the southern continent in the zonal model was supposed to be inhabitable, if inaccessible. The poor brethren, for whose edification he wrote, would have to wait for the fullness of time to find out how it all fitted in.

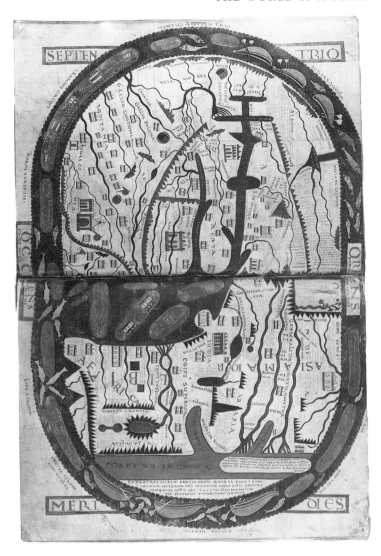

8.4. Beatus, world map from Saint-Sever. Size of map 570 × 370 mm. BN MS lat.8878, between fols 45 and 46, eleventh century. Drawn by Stephanus Garsia for Gregory, abbot of Saint-Sever in Gascony. Reproduced with north at top.
Courtesy of the Bibliothèque Nationale, Paris.

The largest and most detailed map of the Beatus series is in the manuscript made at the Abbey of Saint-Sever in Gascony in the mid-eleventh century. The scribe signs his name, Stephanus Garsia, and dedicates his work to his abbot, Gregory (1028–72).[30] The map is drawn as an oval with the cardinal directions and the names of the winds indicated around the edge. At the top in the Garden of Eden, Eve is in the very act of plucking the fatal apple, while Adam stands by, and the snake, wound around the trunk of the tree, looks on. Sausage-shaped islands occupy the outer ocean, along with the characteristic fish and boats. Others appear in the

[155]

Mediterranean, the largest of which are Sicily, Crete, and Cyprus. Some of the islands, such as Sardinia and Britain, are labelled with their dimensions in miles in a tradition that goes back to Pliny. City symbols crowd western Europe, northern Africa and Asia Minor, while the rest of the world is filled with lengthy quotations, mostly from Isidore, about the wonders to be found there. Numerous rivers are shown, unlike the simpler maps of Branch II, as well as lengthy mountain chains. The scribe, hoping to please his patron, has drawn the humble church of Saint-Sever as large as the city symbols of Rome and Constantinople. In the south the 'Red Sea', coloured red, cuts off the continent of Africa and branches into two gulfs in the east, the Arabian and Persian Gulfs. The island of Taprobane, bearing a long inscription, floats in the eastern part of this sea. Beyond the sea the fourth continent is represented as a small sliver of a circle covered with text from Isidore: 'In addition to the three parts of the world a fourth part lies across the interior ocean in the south which is unknown to us on account of the heat of the sun. In these regions the antipodes are reported, in story, to dwell.'[31]

With 270 names the Saint-Sever world map contains the most geographical detail of all the maps in this tradition. Its quality has led some scholars to think it might be a fairly faithful copy of a Roman map, but the large number of medieval names (50) and the enlargement and special emphasis on Gascony would lead one to conclude that it is a local and contemporary production.[32] Its large size (370 × 570 mm.) perhaps led to its separation from the book, to which it was restored in the nineteenth century. It may have served for a while as a wall map for readers in the Saint-Sever library.

An interesting feature of some Beatus manuscripts is that they contain another map, a small T–O placed in the genealogical tables at the front.[33] The T–O appears next to Noah and holds a brief text, naming Noah's sons and describing the climate of the land each inherited: Asia is temperate, Europe frigid, and Africa, called 'Libia' in these sketches, is hot. The presence of these small icons indicates that the T–O was a form used for shorthand purposes but not regarded as the exclusive model of the earth. Even in maps as abstract as some of the Beatus maps, the T–O form is not strictly followed. In the Saint-Sever map, for example, the O is an oval and the positioning of the Nile and the Black Sea complex do not at all suggest a cross bar of the letter T. In others, such as the one in London, the earth takes the form of a rectangle and the Nile flows in from the west. (See fig.1.6.)

Despite the variations in Beatus world maps, is there a common ancestor? Certainly the maps vary, particularly in their shape, as we have rectangles, circles, ovals, and, in one case, a four-leaf clover. The lack of importance of shape, however, can be seen in the relationship between the Gerona (975) and Turin (early twelfth century) maps. The latter was copied directly from the former and, though nearly all the features on the two maps are exactly the same (the placement and number of mountains, the configuration of rivers), Gerona is rectangular and Turin is circular. The artist in Turin may have altered the shape to conform to more modern conventions, or perhaps he was simply making room for four picturesque wind figures, puffing on horns and riding on inflated goatskins.

The most striking common feature is the inclusion of the fourth continent in some form or another, which is rare in other medieval maps of the ecumene. Although the Apostles appear in person only on three maps, the places to which they were sent appear on nearly all of them. Paradise is also present on all maps, though not in the same form. The manuscripts of Branch II have a picture of Adam and Eve, but Branch I manuscripts have a more abstract shape with the four rivers. A small but perhaps significant detail is the presence of fish in the ocean border on nearly every map. This form of ornamentation seems have struck every copyist's fancy and may be an indication that, whatever else he or she may have been using as a model, at least one came from the Beatus tradition.

In his most recent article, which deals specifically with the descent and copying of the map, John Williams suggests that the map of Magius may be the closest to Beatus's original. Magius, a creative artist, was not particularly interested in cartography. While altering the style of the other illuminations, he may have been content to copy the map without remaking it. In addition, its rectangular form suggests the 'field of the world', the phrase with which Beatus introduces the map. It is also similar in shape to the Albi map, one of the few maps of equal antiquity. When subsequent scribes changed the map form to an oval or circle and added other embellishments, these may have been considered improvements. An example is the change of form when the Gerona map was copied in Turin. Thus, Williams proposes, original illustrations may not always be the most apt, and the appearance of the heads of the apostles on the map at Burgo de Osma and Lorvâo could have been a felicitous invention of the eleventh century.[34]

As for the source of the Beatus maps, Williams reminds us of the dependence of the text on a fifth- or sixth-century copy of the fourth-century commentary of Tyconius, a North African. One piece of evidence for his African sources is the translation of the Bible he uses, which is not the Vulgate, but an earlier African version.[35] It is Williams's hypothesis that the map could have come to Beatus along with Tyconius's commentary, which was apparently illustrated. In this case there is a tantalizing link to Orosius, a geographical writer, originally Spanish, who worked in Africa. Could the Beatus map be a version of Orosius's lost map? Menendez Pidal's thesis, that the Beatus maps were descended in a direct line from Isidore, has been somewhat shaken by the discovery that the primal Isidore map, Vatican Library, MS lat.6018, can no longer be associated with Isidore. If there is a common ancestor between Beatus and the Vatican map, it remains unknown.[36]

The Book of the Apocalypse is a book about time, specifically the end of time, but also about the measurement of time in hours, days, and years, which acquire increasing significance as the end draws near. In Book IV Beatus speculates on when that end will come, although he admits that this is a dangerous activity, condemned by both Jesus and St Augustine. Here he calculates that the sixth or last age of the world will end in 838 of the Spanish era, or 800 AD, six thousand years from the creation of Adam, just 25 years from his own day.[37] In some versions of the commentary, those thought to be copied from the first edition, the current date is given as 776 AD. Other copyists updated this to include their own present year. The alert reader will have already noted unusually specific dates for many of the manuscripts in this series.

The documents which were added to Beatus's commentary also had a temporal significance. The Book of Daniel is not only a prophecy but contains one of the primary tools of medieval historical thinking, the progression of the four empires. The genealogical tables which are appended to the front of many of the manuscripts are a history in terms of human generations. These tables not only list the ancestors of Christ as far back as Adam, but give snippets of historical text and include the Roman emperors up to the time of Jesus. Isidore's text on the degrees of relationship also relates to time, particularly as he notes that these will become meaningless at the Last Judgement.

The depiction of time on the Beatus maps is finely tuned to the ideas presented in his commentary. The comparison of the world to a field may have led to the rectangular shape of one series of the maps. Adam and Eve are shown at the moment of their sin, either in the act of taking the apple or guiltily clutching their fig leaves. Their previous existence in Eden was timeless, but now, with the introduction of sin, death enters, and with it, time. Time progresses through the medium of the biblical narrative and the conquests of the great empires of Alexander and Rome. Finally the coming of Jesus and the dispatching of the Apostles to their mission fields in all parts of the world will bring time to an end, once all souls are converted.

The presence of the fourth continent is ambiguous. Beatus

does not mention it in the commentary, but then there is very little on geography in his exposition. The continent could have been simply an ornament to the map, modelled on an example. If it were truly uninhabited, its presence would be irrelevant to the progress of Christian history. However, if people lived there, the end could not come until they, too, no matter how monstrous, were given the opportunity of salvation. In this case, the world had a long, perhaps an infinite, time to endure, despite Beatus's dire words in Book IV, that God was coming to ask us how we had used the talents which he had given us, and that eternal rewards and punishments would be distributed according to our merits.[38]

THE WORLD AS AN ARK

Hugh of St-Victor distinguishes himself as an author who designed (or described) two maps, one geographical and the other purely visionary. The latter has always been well-known, but the former was recently resurrected from oblivion by the French scholar, Patrick Gautier Dalché.[39] Hugh (1096–1141), originally from Saxony, came to Paris in the early twelfth century and became a teacher and eventually the master of the school at the abbey of St-Victor. Among his theological works is a treatise on the liberal arts, the *Didascalicon*, and a work of history, the *Chronicon*, as well as commentaries on the Bible. Although a mystic, Hugh believed that one must first know facts, before one can ascend to the higher truth of allegory. 'The significance of things,' he wrote, 'is far more excellent than that of words, because the latter was established by usage, but Nature dictated the former. The latter is the voice of men, the former the voice of God speaking to men.'[40] Among the subjects to be studied, he particularly emphasized the role of sacred history, 'from which, like honey from the honeycomb, the truth of allegory is extracted'.[41] The study of place was essential to the study of history, and Hugh opens the *Chronicon* by urging his students to consider the three aspects of history: time, place, and the actors.

In *De Arca Noe Mystica* (1128/29) Hugh begins with the familiar concept of Noah's ark as a symbol of the Church.[42] As the ark saved Noah and his family from the waters of the Flood, the church will save believers from death and the destruction of the final judgement. At the end of this little treatise Hugh describes a cosmic diagram, encircling the rectangular form of the ark with a three-tiered representation of the universe. In the centre he places a *mappamundi*, which he fills with 'countries, mountains, rivers, castles, and fortified

places, and Egypt in the south and Babylon in the north'. Egypt is chosen, as he explains elsewhere in the treatise, because it is the place of liberation, while Babylon represents captivity.[43] Paradise, identified with the bosom of Abraham, is placed at top (east) of the map. The Last Judgement is in the west, with the elect to the right and the damned to the left. Hell is located in the north, the realm of eternal cold. Other than this, Hugh is rather vague about the contents of his 'map', as he is more anxious to move on to show the marvelous symphony of elements, both temporal and spatial.

Surrounding the sphere figure of the earth is another sphere which is the sphere of the air. Here can be found the four seasons, personified, and the four corresponding senses and qualities. Also in the sphere of air are the twelve winged figures, representing the winds, four cardinal winds, each with two 'acolyte' winds. The acolytes have only one trumpet each, while the cardinal winds are blowing on two. The third sphere is that of ether, occupied by the twelve months and the signs of the zodiac. Christ in majesty is enthroned with his shoulders above the universe, his feet below, and his arms outstretched to embrace the whole. He is flanked by two seraphim who shade him with their wings, while a hierarchy

8.5. World diagram, after Hugh of Saint-Victor, *De Arca Noe Mystica*. The world is embraced by God with a row of small medallions descending from his mouth (the Word), illustrating the six days of Creation. The last of these is Paradise, represented in the eastern part of the world. Europe and Africa are shown, and Asia is divided, for theological reasons, into Egypt and Bablyonia. Symbols around the earth indicate the seasons, the qualities, the months of the year and the signs of the zodiac. Reconstructed from Hugh's text by Danielle LeCoq and Jean-Pierre Magnier in *Géographie du Monde au Moyen Age et à la Renaissance*, ed. by Monique Pelletier (Paris, 1989), pp. 13–14.

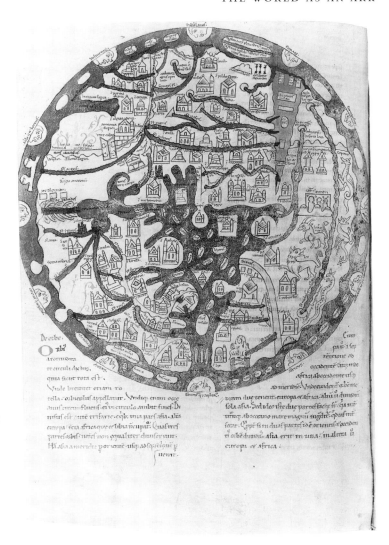

8.6. Map from Isidore's *Etymologies*. A rare example of a detailed world map placed as an illustration in Isidore's encyclopedic text. Patrick Gautier Dalché proposes it as a realization of the *Descriptio mappa mundi* of Hugh of Saint-Victor, 1130–5. Diameter of map 266 mm. MS Clm.10058, fol. 154ᵛ, northern France, twelfth century.

Courtesy of the Bayerische Staatsbibliothek, Munich.

of nine ranks of angels is arranged below. A series of six small medallions, lined up between the top of the earth (creation of light) and the centre (Adam), illustrate the six days of Creation, thus linking, according to Hugh's vision, the moment of Creation with the end of time.

Several scholars have reconstructed Hugh's diagram, as the original has long since disappeared.[44] A number of its features can be readily found in surviving medieval maps, for the winged winds appear in the Henry of Mainz map, and God embraces the earth in both the Ebstorf world map and the Psalter map. The correlation of elements of space and time, such as the seasons, elements and qualities, are recognizable

[161]

from diagrams dating back to Isidore's *De natura rerum* and reproduced in countless manuscripts on astronomical subjects.

Hugh's other map is more mundane. Describing the map in a class lecture, here he limits himself strictly to terrestrial phenomena. For example, the earthly Paradise, present on so many other medieval maps, is not included. In the treatise uncovered by Gautier Dalché, Hugh lists 'countries, mountains, rivers, etc.' by name,[45] organizing them into categories and adding little tag-lines to make them stick in his students' memories. For example, he mentions the serpents who guard the mountain of gold on a promontory of India in the Red Sea, and that Spain is shaped like a triangle.

The map he was describing no longer exists, but Gautier Dalché thinks that it resembled a map found in a copy of Isidore's *Etymologies*, now in Munich, but originally made in the neighbourhood of Paris around the years 1130–5.[46] As noted above, it is unusual to find such a detailed world map in the *Etymologies*. This one was plainly copied at the same time as the text, which surrounds it, and comes at the beginning of Book XIV, though before chapter 2, *De orbe*, instead of chapter 3, *De Asia*, where the T–O usually appears. However, its relation to Isidore is slight – it contains none of the passages from the *Etymologies* which ornamented other medieval maps, but instead has numerous references unique to Hugh's *Descriptio*, which, Gautier Dalché postulates, was delivered in front of the larger original of this map. Examples of the fidelity to Hugh's words include a careful separation and naming of the various parts of the Mediterranean, three islands or pillars (instead of two) in the strait of Cadiz, and the range of the Alps stretching from the toe of Italy to the source of the river Drave.

Otherwise the map follows most of the conventions of the twelfth century. The whole, a creation in vivid green and red, is surrounded by the twelve winds, represented as blowing heads. The earth's surface is crowded with buildings, symbols for cities. Only in the far north and far south (where there are dragons) do these signs of human habitation cease. The course of the Nile in Africa appears in two manifestations, one as a long river running parallel to the southern coast of Africa and another flowing from a source near the Red Sea to the Mediterranean. Not shown is its disappearance and re-emergence from the desert sands. A triangular Sicily stands out among the various islands of the Mediterranean, while islands are ranged around the rim in a regular pattern. Taprobane (Sri Lanka) is divided literally into two islands with one inscription apiece signifying the part dominated by cities and that occupied by wild beasts. The Red Sea is coloured bright red (there is no Persian gulf), and the Caspian Gates are really doors in the middle of the Caucasus range.

Although the Munich map has little in common with Isidore's text, Hugh and Isidore had a common purpose, which was to aid their readers (or hearers) in the study of scripture. Hugh goes further to say that a map alone is not enough, for the mere images of things are meaningless without the interpretation. Hence his text.[47]

Thus Hugh found two diagrams useful in presenting his conception of the world. Where they may seem in part contradictory, for Hugh one simply took up where the other left off. The geographical-style map of the *Descriptio* was the beginning, 'things in themselves'. For the higher meaning one turned to his other diagram, the earth as the scene of the salvation of the human race.

CONCLUSION

The visionary maps of the Middle Ages attempted to reconcile a Christian theological view of the world with the hard facts of physical reality. This project involved placing the earth in both its cosmic and historical contexts. In the cosmic view, the earth was at the centre of the universe and also its lowest point, surrounded by spheres of increasing light and purity as one ascended to the heaven of angels and the presence of God himself. The historical perspective was important for the Christian religion, unlike a religion such as Hinduism, which views time as cyclical. Significant events on the Christian timeline included the Creation, the Flood, the revelation of God to Abraham, the liberation of the Israelites from Egypt and the giving of the law on Mount Sinai, and finally the coming of the Messiah, all of which could be shown on the map. According to St Paul the sacrifice of Christ brought time to an end, but those who lived after him, continuing to experience the travails of temporal existence, struggled to place events in a proper context. The mission of the Apostles, the conversion of the peoples of the world (whether by force or persuasion), and the lives of the saints might all be plotted on a map of the world. Such places on the map showed not only points of spiritual significance, but also indicated the progress of the human race toward its ultimate end, the Last Judgement.

Conclusion

Medieval world maps were philosophical, religious, and historical documents, as well as being concerned with the depiction of space. Taking from the Greco-Roman inheritance, medieval mapmakers envisaged an *ecumene* divided into three continents and surrounded by ocean. They also inherited a zonal model of the earth, which postulated the existence of three other land masses, one in each quarter of the globe, but since these were unexplored, mapmakers were generally content to depict their own world. Whether another, more detailed, map of the world was handed down to them from Rome, we do not know.

In the early years of the Middle Ages there was an effort not only to preserve the classical heritage but also to recast it in a Christian mould. Thinkers such as Jerome, Augustine, Orosius, and Isidore were key figures in this process, but it was not until after the Roman Empire was physically destroyed, along with most of its libraries, that a real restructuring of the world view took place. This was in the era of Charlemagne, when the resources of the Carolingian state and church were marshalled to reach a new synthesis of European thought in all areas. The industrious copying and preservation of what classical literature had survived was an important aspect of this process, but new areas of knowledge were also explored such as the computus, the science of time.

The world map, as it emerged from the Carolingian renaissance, took several forms. One was a T superimposed upon an O, a simple icon denoting the ecumene, or the inhabited portion of the earth, and its three continents. Another was the zonal map, descended from the Greeks, which depicted a globe divided into five climates and, usually, four land-masses, washed by the ocean and swept by its tides as they travelled to the poles and back again. These two forms appeared in scientific manuscripts, histories, even works of literature, wherever a simple rendering of the earth might be wanted. The more detailed world map could be based on either of these forms, or it could take another shape, driven by the demands of geographical realities. Until the twelfth or thirteenth century there is no universal model, though there is wide agreement on certain features.

In depicting the world, medieval mapmakers tried to show

the significance of places as well as their location. They were particularly interested in scenes of memorable religious and historical events. Thus Jerusalem, a provincial city of little importance in the Roman Empire, particularly after its devastation in the first century AD, became a place of great significance as the scene of Christ's execution and resurrection. Gradually it migrated to the centre of medieval maps, not as a geographical fact (though on the surface of a spherical earth the centre could be any point), but as a statement of its spiritual centrality. This was the vision of Dante, who saw Jerusalem as the centre, balanced on the opposite side of the globe by Mount Purgatory, with the earthly Paradise on its summit, out of the reach of sinful humanity.

In making a map, it is difficult to pull together the disparate facts on the ground with abstract ideas of the meaning of the whole. Medieval mapmakers tried to do this with varying degrees of success. In particular, the representation of the passage of time posed a problem: how to show the sequence of events when everything appears simultaneously on the map? The problem was usually addressed (if not solved) by blocks of text, either on the map itself or surrounding it, explaining how the various features were to be interpreted. Probably these written explanations were supplemented by verbal ones now inaudible to us. Thus medieval maps frequently appear in a historical or temporal context, where map and text together elucidate the whole.

By the fourteenth century, when this study ends, the world of maps began to undergo a revolution. Already the first nautical charts based on compass readings had appeared. Their accurate delineation of familiar coastlines were a revelation, and within the next century these forms were incorporated into world maps. Also about this time a manuscript of Ptolemy's *Geography* was discovered in Constantinople. Though it lacked the maps, the text contained directions for projecting the curved earth's surface on a plane and described a method of locating places accurately according to latitude and longitude. These new tools were to change cartography from the province of artists and theologians to that of the geometer.

These technical developments and new tools were driven by an increase in travel and trade, expanding the world view of the Middle Ages and creating the need for more practical maps. The terrible plague of the middle of the fourteenth century, itself spread by the increased contact among the world's peoples, slowed developments on all fronts, including that of cartography. But by the beginning of the fifteenth century Europe was again venturing out, armed with increasingly useful maps. The old maps which drew together theology, science, and history in a single work had seen their culmination in the great *mappae mundi*, of which Hereford Cathedral's map is the best surviving witness. The Catalan World Atlas of the next century (1375) shows an impressive attempt to integrate new cartographic knowledge with the old format. From this point forward, however, the cartographic mainstream flowed into other channels, more devoted to the present than the past.

PREFACE

1. John K. Wright, *Geographical Lore at the Time of the Crusades* (New York, 1925), ch. xi on cartography and pp. 43, and 71. C. R. Beazley titles his book *The Dawn of Modern Geography* (3 vols., London and Oxford, 1897, 1901, 1906), I, viii, 70, 24–5, 399, and *passim*.

2. Matthew Edney, 'Theory and the History of Cartography', *Imago Mundi*, 48 (1996), 187.

3. See J. B. Harley, *Maps and the Columbian Encounter* (Milwaukee, 1990), pp. 135–6.

4. For an example of one of these maps, used in British schoolrooms for over a century, see Peter Whitfield, *The Image of the World* (London, 1994), pp. 124–5.

5. Patrick Gautier Dalché, 'De la glose à la contemplation: Place et fonction de la carte dans les manuscrits du haut moyen âge', *Testo e immagine nell'alto medioevo*, Settimane di Studio del Centro Italiano di Studi Sull'Alto Medioevo (Spoleto, 1994), XLI, 698–702, and n.24. He proposes a new, revised edition of Destombes's catalogue.

6. See Anna-Dorothee von den Brincken, 'Mappa mundi und Chronographia', *Deutsches Archiv für Erforschung des Mittelalters*, 24 (1968), 118–86.

I. INTRODUCTION TO MEDIEVAL MAPS

1. For the destruction at Hanover in the bombardment of 8/9 October 1943 see Dieter Brosius, 'Die Ebstorfer Weltkarte von 1830 bis 1943', in *Ein Weltbild vor Columbus: Die Ebstorfer Weltkarte*, ed. by Hartmut Kugler with Eckhard Michael, Interdisciplinary Colloquium 1988 (Weinheim, 1991), pp. 39–40. Wesley Stevens estimates that perhaps one-fifteenth of all medieval manuscripts survive. See 'Computer databases for early manuscripts', *Encyclopedia of Library and Information Science*, LVI, Suppl. 19, ed. by Allen Kent and Carolyn M. Hall, 86.

2. For example, Matthew Paris's world map, Cambridge, Corpus Christi College, MS 26, p. 284. Matthew notes on his drawing: 'This is a reduced copy of the world-maps of Master Robert Melkeley and Waltham [Abbey].'

3. L. D. Reynolds and N. G. Wilson, *Scribes and Scholars: a Guide to the Transmission of Greek and Latin Literature*, 3rd edn (Oxford, 1991), pp. 52–3 and 92–4.

4. Michael Andrews, 'The study and classification of medieval mappaemundi', *Archaeologia* LXXV (1925–6), 61–76: a good part of his article is translated by Destombes, who adds his own classification afterwards. *Mappemondes, AD 1200–1500*, ed. by Marcel Destombes, Catalogue prepared by the Commission des Cartes Anciennes de l'Union Géographique Internationale (Amsterdam, 1964), pp. 9–15, 16–17.

5. David Woodward, 'Medieval Mappaemundi', in *Cartography in Prehistoric, Ancient, and Medieval Europe and the Mediterranean, History of Cartography*, ed. by J. B. Harley and David Woodward (Chicago, 1987), I, 294–9.

6. A list of other manuscripts containing more than one map form may be found in Pascal Arnaud's interesting article, 'Plurima Orbis Imago: Lectures conventionelles des cartes au moyen âge', *Médiévales* XVIII (spring 1990), 47 n.26.

7. Wesley M. Stevens, 'The Figure of the Earth in Isidore's "De Natura Rerum"', *Isis*, LXXI (1980), no. 257, 268. For the nineteenth-century origin of the idea that medieval people thought the earth was flat, see Jeffrey Burton Russell, *Inventing the Flat Earth* (New York, 1991).

8. Book IV, 36 and 42. Herodotus goes on to say that Asia is the same size as Europe in this configuration, whereas he thinks Europe is as large as Asia and Africa added together. *The Persian Wars*, trans. by George Rawlinson (New York, 1942), pp. 304–6.

9. It seems to function this way in copies of Isidore's *Etymologies*, as a marker for the beginning of Book XIV chapter 3. Pascal Arnaud calls the T-O 'a pure ideogram'. 'Plurima Orbis Imago', p. 51.

10. This is P. D. A. Harvey's term in *Medieval Maps* (London, 1991), p. 19, an excellent introduction to the subject with colour illustrations of some of the most important maps.

11. Noted and explained by Marcia Kupfer, 'Medieval World Maps: Embedded Images, Interpretive Frames', *Word and Image* X, no. 3 (July–Sept. 1994), 265. The poems may be found in their entirety in L. Traube, ed., *Monumenta Germaniae Historiae, Poetae Lat. Aevi Carolini*, III (Berlin, 1896), 296–8.

12. A square with a T in it can be seen in a ninth-century manuscript of Orosius' work: St Gall Stiftsbibliothek, Cod. 621, p. 35. Two examples of an Isidore with two schematic drawings on the same page are Vatican, Bib. Apos., MS reg. lat.

239, fol. 76ᵛ (twelfth century) and Paris, Bibliothèque Nationale, MS lat. 7590, fol. 130ʳ (thirteenth century).

13. Gerald R. Tibbetts, 'Later Cartographic Development', *Cartography in the Traditional Islamic and South Asian Societies, History of Cartography*, vol. II ed. by J. B. Harley and David Woodward (Chicago, 1992), 146–8. Tibbetts says that the earliest extant map of this type dates from the late twelfth century.

14. These are Albi (Bib. Mun. MS 2); Vat. Bib. Apos., MS lat. 6018; the Anglo-Saxon map (British Library, Cotton MS, Tib. B.V. 1); Cosmas Indicopleustes (Vat. Bib. Apos., MS gr. 699); Isidore, Munich, Bayerische Staatsbibliothek (Clm. 10058); Guido Pisano (Brussels, Bib. Roy., MS 3897–3919); Henry of Mainz (Cambridge, C.C.C. MS 66); and Naples (Bib. Naz., Cod. IV, F.45). Destombes's classification system impels him to exclude from this category a number of highly de-tailed and geographical maps, such as the entire Beatus group, and zone-based maps by Lambert of St Omer and the monks of Ripoll (Vat. Bib. Apos., MS reg. lat. 123). There are many medieval maps now known to us which were not found at the time of the compiling of Destombes's catalogue. Indeed it was his hope that many more maps would be found. There is currently a project afoot to issue an updated version of this work.

15. For the latest word on the Beatus stemma, see John Williams, *The Illustrated Beatus: a Corpus of the Illustrations of the Commentary on the Apocalypse* (London, 1995), I, 50–3.

16. Gerald R. Tibbetts, 'The Beginnings of a Cartographic Tradition', in *History of Cartography*, II. 1, 106–7.

17. Konrad Miller, *Mappaemundi: die ältesten Weltkarten*, (Stuttgart, 1895–8), VI, contains the reconstructions. His version of Orosius is roundly criticized by Yves Janvier, *La géographie d'Orose* (Paris, 1982), ch. 3.

18. These are the Recensions A and B which have made such a puzzle for Ptolemy scholars. For a brief and clear introduction to the problem, see O. A. W. Dilke, 'Cartography in the Byzantine Empire', *History of Cartography*, I, 269–72.

19. *Confessions*, XII.22. For a modern attempt to map the Biblical view of the physical world, see Gerald A. Danzer's drawing in *Mapping Western Civilization* (New York, 1990), p. 18.

20. See, for example, the Sallust maps in Leipzig, Stadtbibliothek (eleventh century), Cod. XL, and

Vienna (fourteenth century) shown by Miller, *Mappaemundi*, III, figs 43 and 44.

21. Paris, B.N., MS lat. 8878. See Konrad Miller's discussion of this point, I, 61–70.

22. According to William Stahl, geography was not a highly developed field of classical science: *Roman Science: origins, development and influence to the later Middle Ages* (Madison, 1962), p. 221. Even Ptolemy's brilliant work, 'a superb exposition of the mathematical principles of cartography', was based on 'shoddy data accumulated mainly from the dead reckoning of travelers on land and sea'. (p. 125)

23. Claude Nicolet, *Space, Geography and Politics in the Early Roman Empire* (Ann Arbor, Mich., 1990).

24. Kai Broderson, *Terra Cognita: Studien zur Römischen Raumerfassung* (Hildesheim, 1995), pp. 269–72.

25. Harvey, *Medieval Maps*, pp. 7–9, gives a number of examples of text being used where a map would seem more appropriate to us.

26. On this point see Armin Wolf, 'Ikonologie der Ebstorfer Weltkarte und politische Situation des Jahres 1239', *Ein Weltbild vor Columbus: Die Ebstorfer Weltkarte*, ed. by Harmut Kugler and Eckhard Michael (Weinheim, 1991), pp. 91–103. But Patrick Gautier Dalché disagrees: *La 'Descriptio mappemundi' de Hughes de Saint-Victor* (Paris, 1988), pp. 181–2.

27. See Peter Barber's recent article 'The Evesham World Map: a Late Medieval English View of God and the World', *Imago Mundi* XLVII (1995), 13–33.

28. For Eumenes' lecture see Claude Nicolet, *Space, Geography and Politics in the Early Roman Empire* (Paris, 1988), pp. 111–12. For Hugh's see Patrick Gautier Dalché, *La 'Descriptio Mappemundi' de Hughes de Saint-Victor* (Paris, 1988), pp. 54–5. For St Bernardino, see Marcia Kupfer, 'The lost wheel map of Ambrogio Lorenzetti', *Art Bulletin* LXXVIII, 2 (June 1996), 288.

29. Charles H. Hapgood, *Maps of the Ancient Sea Kings: Evidence of Advanced Civilization in the Ice Age*, rev. edn (New York, 1979). See succinct discussion of this point by Tony Campbell, 'Portolan Charts from the late 13th Century to 1500', in *History of Cartography*, I, 380–1.

30. A facsimile has been published by Georges Grosjean, ed. *Mappamundi: the Catalan Atlas for the Year 1375* (Zurich, 1978). The manuscript is in the Bibliothèque Nationale, Paris, MS Esp. 30.

31. Tony Campbell, *The Earliest Printed Maps* (London, 1987), nos. 77 and 213.

32. Of course, not all monks remained in their cloister, as Chaucer was to observe:

Ne that a monk, whan he is recchelees
Is likned til a fissh that is waterlees –
This is to seyn, a monk out of his cloystre.
But thilke text heeld he nat worth an oystre;
     – *General Prologue*, ll. 179–82

Franciscan friars were sent on a mission to Tartary in the thirteenth century, and even a Benedictine such as Matthew Paris travelled to Norway to settle affairs in a disturbed fellow monastery. However, journeys had been frowned upon by St Benedict, and Serafín Moralejo suggests that the presence of a world map in such a remote site as the rock-hewn church of San Pedro de Rocas in Galicia might have served the purpose of spiritual pilgrimage. See 'El Mapa de la Diáspora Apostólica en San Pedros de Rocas', *Compostellanum* XXXI (1986), 315–41, especially his conclusions.

33. Burchard of Mount Sion, *A Description of the Holy Land* (1280), trans. by Aubrey Stewart, *Library of the Palestine Pilgrims' Text Society* (New York, 1971; repr. from the London edition of 1896), 2–3.

34. *History of Cartography*, I, xvi.

35. See Fig. 5.5 for a veritable symphony of fours – winds, elements, humours, seasons, ages of man, cardinal directions, etc. A full account of these correspondences is to be found in Anna C. Esmeijer, *Divina Quaternitas: a Preliminary Study in the Method and Application of Visual Exegesis* (Amsterdam, 1978).

36. See for example several of the manuscripts of the Beatus Commentary. In addition to the larger world maps they contain, some also have a small T–O accompanying the introductory genealogy: Gerona Cathedral, MS 7, fol. 10ᵛ; Madrid, Bib. Nac., MS Vitr. 14–2, fol. 12ᵛ; Paris, B.N., MS lat. 8878, fol. 7ʳ; Turin, Bib. Naz. Univ., MS I.II.I, fol. 9ᵛ. The Manchester manuscript (John Rylands Library, MS lat. 8) has no large map, but has a genealogy with a T–O on fol. 8ᵛ.

37. On the earthly paradise as represented on medieval maps, see Alessandro Scafi's forthcoming work to be published by the British Library in this series. Also Fred Plaut, 'Where is Paradise? The Mapping of a Myth', *Map Collector* 29 (Dec. 1984), 2–7.

38. *Natural History*, Book VII.2. Pliny's sources included Herodotus and various accounts of the travels of Alexander in the East, including Alexander's alleged letter to Aristotle. For a modern edition see W. Walter Boer, *Epistola Alexandri ad Aristotelem* (Meisenheim, 1973).

39. Plutarch in the first century AD refers to 'geographers, when they come to deal with those parts of the earth which they know nothing about, crowd them into the margins of their maps with the explanation, "Beyond this lie sandy, waterless deserts full of wild beasts", or "trackless swamps", or "Scythian snows", or "ice-locked sea."' 'Life of Theseus', *Rise and Fall of Athens*, I, trans. by Ian Scott-Kilvert (Baltimore, 1960), 13.

40. Job 40.15.

41. For a further analysis of monsters on the margins of the known world and comments on the Psalter map, see Michael Camille, *Images on the Edge: The Margins of Medieval Art* (Cambridge, Mass., 1992), pp. 14–16.

2. ILLUSTRATED HISTORIES

1. See Anna-Dorothee von den Brincken, 'Mappa mundi und chronographia: Studien zur *imago mundi* des abendländischen Mittelalters', *Deutsches Archiv für Erforschung des Mittelalters* XXIV (1968), 118–86.

2. C. M. C. Green argues that the Cyrus of Herodotus was Sallust's model for Jugurtha. See 'De Africa et eius incolis: the function of geography and ethnography in Sallust's *History of the Jugurthine War*', *The Ancient World* XXIV (1993), 2, 192.

3. See for example Oxford, Bodleian Library, MS Rawlinson G.44 (eleventh century). Even the map on fol. 17ᵛ is surrounded by notes from Cincius, *On Military Science*, stating the relative sizes of a legion, a centurion, a cohort, etc.

4. Beryl Smalley, 'Sallust in the Middle Ages', in *Classical Influences on European Culture, 500–1500*, ed. by R. R. Bolgar (Cambridge, 1971), p. 170.

5. Sallust, *War with Jugurtha*, Loeb Classical Library (Cambridge, Mass.), p. 169.

6. Birger Munk Olsen, *L'étude des auteurs classiques aux trois volumes* (Paris, 1982 *et. seq.*), II, 'Sallust'. Marcel Destombes, *Mappemondes* (Amsterdam, 1964), lists 89 Sallust maps ranging from the tenth to the fifteenth centuries. Stephen

Schierling of Louisiana State University has found seven additional Sallust maps in the Vatican Library alone. My thanks to Professor Schierling, who sent me a copy of his work in progress.

7. The oldest manuscript is Paris, B.N., MS lat. 16024 (ninth century). One of several tenth-century manuscripts with a map is Paris, Bib. Nat., MS lat. 5748.

8. Both Destombes, p. 66, and Miller, *Mappaemundi*, III, 115, agree that these are the most numerous.

9. In Florence, Bib. Marucell., MS C.128 (fourteenth century), fol. 27[r], and Bibl. Riccard., MS 687 (fifteenth century), fol. 43[r], Asia is on the bottom half of the circle. In Florence, Bib. Laur., Plut. 89.inf. 20.3 (fifteenth century), fol. 43[r], Europe constitutes the top half, while Asia and Africa are below. Vat., Bib. Apos., MS reg. lat. 1574, twelfth century, is south-orientated.

10. Vat., Bib. Apos., MS reg. lat. 571, fol. 71[v].

11. For these analogies, see Anna C. Esmeijer, *Divina Quaternitas* (Amsterdam, 1978), pp. 61, 151, and *passim*. She does not mention this particular manuscript.

12. These are tenth-century Codex Amiatinus no. 3 in the Bib. Laur. in Florence, fol. 170[r] (Miller, *Mappaemundi*, III, 112), Berlin Deutsche Staatsbibliothek, Cod. theol. lat. fol. 149, fol. 27[r] (Kamal, no. 753.4), Vat., Bib. Apos., MS lat. 4200, f.109[r], twelfth century (Destombes, 38, and Kamal, no. 754.1), and Naples, Bib. Nat. Cod.IV.F.45 (Kamal, no. 754.4). The first of these is a simple T–O, and it is unclear why Miller identified it with Sallust. The others are clearly Sallust-type. Prince Youssouf Kamal, *Monumenta cartographica Africae et Aegypti* (Cairo, 1926–51), 5 vols. Prince Kamal commissioned a huge project to identify maps of Africa, which includes drawings of all maps and transcripts and translations of their text. In the course of this activity a number of new world maps were uncovered.

13. In Bolgar, *Classical Influences on European Culture, 500–1500* (Cambridge, 1971), p. 171.

14. For example, London, B.L., Harl. MS 4865 (fourteenth century), fol. 38[v].

15. Florence, Bib. Laur., MS Plut. 45.2 (thirteenth century).

16. *Inferno*, IV, 88–90.

17. Modern works on the *scholia* do not discuss the illustrations. See Johann Endt, 'Isidorus und die Lucanscholien', *Wiener Studien* XXX (1908),

294–307; Hermannus Usener, *M. Annaei Lucani Commenta Bernensia* (Hildesheim, 1967, repr. of 1869 edn). One who does discuss the maps, though briefly, in the context of Lucan scholia is Eva M. Sandford, 'The Manuscripts of Lucan: Accessus and Marginalia', *Speculum* IX (1934), 293–5. A list of maps in Lucan manuscripts may be found in Destombes, *Mappemondes*, pp. 39, 74–8.

18. Florence, Bib. Laur., MS S. Croce 24.sin. 3 (twelfth century), fol. 83[r], includes synonyms for some of the wind names used by Lucan as well as the characteristics of each wind.

19. Oxford, Bodl. Lib., MS lat. class. d.14, fol. 137[r].

20. Olsen, *L'étude*, II, 326. The manuscript is Copenhagen, Fabricius 83.

21. Paris, B. N., nouv. acq. lat. 1626.

22. These are examples from Isidore's *De natura rerum*.

23. Virgil, *Eclogues, Georgics, Aeneid I–VI*, trans. by H. Rushton Fairclough, Loeb Classical Library, rev. edn (Cambridge, Mass., 1974), pp. 96–9.

24. For example, Vat. Bib. Apos., MSS lat. 1573, eleventh century, fol. 13[v]; lat. 3252, ninth century, fol. 29[v]; lat. 1575, twelfth century, fol. 18[r]; 3251, eleventh century, fol. 19[v].

25. Macrobius, *Commentary on the Dream of Scipio*, trans. and intr. by William Harris Stahl (New York, 1950 and 1992), pp. 200–10. Macrobius is particularly eager to resolve an apparent contradiction between Cicero's text and that of Virgil.

26. In his preface Jerome says that Eusebius provided a *Chorographia*, which can mean either a verbal description or a map. He goes on to say that Eusebius' work was illustrated with a map of Jerusalem and a drawing of the temple. Jerome, 'Prefatio', *Liber de situ et nominibus locorum hebraicorum*, in *Patrologiae Cursus Completus*, series latin ed. by J.-P. Migne (Paris, 1845), xxiii, 859–60.

27. O. A. W. Dilke, 'Cartography in the Byzantine Empire', in *History of Cartography*, I, 264–5. He provides a photograph of the entire mosaic, which is in fragments, and a detail.

28. London, B.L., Add. MS 10049. The text is published in Pauli de Lagarde, *Onomastica Sacra: Studia et Sumptibus Alterum Edita* (Göttingen, 1887), 118–90. P. D. A. Harvey is currently working on these interesting maps.

29. But David Woodward disagrees, saying that the Asia map is among several works 'mistaken for fragments of world maps'. *History of Cartography*, I, 292.

30. For an excellent discussion of the maps and a list of all the place names and legends, see Konrad Miller, *Mappaemundi: Die ältesten Weltkarten* (Stuttgart, 1895–8), III, 1–21.

31. Lagarde, pp. 118–19.

32. Lagarde, p. 155. Genesis 2.10–12.

33. Lagarde, p. 150.

34. Miller, III, 2. Patrick Gautier Dalché, *La 'Descriptio Mappe Mundi' de Hugues de Saint-Victor* (Paris, 1988), p. 70, n. 60.

35. *Confessions*, I.16–19. A good brief account is by Philip Levine, 'The continuity and preservation of the Latin tradition', in *The Transformation of the Roman World*, ed. by Lynn White (Berkeley, Calif., 1966), pp. 219–22.

36. From the dedication. Orosius, *Seven Books of History Against the Pagans*, trans. by Irving W. Raymond (New York, 1936), p. 30.

37. Orosius, I.1.

38. Yves Janvier, *La géographie d'Orose* (Paris, 1982), pp. 165–8 and 253. For the lack of fit between names in the geographical chapter and elsewhere in the history, see p. 138.

39. These are two from the eighth century (Albi, Bibl. Mun., MS 29, and St Gall, Stiftsbibliothek, Cod. 621), one from the thirteenth century (Paris, B.N., MS lat. 17543), and one from the fifteenth century (Tours, Bib. Mun., MS 973). Destombes, pp. 46, 172, 186.

40. The St Gall, Cod. 621, map is much simpler. Destombes describes it as tripartite T–O, surrounded by the winds.

41. For a complete table of contents, see Colette Jeudy and Yves-François Riou, *Les manuscrits classiques latins des bibliothèques publiques de France* (Paris, 1989), I, 10–13. For a complete list of place names on the map, see Fr. Glorie, *Itineraria et alia geographica*, in *Corpus Christianorum*, series latina, CLXXV (Turnhout, 1965), 468–94.

42. The first two short works can be found in Alexander Riese, *Geographi Latini Minores* (Heilbronn, 1878), 131–3, 141–4. The last appears under the title 'De urbibus Gallicis (Glossae)', in *Itineraria et alia geographica*, ed. by F. Glorie, *Corpus christianorum*, series latina, CLXXV (Turnhout, 1965), 409–10.

43. Konrad Miller tried to reconstruct Orosius' map from his text in vol. VI. His efforts are severely criticized by Janvier, 59ff.

44. *The Old English Orosius*, ed. by Janet Bately, for the Early English Text Society (London, 1980). On the map question, see her introduction, pp. lxiii–lxx.

45. Woodward, 'Medieval Mappaemundi', in *History of Cartography*, I, 347. He is more cautious on p. 301.

46. John Williams, 'Isidore, Orosius and the Beatus Map,' *Imago Mundi*, 49 (1997). My thanks to Dr. Williams for sharing the draft of his article with me.

47. This is also true of the Peutinger itinerary map. The intent appears to be to show the original homeland, insofar as it was known, of each of these tribes.

48. There is much dispute on this important topic. For a proponent of the continuity hypothesis, see Pierre Riché, *Education and Culture in the Barbarian West*, trans. by John J. Contreni (Columbia, SC, 1976).

49. The numbers are from Otto of Freising, *The Two Cities: a Chronicle of Universal History*, trans. by Charles C. Mierow (New York, 1928), v.31, and vi.22, pp. 353 and 383.

50. Dante, *Monarchy* (Westport, Conn., 1979), esp. Book III and Letter VI, p. 103.

51. O. A. W. Dilke has a nice close up of this scene in his 'Maps in the service of the state', in *History of Cartography*, I, 206, fig. 12.4. The inscription on the map's border notes that the three geographers actually worked for Julius Caesar. See Claude Nicolet and Patrick Gautier Dalché, 'Les "Quatre Sages" de Jules César et la "mésure du monde" selon Julius Honorius', *Journal des Savants*, 1987, 157–218.

3. THE NATURE OF THINGS

1. In one of his sermons Caesarius of Arles (470–542) explained that the ignorant cannot rise to the level of the learned, so the learned must lower themselves to the ignorance of the simple. Quoted in Pierre Riché, *Education and Culture in the Barbarian West*, trans. by John J. Contreni (Columbia, SC, 1976), p. 92 and note.

2. *Confessions*, VIII.2, where he describes the sensation in the church at the baptism of the eminent

and learned Victorinus. The sensation created by Augustine's own conversion can well be imagined.

3. *Commentary on the Dream of Scipio by Macrobius*, trans. and introduced by William Harris Stahl (New York, 1952 and 1990), p. 175. In his excellent edition Stahl also reproduces diagrams. A copy of the *mappa mundi* from an early printed edition appears between pp. 214 and 215.

4. Jacques Fontaine, who has studied Isidore's sources, warns us that he had not actually read everyone he quoted. Indeed, some of his quotations were at third and fourth hand. See Fontaine's thoughtful chapter on Isidore's library in *Isidore de Seville et la culture classique dans l'Espagne Wisigothique* (Paris, 1959), pp. 735–62.

5. Jacques Fontaine, 'La diffusion carolingienne du *De natura rerum* d'Isidore de Seville d'après des manuscrits conservés en Italie', *Studi Medievali*, ann. 7 (1963), fasc. 1, 108–27, esp. p. 125.

6. I owe this observation to Bruce S. Eastwood, 'The Astronomies of Pliny, Martianus Capella and Isidore of Seville', in *Science in Western and Eastern Civilization in Carolingian Times*, ed. by P. L. Butzer and D. Lohrmann (Basel, 1993), pp. 161–80, esp. p. 174.

7. Wisdom of Solomon 7.17–19.

8. Isidore, *De natura rerum*, XIV, 2.

9. On this long recension and the stemma of the manuscripts see Jacques Fontaine, *Isidore de Séville Traité de la nature* (Bordeaux, 1960), pp. 39–42. Fontaine concludes that ch. 48 is 'probably Isidore.' (p. 44). Wesley Stevens discusses an additional English edition of Isidore, which varies in a number of ways from the versions discussed by Fontaine. Examples are London, B.L., Cotton MS, Vitellius A.XII (end of the eleventh century), fols 46–64; London, B.L., Cotton MS Domitian I; and Exeter Cathedral, MS 3507 (both second half of the tenth century). Cotton MS Vitellius A.XII contains six of Isidore's diagrams, including the map. The text on the map is a list of provinces, unlike the text on continental manuscripts, given below.

10. For a manuscript with ch. 48 but without a map see Vatican, Bib. Apos., MS Pal. lat. 1448 (*c.* 810, Trèves).

11. Ambrose, *Hexameron*, trans. by John J. Savage, in *The Fathers of the Church* series (New York, 1961), pp. 1–283. Augustine, *City of God* and *Literal Commentary on Genesis*.

12. Isidore, *DNR*, VII.6.

13. Isidore, *DNR*, XII.1–2. Isaiah 51.6.

14. Isidore, *DNR*, XVIII.6.

15. Gregory of Tours, *De cursu stellarum*. See Stephen C. McCluskey, 'Gregory of Tours, Monastic Timekeeping and Early Christian Attitudes Toward Astronomy', *Isis*, LXXXI (1990), 9–22. He notes that the Cygnus is renamed the Greater Cross, the Dolphin the Lesser Cross, Lyra Omega. More successful was calling Ursa Major the Wain. Another attempt was apparently made in the seventeenth century. See Andreas Cellarius, *Harmonica Macrocosmica*, which in 1660 turned the zodiac into the twelve apostles and populated the skies with Abel, Eve, St Benedict, and King David, as well as Noah's ark and the crown of thorns. Ursa Major has become St Peter's bark. For a colour reproduction, see Peter Whitfield, *The Mapping of the Heavens* (London, 1995), pp. 92–3.

16. Isidore, *DNR*, XLV.1–2.

17. Fontaine reproduces the seven illustrations from an eighth-century manuscript now Munich, Bayerische Staatsbibliothek, MS Clm. 14,300. They follow pp. 190, 202, 210, 212, 216, 260, and 296 in his book. In this manuscript the *rotae* have human figures in their centres. See Bernard Teyssedre, 'Les illustrations du *De natura rerum* d'Isidore: un exemple de survie de la figure humaine dans les mss. précarolingiens', *Gazette des Beaux-Arts*, 6th series, LVI (1960), 19–34. Teyssedre is mostly interested in style, but notes that the models show: 'According to Isidore, every phenomenon had two faces: natural and moral.'

18. See, for example, Vatican MS Pal. Lat. 834, fol. 68 (ninth century). Here, however, all the moon drawings look the same, though each 'phase' is given a fancy Greek name.

19. Vatican, Bib. Apos., MS Pal. lat. 1448 is one of these. Although it describes itself on fol. 19ᵛ as '*Liber rotarum sancti Isidori episcopi*', no *rotae* were ever drawn.

20. '*Inscriptiones extra circulum positas neglexi, quibus auctor regiones caeli quattuor ad figuram inepte conceptam accommodare frustra contendit.*' Fontaine, *Traité*, 210 *bis*.

21. For the best summation of the controversy see Wesley M. Stevens, 'The Figure of the Earth in Isidore's *De natura rerum*', *Isis*, LXXI (June 1980), 268–77. For a contrary view and a general course of Isidore-bashing, consult Ernest Bréhaut, *An Encyclopedist of the Dark Ages: Isidore of Seville* (New York, 1912; reissued 1968), pp. 50–5.

22. Gestures to indicate numbers up to one thousand are shown in Vatican, Bib. Apos., MS urb. lat. 290, fols 31ʳ–31ᵛ.

23. Bruce Eastwood calls them 'clever mnemonics'. See his 'Plinian Astronomy in the Middle Ages and Renaissance', in *Science in the Early Roman Empire: Pliny the Elder, His Sources and Influence*, ed. by Roger French and Frank Greenaway (Totowa, NJ, 1986), p. 204.

24. Harry Bober, 'In Principio: Creation before Time', in *Essays in Honor of Erwin Panofsky*, ed. by Millard Meiss (New York, 1961), I, 13–29. Plato, *Timaeus*, 54–6.

25. Isidore, *DNR*, XI.1.

26. Vatican, Bib. Apos., MS Pal.lat. 834 (ninth century, Rhineland), fol. 60, shows an alternative model in the margin.

27. Baltimore, Walters Art Gallery, MS 73 (late twelfth century, English), fol. 1ᵛ, and London, B.L., Cotton MS, Tiberius E.IV (twelfth century, English), fol. 30ʳ.

28. This text can be found on the map in the following manuscripts of Isidore's *De natura rerum* (and doubtless others): Florence, Bib. Laur., MS Plut. 29.39, fol. 19ᵛ; Rouen, MS 529, fol. 91ᵛ; Bern, Burgerbibliothek, MS 417, fol. 98ᵛ (illustrated in I, fig. 18.43); Vatican, Bib. Apos., MS Pal. lat. 834, fol. 90ᵛ; Bamberg, Cod. misc.1 (H.1.IV.17), fol. 43ᵛ; Vat. Bib. Apos., MS reg. lat. 1573, fol. 112ᵛ. The most noticeable variation is that two of these (Bern, MS 417, and Vat. Bib. Apos., MS reg. lat.1573) read 'post conversionem' instead of 'post confusionem'.

29. See some antique examples in the illustrations to Jurgis Baltrusaitis' article 'L'image du monde céleste du IXe au XIe siècle', *Gazette des Beaux-Arts*, ser. 6, XXI (1939), 137–48.

30. J. H. Waszink, *Timaeus: a Calcidio Translatus Commentarioque Instructus* (London, 1975), includes drawings of the diagrams, most of which are more scientific than Isidore's. It is possible that the triple cube (on p. 69) was the source of Isidore's creation of the 'cube of elements'.

31. See an example of an Egyptian calendar *rota* in a wall painting now at the Metropolitan Museum in New York in David Bergamini, *The Universe* (New York, 1966), p. 19.

32. *De natura rerum* continued to be popular in the early modern period. There were ten printed editions between 1477 and 1577. Bréhaut, p. 18.

33. Isidore, *Etymologiarum sive Originum*, ed. by W. M. Lindsay (Oxford, 1911), I.29. The work is published in two vols, with Books I–X in vol. I and XI through XX in vol. II. There are no page numbers. References will be to Isidore, book and ch. number, and all translations are mine.

34. L. D. Reynolds and N. G. Wilson, *Scribes and Scholars: a guide to the transmission of Greek and Latin literature*, 3rd. edn (Oxford, 1991), p. 84.

35. Bréhaut, p. 76. 'his version of secular knowledge . . . poor as it was . . . [without it] the Middle Ages would have been a great deal poorer.'

36. Lindsay includes drawings of all three, but eliminates the head, arms, and feet of the humanoid diagram. For a manuscript with a human diagram, see Florence, Bibl. Laur., MS Conv.Sopp. 319 (thirteenth century, Vallambrosa), fol. 63ᵛ. For a manuscript with multiple versions, see Bern, Burgerbibliothek, Cod.263 (ninth century), fols 13ᵛ–14ʳ.

37. As far as can be gathered from Destombes's catalogue, out of approximately 150 manuscripts of *Etymologies*, over a hundred have this simple icon, sometimes supplemented with the triangle-in-a-square with the names of Noah's sons. Miller, VI, 57.

38. Paris, B.N., MS lat.10293 (twelfth century), fol. 139ʳ, for one. Destombes has a photograph of this manuscript, pl.B.II.b. Alongside is written the text '*Ecce sic diviserunt terram filii noe post diluvium.*' (This is how the sons of Noah divided the earth after the Flood.)

39. Examples are London, B.L., MS Harl. 2660 (twelfth century), fol. 123ᵛ, St Gall, Stiftsbibliothek, MS 236 (tenth century), p. 89, Columbia University Library, MS Plimpton 125 (twelfth century, north Italy, Bobbio), fol. 115ʳ.

40. These are MS 25, fol. 204ʳ, and MS 76, fol. 108ʳ. My thanks to John Williams, who sent me copies of these two maps. Another map of this format is Florence, Bibl. Laur., Plut.27.sin.8 (Spanish, thirteenth century), fol. 64ᵛ, reproduced by Destombes, pl. C, III.c. A helpful drawing is presented by G. Menendez Pidal, who also discusses this map in 'Mozárabes y asturianos en la cultura de la Alta Edad Media en relación especial con la historia de los conocimientos geográficos', *Boletín de la Real Academia de la Historia*, CXXXIV (1954), 137–291, esp. p. 184.

41. On Sciapods, see Serafín Moralejo, 'World and Time in the Map of the Osma Beatus', in *Apocalipsis Beati Liebansis. Burgi Oxomensis, II: El Beato de Osma. Estudios*, ed. by John Williams (Valencia, 1992), 151–79, esp. 147–9. The source

of the terms 'terra de pedes latos' is unknown. For an intelligent discussion of this problem, see John Williams, 'Isidore, Orosius and the Beatus Map', *Imago Mundi*, 49 (1997).

42. Paris, B.N., MS lat. 8878 (eleventh century). The map has been removed from the manuscript and is not shown to researchers because of its fragility. A large facsimile accompanying Miller's work can occasionally be found. The map is so large that most reproductions, including the one available in Paris, render the legends on it illegible. One must rely on Miller's transcriptions of them in his vol. III.

43. *Etym*, XIV.v.17. Another note on these people is found in IX.ii.133. Here Isidore seems to be describing people in the southern half of the western hemisphere, and he is sceptical of their existence, attributing the stories about them to 'poets'. See Moralejo, 'World and Time', 147–53.

44. *Etym.*, XIV.iv.10. Isidore takes this passage from Augustine, *City of God*, XVIII.9, who, however, uses it sarcastically to mock Athens's superstition about how the city got its name. The best and most complete work on Isidore's sources is Hans Philipp, *Die historisch-geographischen Quellen in den Etymologiae des Isidorus von Sevilla*, in *Quellen und Forschungen zur alten Geschichte und Geographie*, ed. by W. Sieglin (Berlin, 1912–13), XXVI and XXVIII. For this reference see II, 112.

45. *Etym*. XIV.iii.33 and 37.

46. *Etym.*, XV.66–7. Philipp thinks that Braulius, who was bishop of Saragossa, inserted the note on the martyrs out of patriotism (Philipp, II, 192). As for the destruction of Cartagena, it had been reconquered by the Visigoths from the Byzantine Empire around 620. Isidore's reference, however, seems to be to the two-centuries-old attack and destruction. His family, who was from Cartagena, had probably fled Justinian's army in 555. He could only rejoice at his own king's reconquest. See Kenneth Baxter Wolf, *Conquerors and Chroniclers of Early Medieval Spain* (Liverpool, 1990), pp. 13–14.

47. *Etym.*, XIV.v.2. Also on Afer, see IX.ii.115.

48. *Etym.*, XIV.iii.3.

49. *Etym.*, XIV.iii.21.

50. *Etym.*, XIV.iii.35 and viii.5. For Delos, XIV.vi.21. Isidore says (*Etym.*, XIII.xxii, *De diluviis*) that there were three floods, of which Noah's was the first. He takes his information from Orosius, Book I. See Philipp, II, 139.

51. Philipp thought not (I, 12), arguing that Isidore's descriptions are graphically confusing and more consistent with written sources. Still it is hard to imagine that Isidore would not have had a map available in his well-equipped library. See similar comments on the geographical description of Dionysius Periegetes by Christian Jacob, 'L'oeil et la mémoire: sur la Périégèse de la Terre habitée de Denys', in *Arts et Légends d'Espaces*, ed. by Jacob and Frank Lestringant (Paris, 1981), pp. 21–98, esp. pp. 38–44. Jacob asserts that while one could hardly make a map from Dionysius' description, it was most probably 'une ekphrasis de carte' (p. 38).

52. *The Nature of Maps: Essays Toward Understanding Maps and Mapping* (Chicago, 1974), p. 50.

53. Fontaine, ed., *Traité*, pp. 44–5. He does not discuss the connection with the *Etymologies*.

54. Modern editions of these works are now available in the *Corpus Christianorum*, series latina, ed. by Charles Jones. For *De temporibus* (Turnhout, 1975), CXXIII–C, 580–611. *De natura rerum* (Turnhout, 1980), CXXIII–A, 173–234.

55. Quoted by Jones, *Bedae Opera de Temporibus*, 129. See this book for an excellent though brief chapter, 'Bede's Use of Natural Science', 125–9.

56. Ed. by Charles W. Jones, *Corpus Christianorum*, series latina (Turnhout, 1977), CXXIII–B.

4. SPACE AND TIME IN THE COMPUTUS MANUSCRIPTS

1. *Bedae Venerabilis Opera*, part 1, *Opera didascalica*, ed. by Charles W. Jones, *Corpus Christianorum*, series latina, CXXIII A (Turnhout, 1975), preface, p. xiv.

2. David C. Lindberg, *The Beginnings of Western Science: the European Scientific Tradition in Philosophical, Religious, and Institutional Context, 600 BC to AD 1450* (Chicago, 1992), p. 159. For his opinion of medieval science, see pp. 156–7. In Lindberg's case, he is rushing to get to the twelfth century. Also see Timothy Ferris, *Coming of Age in the Milky Way* (New York, 1989), pp. 42–5, for a popular view of the benighted Middle Ages: 'The proud, round earth was hammered flat. Likewise the shimmering sun.

Behind the sky reposed eternal Heaven, accessible only through death.'

3. C. S. Lewis, *The Discarded Image: an Introduction to Medieval and Renaissance Literature* (Cambridge, 1964), pp. 98–100, 112–21, and *passim*.

4. Quoted by Bede, *A History of the English Church and People*, trans. by Leo Sherley-Price (London, 1968), v.21, p. 322.

5. Bruno Krusch, *Studien zur Christlich-Mittelalterlichen Chronologie: Der 84jährige Ostercyclus und seine Quellen* (Leipzig, 1880), p. 279.

6. Pachomius was a fourth-century Egyptian monk with no known connection to the Easter controversy. How he came to be linked with this story is explained by Maura Walsh and Dáibhí O Cróinín in *Cummian's Letter, De Controversia Paschali* (Toronto, 1988), pp. 43–4. See also Charles W. Jones, 'A Legend of St Pachomius', *Speculum* XVIII (1943), 198–210.

7. Charles W. Jones, *Bedae Pseudepigraphia: Scientific Writings Falsely Attributed to Bede* (Ithaca, New York, 1939), p. 1. For the importance of computus to church organization and ideas of order see Faith E. Wallis, 'Images of Order in the Medieval Computus', in *Ideas of Order in the Middle Ages*, ed. by Warren Ginsberg (Binghamton, New York, 1990), pp. 45–68.

8. Kenneth Harrison, 'Luni-Solar Cycles: Their Accuracy and Some Types of Usage', in *Saints, Scholars and Heroes*, ed. by Wesley M. Stevens and Margot H. King (Collegeville, Minn., 1979), pp. 65–78, esp. p. 65.

9. Charles W. Jones, *Bedae Opera de Temporibus* (Cambridge, Mass., 1943), p. 59, for a narrative account. Bruno Krusch, *Studien* I, 245–78, for the original documents.

10. Jones, *Bedae Opera de Temporibus*, p. 34.

11. For a lengthy account of the work of Victorius and Dionysius, see Jones, *Bedae Opera de Temporibus*, pp. 61–75.

12. Bede, *History*, I.30, gives a copy of the letter from Pope Gregory to the Abbot Mellitus on his departure for England in 601, dealing with the issue of pagan temples and customs.

13. Cummian's letter to the abbot of Iona in 633, in Walsh and O Cróinín, pp. 75 and 95.

14. See *De temporum ratione*, ch. LI, '*Quomodo errent quidam in primi mensis initio*', in which he attacks Victorius of Aquitaine: ('I beseech you,

brother Victor . . . ') on the issue of the beginning of the first month.

15. 'Admonitio generalis', *Monumenta Germaniae Historica, Capitularia Regum Francorum* (Hanover, 1883), I, 60. Bernhard Bischoff, *Manuscripts and Libraries in the Age of Charlemagne*, trans. and ed. by Michael Gorman (Cambridge, 1994), p. 108.

16. For a full discussion see Jones, *Bedae Opera de Temporibus*, pp. 34–54. Source of table: Bruno Krusch, *Studien zur Christlich-Mittelalterlichen Chronologie*, I, 69.

17. Bede, *DTR*, LIII. Jones, *Bedae Opera de Temporibus*, note, p. 387.

18. Eusebius, *History of the Church*, V. 23–5.

19. Jones cites the indiction as an Egyptian invention, adopted by Constantine in 312 and used by both the Eastern and Western empires. Bede thought the original indiction was based on a census cycle. See *De temporum ratione*, ch. XLVIII, '*De indictionibus*' and Jones's notes, *Bedae Opera de Temporibus*, pp. 382–4.

20. Reginald L. Poole, *Chronicles and Annals* (Oxford, 1926), pp. 10–14. This is an excellent little handbook for the student of medieval history.

21. For a complete discussion of this issue, see Johannes Heller, 'Über den Ursprung der sogenannten spanischen Aera', *Sybel's Historische Zeitschrift*, XXXI (1874), 13–32.

22. Jones, *Corpus Christianorum*, series latina, CXXIIIA, xiii-xiv.

23. These are Brussels, Bib.Roy., MS 5413–22, fols 77ᵛ–107ᵛ (ninth century, north France), and Vat. Bib. Apos., MS reg. lat. 1260 (ninth/tenth/eleventh century, possibly Fleury), fols 87ᵛ–99ᵛ. On the Irish computus, see Walsh and O Cróinín, *Cummian's Letter*, pp. 101–12.

24. Vat. Bib. Apos., MS reg. lat. 2077, fols 79 ff. (eighth century). Charles W. Jones, 'Preface', *Beda Venerabilis Opera*, part 1, *Didascalica* (Turnhout, 1975), *Corpus Christianorum*, series latina, CXXI-II-A, p. xiii and n. 3.

25. Discovered in the course of Prince Youssouf Kamal's researches into maps of Africa, *Monumenta cartographica* (Rome, 1928), III, no. 528. It was first written up by Richard Uhden, 'Die Weltkarte des Isidorus von Sevilla', *Mnemosyne: Bibliotheca Classica Batavia*, 3rd ser., 1935–6, 1–28. fol. Glorie corrects some of Uhden's place names in *Itineraria et Alia Geographica, Corpus Christianorum*, series latina, CLXXV (Turnhout, 1965), 455–66. Each of these contains a photo-

graph of the map, as does Marcel Destombes, pl. xix.

26. The identification on the title-page is signed 'L.H.' for Lucas Holst, who was librarian at the Vatican in the seventeenth century. The hand-written catalogue, however, from the eighteenth century identifies the opening document as 'Vocabularium sine nomine auctoris, ordine alpha-betico' (Anonymous vocabulary in alphabetical order). Thanks to Patrick Gautier Dalché for pointing out this identification for me.

27. J.-P. Migne, ed., Patrologiae Cursus Completus, Series Latina, L, 811. This excerpt stops at 'Joses', in mid-alphabet. The preceding six folios contain various other excerpts from Eucherius' work, 'Instructionum in libri duo', explaining Greek and Hebrew words, reproduced in PL, L, cols. 773ff. Eucherius was bishop of Lyons from 432 to 441 and died in 449.

28. On Egyptian days, see Lynn Thorndike, A History of Magic and Experimental Science During the First Thirteen Centuries of Our Era (New York, 1923), I, 685–9. The identity of these days varies from one document to another.

29. Uhden calls these 'very surprising', and suggests that they might represent the sun and the moon (p. 3). Glorie does not discuss them. A four-teenth-century manuscript of Isidore's De natura rerum shows a simple world map surrounded by the phases of the moon (Paris, B.N., MS lat. 6414, fol. 11^r), listed by Destombes, p. 61.

30. Glorie, Itineraria, p. 461 and n. 131.

31. See various readings in Glorie, p. 463, n. 184/185.

32. Uhden, 'Die Weltkarte des Isidorus von Sevilla', p. 6.

33. This river, now known as the Barada, flows through Damascus. In ancient times its classical name was Chrysorrhoas. In the Bible it is called the Abana, II Kings 5.12.

34. Glorie gives references for each name. He also tries to guess what some of the anonymous c's and misspellings represent.

35. An excellent colour illustration of this map can be found in P. D. A. Harvey, Medieval Maps (London, 1991), fig. 16. This map has been inter-estingly discussed by Patrick Gautier Dalché, who thinks it may be the model for Hugh of St. Victor's geographical lecture. See La 'Descriptio Mappe Mundi' de Hugues de Saint-Victor (Paris, 1988), pp. 81–5. Other exceptional Isidore maps include a thirteenth-century zonal map in Heidelberg

(Cod.Salem IX.39, fol. iv^r), where it serves as a frontispiece, while a smaller map is found on fol. 91^r; and Paris, B.N., MS lat.7676, fifteenth century, which looks like a Sallust map.

36. Jones, Bedae Venerabilis Opera, Corpus Christianorum, series latina, CXXIII–B (Turnhout, 1977), 241–56.

37. In chs.XLV-LXII he goes through the columns of the table and explains each one. The reference to the calendar is in ch. XLI, where he speaks of the extra day of leap year being 'on the same line as the sixth of the kalends of March' or 24 February. Jones, CXXIII–C (Turnhout, 1980), 549 and 565.

38. Jones, 'Kalendarium sive Martyrologium Quasi Bedae Cura et Opere', Bedae Venerabilis Opera, Corpus Christianorum, series latina (Turnhout, 1980), CXXIII–C, 567–78. Illustrations, for example, B.L., Cotton MS, Julius A.VI, tenth century, fols 3^r–8^v. In an early manuscript in Vienna, the labours are all put together on a single page. This is Wien, Oesterreichische Nationalbibliothek, MS lat. 387, fol. 90^v. A colour reproduction can be found in Eva Irblich, Karl der Grosse und die Wissenschaft (Wien, 1994), p. 111. For the calendar in B.L., Cotton MS, Tiberius B.V.1, see Patrick McGurk, An Eleventh-Century Anglo-Saxon Illustrated Miscellany (Copenhagen, 1983), pp. 40–50.

39. Bischoff, Manuscripts and Libraries, p. 108 and note 78. Vat. Bib. Apos., MS reg.lat. 309, Paris B.N., n.a. lat. 456 and 1615, Munich, Bayerische Staatsbibliothek, MS Clm. 210, Vienna, O.N. MSS lat. 387 and 12600, Vat., Bib. Apos., MSS lat. 643 and lat. 645. For the contents of Vat. MS reg.lat. 309 see Andreas Wilmart, Codices Reginenses Latini in Bibliothecae Apostolicae Vaticanae Codices Manu Scripti Recensiti (Vatican, 1945), II, 160–74. For the three- and seven-book analysis, see Patrick McGurk, 'Carolingian Astrological Manuscripts', in Charles the Bald: Court and Kingdom, ed. by Margaret Gibson and Janet Nelson (Oxford, 1981), pp. 317–32, esp. 320–2. The Vienna and Munich manuscripts are the three-book compilations, while the others are divided into seven books.

40. I have looked at the Paris manuscript and at a microfilm of Vat., Bib. Apos. MS reg.lat.309, but have not seen the others. The maps in Munich and Vienna are listed in Destombes's catalogue.

41. Wallis, 'MS Oxford St John's 17' pp. 403–53.

42. See Harry Bober, 'An Illustrated Medieval School-book of Bede's "De Natura Rerum"',

Journal of the Walters Art Gallery, XIX–XX (1956–7), for a selection of these writings in an eleventh-century English manuscript. On the York excerpts, see Bruce Eastwood, 'Plinian Astronomy in the Middle Ages and the Renaissance', in *Pliny the Elder: His Sources and Influence*, ed. by Roger French and Frank Greenaway (Totowa, New Jersey, 1986), pp. 201–2 and n.40.

43. Jones, *Bedae Opera de Temporibus*, p. 218. This characteristic of Bede is also noted by John Murdoch, *Album of Science* (New York, 1984), p. 57. That Bede was not opposed to diagrams altogether, however, is shown by his use of drawings, taken from Adamnan's work, in *De locis sanctis*.

44. William Harris Stahl, *Martianus Capella and the Seven Liberal Arts* (New York, 1971), I, 52.

45. J. H. Waszink, *Timaeus a Calcidio Translatus Commentarioque Instructus* in *Plato Latinus*, ed. by Raymond Klibansky (London, 1975), IV.

46. The eclipse diagrams appear on pp. 140 and 143, and the orbits of Mercury and Venus on pp. 158 and 162.

47 Waszink, 114.

48. Vat. Bib. Apos., MS reg.lat.123, fols 205ᵛ–218. See Waszink on this manuscript, pp. cxxiii–iv.

49. M. and R. Mostert, 'Using Astronomy as an Aid to Dating Manuscripts: the Example of the Leiden Planetarium', *Quaerendo*, 20 (1990), 248–61. This dating replaces a previous theory that the date was 28 March 579. See Bruce Eastwood, 'The Astronomies of Pliny, Martianus Capella and Isidore of Seville in the Carolingian World', in *Science in Western and Eastern Civilization in Carolingian Times*, ed. by P. L. Butzer and D. Lohrmann (Basel, 1993), p. 173.

50. Eva-Maria Engelen, *Zeit, Zahl und Bild: Studien zur Verbindung von Philosophie und Wissenschaft bei Abbo von Fleury* (Berlin, 1993). Bruce S. Eastwood, 'Origins and Contents of the Leiden Planetary Configuration, MS Voss Q–79, fol. 93ᵛ: an Artistic Astronomical Schema of the Early Middle Ages', *Viator* XIV (1983), 1–39. Ranee Katzenstein and Emilie Savage-Smith, *The Leiden Aratea: Ancient Constellations in a Medieval Manuscript* (Malibu, Calif., 1988).

51. According to Stahl, Capella's work was illustrated early on, perhaps in its original form. Stahl, *Martianus Capella*, I, 245–9. For an example, see Paris, B.N., MS lat. 5239, fol. 143ᵛ, tenth century.

52. Bober, p. 69.

53. Pliny, *Natural History*, II, 99.

54. This is Paris, B.N. MS n.a. lat. 1615, fol. 175ᵛ. The tidal *rota* is on fol. 170ᵛ. Other manuscripts with identical diagrams are London, B.L., MS Harl 3017, fol. 135ʳ; Paris, B.N. MS lat. 5239, fol. 142ʳ. All are ninth century, from Fleury.

55. Paris, B.N., MS lat. 5543, ninth century, Fleury, fol. 139ʳ.

56. Arno Borst claims that the original figures were calculated for Italy and 'went astray north of the Alps'. *Ordering of Time* (Chicago, 1993), p. 54.

57. Paris, B.N., MS n.a.lat. 1618, fol. 88ᵛ. The original manuscript is tenth century – the scribe writes perhaps a century later.

58. Harry Bober, pp. 65–97, with numerous illustrations and a complete analysis of the textual excerpts.

5 · THREE MAPS IN COMPUTER MANUSCRIPTS

1. S. J. Crawford, ed., *Byrhtferth's Manual, AD 1011* (Oxford, 1929), p. 151.

2. Faith Elena Wallis, 'MS Oxford, St John's 17: a Medieval Manuscript in its Context,' University of Toronto dissertation (1985), pp. 610–39.

3. Wallis, p. 706.

4. The original comparison is from *Byrhtferth's Manual*, ed. by Crawford, p. 143.

5. P. D. A. Harvey, *Medieval Maps* (London, 1991), p. 21. 'It may even be that we have here a direct descendant of the world map which Marcus Vipsanius Agrippa, son-in-law of Augustus, compiled at the end of the first century BC and which was probably based on the survey of the world ordered in 44 BC by Julius Caesar.'

6. Patrick McGurk, D. N. Dumville, M. R. Godden, and Ann Knock, *An Eleventh-Century Anglo-Saxon Illustrated Miscellany: British Library Cotton Tiberius B.V.*, Part I, *Early English Manuscripts in Facsimile*, XXI, ed. by Geoffrey Harlow (Copenhagen, 1983), 15–24. On its Canterbury provenance see p. 109 and D. N. Dumville, 'The Catalogue Texts', pp. 55–8.

7. Francis P. Magoun, 'An English Pilgrim-Diary of the Year 990', *Medieval Studies*, II (1940), 231–52.

8. This complex issue is thoroughly studied by McGurk. See pp. 28–30 and *passim*. Early catalogue listings make it possible to reconstruct the manuscript as it appeared at the end of the Middle

Ages at any rate, but the manuscript contains a number of single pages, and its analysis is a challenge.

9. Fol.57ʳ, McGurk, pp. 23–4. '*Incipit liber pergesis [sic] id est de situ terrae Prisciani grammatici urbis Rome Caesariensis doctoris quem de priscorum dictis excerpsit ormistarum sed et huic operi de tribus partibus videlicet Asia Africa Europa mappam depinxerat aptam in qua nationum promontoriorum fluminum insularum que situa atque monstrorum formatur honeste.*' Ornesta (here, ormista) thought to be a generic term for medieval world maps, also shows up on the Hereford map. See David Woodward, 'Medieval Mappaemundi', in *History of Cartography* (cited above, n.1.5), I, 309 n. 113; and G. R. Crone, 'New Light on the Hereford Map', *The Geographical Journal*, 131, part 4 (Dec. 1965), 448, n. 21.

10. McGurk, p. 79. In the note he goes on to say, 'many maps are found in isolation in compilations or encyclopaedias (Vatican Bib. Apos., MS reg. lat. 123, "the Ripoll map") or in loose association with a group of texts (Albi 29, Vat.lat. 6018, British Library, MS Add.10049) or separately (Hereford, Ebstorf).' p. 79, n.2.

11. Miller, VI, 95–101. McGurk, p. 86.

12. Christian Jacob, 'L'oeil et la mémoire', in *Arts et légendes d'espaces*, ed. by Jacob and Frank Lestringant (Paris, 1981).

13. For the complete text of Priscian's poem, see Emil Baehrens, *Poetae latinae minores* (Leipzig, 1879–80), V, 275–312.

14. For a complete list of place-names see Miller, III, 31–5. His list is corrected by McGurk, pp. 86–7, at the end of his chapter devoted to the map, pp. 79ff. Perceptive comments on the map and a good colour illustration can be found in P. D. A. Harvey, *Medieval Maps* (London, 1991), pp. 21–6.

15. Harlow, 'Preface', in McGurk, p. 7.

16. This is also true in Oxford, Bodleian Library, MS Bod.614. For the relationship between these manuscripts and others see McGurk and Knock, 'Marvels of the East', in McGurk, *Eleventh-Century Miscellany*, pp. 88–103.

17. See McGurk, p. 99, for further details and references on this story and its illustration.

18. Ker, *Catalog of Manuscripts Containing Anglo-Saxon* (Oxford, 1959), no. 193.

19. Vat. Bib. Apos., MS reg.lat.123. Oliva was also bishop of Vich and son of the count of Cerdagne. Letters between him and Gauzlin, abbot of St-Benoît-sur-Loire at Fleury survive. Oliva died in 1046, ten years before the manuscript was completed. See Alexandre Vidier, 'La mappemonde de Théodulphe et la mappemonde de Ripoll, IX-XI siècles', *Bulletin de géographie historique et descriptive*, 26 (1911), 285–313, esp. 307ff. The manuscript went to the monastery of St Victor in Marseilles in the late twelfth century.

20. The contents of this manuscript are listed in some detail by Andreas Wilmart, *Codices Reginenses Latini* (Vatican City, 1937), I, 289–92. The map is listed and reproduced by both Prince Youssouf Kamal, III, fasc. 3, 362–4 (no.725) and Marcel Destombes, 48 (no.24.11) and pl. xviii. Other important studies are by A. Vidier (cited in the previous note); and Anna-Dorothee von den Brincken, *Fines Terrae: Die Enden der Erde und der vierte Kontinent auf mittelalterlichen Weltkarten* (Hanover, 1992). The text has been studied by Richard Uhden, 'Specimen Terrae: Landermässe eines unbekannten Geographen aus dem I. Jahrhundert n. Chr.', *Petermanns Mitteilungen*, LXXVII (1931). My account is deeply indebted to Patrick Gautier Dalché, 'Notes sur la "Carte de Théodose II" et sur la "Mappemonde de Théodulf d'Orléans"', *Geographia Antiqua*, III-IV (1994–5), 91–108.

21. Jones, *Bedae Opera de Temporibus*, pp. 371 and 375. The *saltus lunae* was a day skipped over in the lunar calendar in order to bring it into closer correspondence with the solar cycle.

22. There are doubtless other examples of the scribe's own words which may be found by a diligent reader. Patrick Gautier Dalché promises us a complete analysis of this interesting manuscript in the near future. For the work by Bede, see Migne, *PL*, XCI, 1179–90.

23. A Greek work of the third century BC by the poet Aratus. It described the constellations and celestial weather portents and was tremendously popular both in classical and in medieval times. Various Latin translations exist. It was probably illustrated in late antiquity, and continued to be illustrated in a classical style right through the Middle Ages.

24. Macrobius, *Commentary on the Dream of Scipio*, I, xxi. The Leiden manuscript is Bibliothek der Rijksuniversiteit, MS Voss.lat.Q.79 (early ninth century). See Eastwood, 'Origins and Contents of the Leiden Planetary Configuration, MS Voss.Q.79, fol. 93v.: an Artistic Astronomical

Schema of the Early Middle Ages', *Viator*, XIV (1983), 1–39; and 'Plinian Astronomical Diagrams in the Early Middle Ages', in *Mathematics and its Applications to Science and Natural Philosophy in the Middle Ages: Essays in Honor of Marshall Clagett*, ed. by Edward Grant and John E. Murdoch (Cambridge, 1987), pp. 141–72. Eastwood mentions the drawing in the Vatican manuscript in 'Plinian Astronomy in the Middle Ages', *Pliny the Elder: His Sources and Influence*, ed. by Roger French and Frank Greenaway (Totowa, NJ, 1986), p. 204 and note 54.

25. Patrick Gautier Dalché, *La 'Descriptio Mappe Mundi' de Hugues de Saint-Victor* (Paris, 1988), p. 94.

26. Leiden, Bibliothek der Rijksuniversiteit, MS Voss.Lat.F.12d, fols 40ᵛ–41ʳ (ninth century). The manuscript is from the region of Orléans, perhaps Fleury. According to Gautier Dalché's analysis the two versions, which are much alike, were both copied from a single source. Gautier Dalché, p. 92.

27. E. Dümmler, ed., *Poetae Latini Aeri Carolini, Monumenta Germaniae Historica* (Munich, 1978), I, 547–48.

28. Either *Etymologies*, III.44 or XIII.6, or from *De natura rerum*, X.

29. A list of place-names appears in Gautier Dalché, pp. 97–8.

30. Vidier, pp. 301–3. Vidier's work is still the most complete analysis of the geographical content of the map. Gautier Dalché gives more information on the surrounding text and its origin. Both reproduce illustrations of the map.

31. The texts on the map are reproduced by Kamal and Gautier Dalché. I am dependent on the latter for his penetrating analysis of the poem and its relationship to the printed edition of Theodulph's works which appeared in 1646, ed. by J. Sirmond. See Gautier Dalché, 'Notes sur la "Carte de Théodose II"', pp. 100–1.

32. This work appears in almost identical form in Migne, *PL*, XCI, 1179–90, though the introductory verse is omitted. The drawing is not reprinted but is indicated in the text '*Deest figura in mss*' (The figure is missing in the manuscript). Altogether three diagrams are called for in this short work. The others are a plan of Jerusalem and Lazarus' tomb. All are introduced by lines in the text, such as '*Huius ergo ecclesiae talis dicitur esse figura*' (Here is the diagram of this church such as it is said to be). Although not in Migne's manuscript, these drawings appear in other manuscripts of this

work. See I. Fraipont, 'Bedae Venerabilis de Locis Sanctis', *Itineraria et alia Geographica*, *Corpus Christianorum*, series latina, CLXXV (Turnhout, 1065), 250–80. A note on p. 256 mentions that the presence or absence of illustrations in various manuscripts.

33. Wallis, 'MS Oxford St John's College 17', pp. 50 and 59.

34. *De natura rerum* is not complete, but begins with ch. XVI. Wallis (p. 506) says the other pages were removed by a vandal.

35. Charles Singer, 'A Review of the Medical Literature of the Dark Ages, with a New Text of About 1110', *Proceedings of the Royal Society of Medicine*, X (1917), 117–27.

36. A complete table of contents for this section can be found in Wallis, pp. 181–2, followed by a detailed analysis.

37. According to Wallis, pp. 216–18. The centre is labelled '*Laterculus secundum Antiochos*', an error for Anatolius, bishop of Laodicea in the third century. The Paschal text in question was actually composed in Ireland in the sixth century and spuriously attributed to Anatolius.

38. Wallis, p. 219.

39. Von den Brincken surmises that the map might have been copied from a north-oriented Byzantine world map written in Greek. The difficulty of shifting its orientation could have led to some of the confusion of placement. 'Gyrus und Spera: Relikte griechische Geographie im Weltbild der Frühscholastik', *Sudhoff's Archiv* 73 (1989), 143.

40. One of Alexander's fabled exploits had involved the receding of the Pamphyllian Sea, off the south coast of Asia Minor, to allow his army to advance.

41. Miller notes that the Ravenna cosmographer gives a total of thirty two (eleven 'patriae' and twenty one 'provinciae') for this area, including Albania, Armenia ' ing a fairly vague concept at this time. See Miller, III, 119.

42. Also described in Deuteronomy 19, and Numbers 35.6. The number of cities varies from three to six, but on the map it is singular.

43. Wallis, p. 220.

44. The only manuscript is Bodl. Lib., MS Ashmole 328. For a modern edition, see S. J. Crawford, ed. and trans. *Byrhtferth's Manual (AD 1011)*, published for the Early English Text Society (Oxford, 1929).

45. Crawford, p. 37.

46. In its most extreme form this thesis argues that the St John's College manuscript was composed at Ramsey in the late eleventh century and sent to Thorney. It was a copy or version of the very text explicated by Byrhtferth. See articles by Cyril Hart, 'The Ramsey Computus', *English Historical Review* 85 (1970), 29–44; and 'Byrhtferth and His Manual', *Medium Aevum* 41 (1972), 95–109. Also Peter Baker, 'Byrhtferth's Enchiridion and the Computus in Oxford', in *Anglo-Saxon England* X, ed. by Peter Clemoes (Cambridge, 1981), 123–42. Wallis disagrees, pp. 11 and 821.

47. Reproduced by Crawford, p. 90.

48. Charles and Dorothea Singer, 'Byrhtferð's Diagram', *Bodleian Quarterly Record*, II, no. 14 (1917), 47–51, with illustrations.

49. This is an almond-shape or mandorla, which surrounds Christ in glory in medieval art. Wallis, p. 815.

50. Wallis, p. 243.

51. Singers, note on fig. 3.

52. Crawford, p. 11.

53. Crawford, after p. 86.

54. B.L. MS Harley 2799 (twelfth century, German), fol. 241^v.

55. This page has been reproduced by John E. Murdoch, *Album of Science* (New York 1984), p. 230, no.207.

56. For an illustration from Bodl. Lib., MS Digby 56, fol. 165^v, see Murdoch, *Album*, p. 80, no. 75.

6. MAPS IN MEDIEVAL HISTORIES

1. *The Peloponnesian War*, trans. by Rex Warner (New York, 1972) II.2. The introduction to the Penguin edition by M. I. Finley has some interesting observations on the Greek dating problem, pp. 21–2.

2. *Eusebii Chronicorum Libri Duo*, ed. by Alfred Schoene (orig. 1875; Zurich, 1967), 2 vols, has double columns with Jerome's Latin version running parallel to the Greek.

3. Although Bede introduced the concept of BC, it was rarely used by others before the fifteenth century. An exception is Lambert of St Omer in the *Liber Floridus*, Ghent, Rijksuniversiteit Bibliotheek, MS 92, fol. 138^v, noted by Anna-Dorothee von den Brincken as a 'rare example', *Fines Terrae: Die Enden der Erde und der vierte Kontinent auf mittelalterlichen Weltkarten* in *Monumenta Germaniae Historica*, XXXVI

(Hanover, 1992), 73. See also Ernst Breisach, *Historiography: Ancient, Medieval and Modern* (Chicago, 1983), p. 92.

4. Examples of chronicle pages from manuscripts are reproduced by Reginald L. Poole, *Chronicles and Annals* (Oxford, 1926), before pp. 5 and 7.

5. Andreas Wilmart, *Codices Reginenses Latini* (Vatican City, 1937), II, 290. Vat. Bib. Apos. reg. lat 123, fols 111^v–125^v 5.

6. Poole, *Chronicles and Annals*, p. 42.

7. V. H. Galbraith, *Historical Research in Medieval England* (London, 1951), p. 8.

8. Bede, *De temporum ratione liber*, ch. lxvi, in *Opera Didascalica*, ed. by Charles W. Jones, *Corpus Christianorum, series Latina* (Turnhout, 1977), CXXIII B, 463–4.

9. Bede, *De temporum ratione*, ch. lxvi, p. 495.

10. Lambert, ch. xix, in Ghent, Rijksuniversiteit Bibliotheek, MS 92, fols 32^v and 232^v. A color reproduction of this page appears in Beryl Smalley, *Historians of the Middle Ages* (London, 1974), p. 33, colour pl. I. See analysis by Danielle LeCoq, 'La mappemonde du *Liber Floridus* ou la vision de Lambert de Saint-Omer,' *Imago Mundi*, 39 (1987), 25–6.

11. Otto, Bishop of Freising, *The Two Cities*, trans. by C. C. Mierow (New York, 1928), p. 123 (Book I.1). This is not to say that Otto did not employ geographical references in his history, but that he eschewed a geographical introduction.

12. A medieval example is Paul the Deacon in his history of the Lombards. See Breisach, p. 106.

13. 'Mappamundi und Chronographia: Studien zur Imago Mundi des abendländischen Mittelalters,' *Deutsches Archiv für Erforschung des Mittelalters* 24 (1968), 126–7.

14. According to a modern geographer, Catherine Delano Smith, a map used as an illustration should make a point, related to the text, with minimum distracting material and in the simplest visual style. Would that all authors heeded this advice! (Personal communication from Catherine Delano Smith.)

15. Walter of Châtillon, *The Alexandreis*, VII, lines 378–430, trans. by R. Relfryn Pritchard (Toronto, 1986), 173–4. For a critical edition of the Latin manuscripts, see Marvin L. Colker, *Galteri de Castellione Alexandreis* (Padua, 1978).

16. David J. A. Ross is the premier scholar in the area of illustrated Alexander manuscripts. See his *Alexander Historiatus: A Guide to Medieval Illustrated Alexander Literature* (Frankfurt-am-

Main, 1988; reprint of 1963 edition). Unfortunately Ross is not much interested in maps, and does not include in his list (pp. 141–5) any of the manuscripts in Destombes's catalogue.

17. Max Manitius, *Handschriften antiker autoren in mittelalterlichen Bibliothekskatalogen* (Leipzig, 1935; reprinted Wiesbaden, 1968), pp. 104–10, lists literally hundreds of these works in the collections of primarily monastic and cathedral libraries.

18. Destombes, pp. 167–72. Pl. VI reproduces the map in Paris, B.N., MS lat.11334, fol. 1[r]. It is 104 mm in diameter.

19. Research on Lambert benefitted from the 150th anniversary of the founding of the University of Ghent in 1967 with the publication of a facsimile of his autograph manuscript: Lambertus, St Audomari canonicus, *Liber Floridus: Codex autographus Bibliothecae Universitatis Gandavensis*, ed. by Albert Derolez (Ghent, 1968). A colloquium held at the time produced a spate of interesting and useful articles. See *Liber Floridus Colloquium*, ed. by Albert Derolez (Ghent, 1973). The codiological analysis is in Dutch, ed. by Albert Derolez, *Lambertus Qui Librum Fecit: Een Codicologische Studie van de Liber Floridus-Autograaf* (Brussels, 1978), with a summary in English on pp. 469–79. The map has been studied by Konrad Miller, *Mappaemundi: Die ältesten Weltkarten*, III, 43–53; Richard Uhden, 'Die Weltkarte des Martianus Capella', *Mnemosyne*, 3rd series, III, 97–124, with fold-out map; and, most recently, by Danielle LeCoq, 'La mappemonde du *Liber Floridus* ou la vision de Lambert de Saint-Omer', *Imago Mundi* 39 (1987), 9–49. Portions of Lambert's geographical texts and a number of his cartographic illustrations appear in Kamal, *Monumenta*, III, 773–84. A discussion of Lambert's geography and map also appears in C. Raymond Beazley, *Dawn of Modern Geography* (London, 1901), II, 570–3, 621–4.

20. Hanns Swarzenski, 'Comments on the Figural Illustrations,' in *Liber Floridus Colloquium*, ed. by Albert Derolez (Ghent, 1973), p. 21. This is Ghent MS 92.

21. Léopold Delisle, 'Notice sur les manuscrits du *Liber Floridus* de Lambert', *Notices et extraits des manuscrits de la Bibliothèque Nationale*, XXXVI-II, no. 2 (1906), 577, quoted by Lefèvre, *Liber Floridus Colloquium*, 5.

22. Yves Lefèvre, in 'Le *Liber Floridus* et la littérature encyclopédique au Moyen Age', *Liber Floridus Colloquium*, ed. by Albert Derolez (Ghent, 1973), pp. 1–9, especially p. 9. Lefèvre tellingly compares Lambert with the better organized, but philosophically similar, works of Honorius of Autun and Herrad of Landsberg.

23. For a complete account of his sources see Derolez, *Lambertus Qui Librum Fecit*, pp. 33–357.

24. LeCoq, 'La mappemonde du Liber Floridus ou la vision de Lambert de Saint-Omer', *Imago Mundi*, 39 (1987), 9–49.

25. The Ghent autograph manuscript has lost its world map, along with the entire gathering which contained it, but the other six illustrated copies retain their maps, and the one at Wolfenbüttel is generally thought to be the closest to the original. For a complete list of manuscripts and their maps, consult Destombes, pp. 111–15. The list of maps here is based on Destombes, but the numbering has been slightly altered.

26. Claude Nicolet and Patrick Gautier Dalché, 'Les Quatre Sages de Jules César et la 'mesure du monde,' selon Julius Honorius'. *Journal des Savants* (1986), 203.

27. The example from the Leiden MS is reproduced in Destombes, pl. XI.

28. A photo of this diagram from the Wolfenbüttel MS, fol. 16[v], appears in von den Brincken, *Fines terrae*, Pl. 27.

29. Now missing from the autograph manuscript in Ghent, although its presence is promised on fol. 28[r]. The oldest manuscripts with the map are Wolfenbüttel, Herzog August Bibliothek, MS Guelf. 1 Gudiana lat. (late twelfth century), fols 69[v]–70[r]; Paris, B.N., MS lat. 8865 (*c.* 1260), fol.62[v]; and Leiden, Bibliotheek der Rijksuniversiteit, MS Voss.lat.Fol.31 (*c*.1290), fols 175[v]–176[r].

30. Wolfenbüttel, fol. 64[v]. A reproduction appears in Derolez, *Lambertus Qui Librum Fecit*, fig. 2.

31. Fol.241[v]. Drawings of this map and a list of places appear both in Miller, III, 45 and LeCoq, p. 29.

32. Miller, III, 61–8, with drawing.

33. Albert Derolez, *Lambertus Qui Librum Fecit*, pp. 474 and 477.

34. J.-M. De Smet, 'La mentalité religieuse du chanoine Lambert', in *Liber Floridus Colloquium*, pp. 11–12. See above p. 100 for a table of Lambert's analogies with the six ages.

35. In Wolfenbüttel MS, fol. 8[v].

36. Miller, III, 52.

37. Richard Uhden, 'Die Weltkarte des Martianus Capella', pp. 99.

38. Fols 275ᵛ–276ʳ, Leiden, MS Voss lat. Fol. 31. Reproduced by Kamal, III, 3, 770.

39. Capella was cited above as source of excerpts on size of earth. For a modern edition of his work see William H. Stahl et al., *The Marriage of Philology and Mercury*, in *Martianus Capella and the Seven Liberal Arts* (New York, 1977), II.

40. Uhden, pp. 99–100. His percentages are on p. 121. Uhden could not resist noting the appearance of a troublesome place-name, Lama or Lana, in the very region from which Krates of Mallos, creator of the zonal map, originally came.

41. Gen.5.24 for Enoch and 2 Kings 2.ll for Elijah. While Elijah's departure is fairly clear, Enoch's may be regarded as a euphemism. However, in his letter to the Hebrews (ll.5) Paul writes 'By faith Enoch was taken so that he did not experience death.'

42. Usually twenty-two. The higher number comes from Aethicus Ister, the only source who refers to thirty-two nations behind the wall. See Beazley, II, 624.

43. 'Hic Antipodes nostri habitant, sed noctem diversam diesque contrarios perferunt et estatem.' (Here dwell our Antipodes, but they endure a different night, contrary days and summer.) This is a hypothetical translation, as words seem to be left out. See Uhden's comparison with Capella's text, p. 104. It should be pointed out that Capella is none too clear himself on this issue. See Stahl, II, 238.

44. LeCoq, p. 42. In the table of contents the genealogy of the counts of Flanders and their history immediately follows the map.

45. LeCoq, pp. 38–42.

46. Suzanne Lewis points out another interesting example of this analogy in Matthew Paris's very similar pictures of Alexander and Christ. Both are enthroned with their feet resting on a lion and a dragon, showing their triumph over disorder. See *Art of Matthew Paris* (Berkeley, California, 1987), pp. 138–9, figs 74 and 76.

47. LeCoq, p. 27. Fols 152ᵛ–162ʳ in the Ghent manuscript deal with Alexander. Also in this group of texts is the *Collatio con Dindimo*, a conversation between Alexander and a wise Brahmin.

48. LeCoq, pp. 20–2.

49. The best modern sources on Honorius are Valerie Flint, 'Honorius Augustodunensis Imago Mundi', *Archives d'Histoire Doctrinale et Littéraire du Moyen Age*, XLIX (1982), 1–151, a critical edition of the work; and Danielle LeCoq, 'La Mappemonde d'Henri de Mayence, ou l'Image du Monde au XIIe Siècle', in *Iconographie Médiévale: Image, Texte, Contexte*, ed. by Gaston Duchet-Suchaux (Paris, 1990), pp. 155–207. LeCoq includes a drawing of the map with a complete list of place names and a key. See also Beazley, *Dawn of Modern Geography*, II, 563–6 and 614–17, and Konrad Miller, *Mappaemundi*, III, 21–7. An article by P. D. A. Harvey, 'The Sawley Map and Other World Maps in Twelfth-Century England', *Imago Mundi*, 49 (1997), has been kindly shared with me by the author.

50. This is the opinion of LeCoq, p. 156. P. D. A. Harvey, however, disagrees.

51. Destombes, nos. 49.13 and 50.12. Flint, on the Henries, pp. 10–13 and n. 1. All of which recalls to me the daunting fact that my college medieval history book had twenty-two Henries in the index: Robert S. Hoyt, *Europe in the Middle Ages* (New York, 1957), pp. 646–7.

52. Prologus, Flint, p. 49. This work contains an extensive introduction with a description of manuscripts, as well as the Latin text of Honorius' work, pp. 48–151.

53. Lefèvre claims that Honorius and Lambert shared a common philosophy, but that Lambert was less well organized. See *Liber Floridus Colloquium*, pp. 7–8.

54. Cambridge, Corpus Christi College, MS 66, from Sawley, Yorks., late twelfth-early thirteenth century. The manuscript has a complex history and has been rebound several times, with some geographical (Pliny) and historical works added to it. The text of Honorius and the map, however, are assumed to have been together since the beginning. The text of *Imago Mundi*, though copied at least half a century after Honorius' death, is a copy of his earliest edition, that of 1110. Valerie Flint's edition is based on that of 1139, the last one under the control of Honorius himself. Flint, p. 44.

55. Christian: 'positionem orbis quasi in tabella nobis describas.' Honorius: 'totius orbis tibi depingi formulam in qua sic oculum corporis valeas reficere sicut visum cordis soles in machina universitatis depascere.' Flint, p. 48.

56. And probably more. Known to have maps are Admont, Stiftsbibliothek, MS 400, fol. 35ᵛ; Göttweig, Stiftsbibliothek, MS 103, fols 1ʳ and 2ʳ; Salzburg, St Peter's Stiftsbibliothek, MS a IX i, fol. 161; Munich, Bayerische Staatsbibliothek, MS

14731, fol. 83^r; Paris, B.N., MS lat.11130, fol. 82^r; Oxford, Bodl. Lib., MS Bodl.e.Mus. 223 (thirteenth century) fol. 185^r; Cambridge, University Library, MS Add.6860 (fourteenth century), fol. 188^r; London, B.L., Cotton MS Cleopatra B.IV, fol. 4^r. These citations come from Flint, pp. 21–35, and Destombes, p. 48 (25.3), p. 170 (49.10), and p. 175 (50.12). The exact location of the maps in relation to *Imago Mundi* and to the other documents each manuscript contains needs further study. All these manuscripts are of the twelfth century, except as noted otherwise.

57. Harvey, 'The Sawley Map,' *Imago Mundi*, 49 (1997).

58. 'The sacred place has never been definitely located and is probably mythical. . . . It has been variously named as a mountain in Thrace, a city on a mountain in India, a city in Caria about 45 miles E of Ephesus, Mount Helicon in Greece, and a remote place in Aethiopia.' Catherine B. Avery, *The New Century Classical Handbook* (New York, 1962), p. 759, 'Nysa'.

59. LeCoq suggests that, if he were in fact English, he might be trying to preserve his anonymity, p. 199.

60. The story is told by John B. Friedman, *The Monstrous Races in Medieval Art and Thought* (Cambridge, Mass., 1981), pp. 72–4.

61. The manuscripts are Brussels, Bibliothèque Royale, MS 3897–3919 (twelfth century) fols 46^v, 53^v; and Florence, Bib. Ricc., MS Cod. 881 (thirteenth century), fol. 20^r. See Destombes, pp. 48 and 167. Guido has also been studied by Miller, III, 54–7; Beazley, II, 632–3; Kamal, no.774; von den Brincken, *Fines terrae*, pp. 62–3, and pl. 20. Harley and Woodward, I, mention him briefly, p. 348, and reproduce his world map, p. 350.

62. From the *Historia de Preliis*. See Ross, *Alexander Historiatus*, 54, on the Brussels manuscript. He mentions several illustrations, but not the maps.

63. Miller, III, 57.

64. On his illustrations see Suzanne Lewis, *The Art of Matthew Paris in the Chronica Majora* (Berkeley: University of California Press, 1987). Ch. 6 deals with his cartography.

65. Richard Vaughan, *Matthew Paris* (Cambridge, 1958), p. 242. The *Chronica Majora* appears in an English translation under the title *Matthew Paris's English History*, trans. by J. A. Giles (London, 1852–4), 3 vols. Matthew's work appeared in several versions in his own lifetime: the *Chronica Maiora*, the *Historia Anglorum* (a short form of the previous work), *Abbreviato Chronicorum*, and the *Liber Additamentorum*, which includes documents not copied out in the main work. For a complete description of the contents of each manuscript consult Richard Vaughan.

66. Perhaps the same map? No other reference to Robert of Melkeley has been found. Waltham Abbey, north of London, appears on Matthew's maps of Britain.

67. On this monument, and whether it could have been a map or not, see Paul Binski, *The Painted Chamber at Westminster* (London, 1986), p. 44. The chamber was completely redecorated after a fire in 1263.

68. This interesting drawing (called the heptarchy) can be found in the British Library, Cotton MS Julius D.VII, fols 49^v–50^r (formerly bound with Cotton MS Claudius D.VI). It was described briefly by Miller, who included a sketch of it, III, 83, attributing it to Matthew. Neither Suzanne Lewis nor Richard Vaughan mentions this diagram.

69. See Eva G. R. Taylor, 'The "De Ventis" of Matthew Paris,' *Imago Mundi*, II (1937), 23–6. He also drew a 12-wind rota for his *Liber Additamentorum*, British Library, Cotton MS Nero D.I, fol. 184^v.

70. This list is taken from Vaughan, pp. 241–2, with some emendations. Reproduced illustrations can be found in J. P. Gilson and H. Poole, *Four Maps of Great Britain Designed by Matthew Paris* (London, 1928); P. D. A. Harvey, *Medieval Maps* (London, 1991), pl. 1, pp. 57, 58, 73 (colour reproduction of part of an itinerary, the two British Library maps of Britain, and the B.L. map of Palestine); Suzanne Lewis, *Art of Matthew Paris*, has a very complete range of black-and-white reproductions of most of Matthew's work in her chapter 'Imagines Mundi: Matthew's Cartography,' pp. 321–76; Richard Vaughan, *The Illustrated Chronicles of Matthew Paris* (Cambridge, 1993) has numerous colour illustrations of the maps in Cambridge and details, distributed so as to illustrate different selections from the *Chronica Maiora*. Complete lists of place-names can be found in Miller, III, 68–94.

71. The suggested attribution is made by Anna-Dorothee von den Brincken, 'Die Klimatenkarte in der Chronik des Johann von Wallingford – ein Werk des Matthaeus Parisiensis?', *Westfalen*, 51

(1973), 47–56. The manuscript is British Library, Cotton MS Julius D.VII, fol. 46^r.

72. Including a map of Britain to which John has added more than sixty names. See P. D. A. Harvey, 'Matthew Paris's Maps of Britain', *Thirteenth-Century England* IV (Woodbridge, England, 1992), 109–10.

73. Pliny, *Natural History*, VI.211–20.

74. For a reproduction of Petrus Alfonsus' map see Harley and Woodward, I, fig.18.73, p.355. The manuscript is Oxford, Bodleian Library, MS Laud Misc. 356, fol. 120. For an excellent account of his life see Dorothy Melitzski, *The Matter of Araby in Medieval England* (New Haven, CT, 1977).

75. See Harvey, 'Matthew Paris's Maps of Britain', for speculation on the order in which the maps were made, pp. 114–16.

76. See Richard Vaughan who definitely assigns this map to Matthew on pp. 240, 241, 245–6, only to cast a doubt on p. 247. The Bible, originally from St Albans, contains textual rubrics and marginal notes in Matthew's hand. The identification of the handwriting on the map with Matthew was made over a century ago by Sir Frederick Madden. Konrad Miller also guessed he was the author, III, 156. On the folio with the map is a copy of his chronicle entry for 1246, listing the grievances of the English church. The folio also contains characteristic notes on cartography. For more detail see Evelyn Edson, 'Matthew Paris's "Other" Map of Palestine', *The Map Collector*, no. 66 (Spring 1994), 18–22, illustrated. An excellent colour reproduction of this map appears in Kenneth Nebenzahl, *Maps of the Holy Land: Images of Terra Sancta Through Two Millennia* (New York, 1986), Pl. 13, p. 39.

77. These notes are helpfully transcribed by Richard Vaughan, p. 240.

78. These maps are thoroughly described by Suzanne Lewis, pp. 347–64.

79. 'Matthew Paris's Maps of Britain', p. 111. The itinerary theory was originally put forward by J. B. Mitchell, 'Early Maps of Great Britain: I. The Matthew Paris Maps', *Geographical Journal* LXXXI (1933), 27–34.

80. What Miller cites as Britain is more likely Britanny, as it appears to be located in the far north-west corner of France.

81. The information is from Isidore, *De Ortu et Obitu Patrum*, ed. by César Chaparro Gómez (Paris, 1985), pp. 203–11.

82. British Library, Cotton MS Julius D.VII, fols 49^v–50^r. This has now been removed from the manuscript and is kept separate, as it is on the verso of one of Matthew's famous maps of Great Britain. Other floral diagrams of the heptarchy appear in BL, Cotton MS Claudius D.VI, fol. 5^v, next to a portrait of King Offa. This diagram is perhaps unfinished as there is only a single line of text ['cenobium st albans']. Below is a note on the size of England. This diagram is reproduced by Lewis, p. 166, fig. 93. Another version of the diagram has King Alfred's face in the centre, as unifier of the once fragmented kingdom, and is the beginning of a genealogy of the English kings. This is Cambridge, Corpus Christi College, MS 26, fol. iv, verso, and is reproduced by Lewis, p. 169, fig. 96. The seven kingdoms are labelled and numbered, and the cardinal diagrams are written in. None of these versions are the same as the one drawn by Konrad Miller, which he claims is to be found on fol. 6^r of Cotton MS Claudius D.VI. See Miller, III, 83.

83. Lewis, *Art of Matthew Paris*, p. 322. Harvey, 'Matthew Paris's Maps of Britain', p. 119, notes that 29% of the place-names on the map of Britain do not appear in the chronicle and that half of these are the names of natural features or of districts.

84. See Oxford, Corpus Christi College, MS 2*, and Richard Vaughan's comments in *Matthew Paris*, p. 240.

85. Vaughan, *Illustrated Chronicles*, p. 196: entry for 1250.

86. John Taylor, *The Universal Chronicle of Ranulf Higden* (Oxford, 1966), examines his sources, pp. 72–88. John of Wales was a thirteenth century Franciscan who assembled a collection of historical anecdotes on which Higden drew extensively.

87. 'Descriptiones locorum, status rerum, distinctiones temporum, successiones regiminum, variationes rituum, decursiones aetatum, qualitates actionum; et in his omnibus varias prorsus supputationes annorum.' Ranulf Higden, *Polychronicon*, ed. by Churchill Babington, in *Chronicles and Memorials of Great Britain and Ireland during the Middle Ages* (London, 1865), XLI, no. 1, ch. 4, pp. 30–40.

88. Taylor, p. 97.

89. Note from Peter Barber of the British Library. The fine edition was BL, Royal MS 14.C.IX, which is discussed below.

90. Huntington Library, HM 132, fol. 4ᵛ. (fourteenth century, after 1352, St Werburgh, Chester). V. H. Galbraith, 'An Autograph MS of Ranulph Higden's *Polychronicon*', *Huntington Library Quarterly*, XXXIV (1959), 1–18. Though Woodward disagrees. See the caption to Pl. 15, I, following p. 106. For a proposed stemma, see Peter Barber, 'The Evesham World Map: A Late Medieval English View of God and the World', *Imago Mundi*, XLVII (1995), 13–33, esp. p. 20.

91. Taylor describes the Higden maps as 'derived from' the T–O model with Jerusalem in the centre (pp. 63–4), but, as we have discussed above, the centrality of Jerusalem is a much later development than the T–O form. And to call these maps T–O is an over-simplification.

92. The form of the Cambridge University Library map is circular, but in other respects it is pure Higden. MS 3077, fol. 11ʳ (English, 1367).

93. BL, Royal MS 14.C.IX (fourteenth century, Ramsay Abbey). The larger map is on fols 1ᵛ–2ʳ, and the smaller one on fol. 2ᵛ.

94. Konrad Miller, *Mappaemundi*, III, 94–109, esp. p. 103. Miller's account, particularly his stemma, is now dated by the discovery of additional manuscript maps, but he is still the only author to give a complete catalogue of place-names and inscriptions. He carefully cites the appearance of the same place-names on other medieval maps and gives literary sources (Pliny, Solinus, etc.) but does not relate them to Higden's text.

95. Personal communication from Peter Barber at the British Library.

96. An example may be found in the Vatican, Bib. Apos., MS reg. lat. 731, opening folios. This map does have highly abstract shapes drawn in for mountains, but no boundaries or coastlines.

97. Destombes, pp. 149–60. Five of the Higden maps are also printed in Kamal, *Monumenta*, IV, fasc. II, 1266–70.

98. College of Arms, Muniment Room 18/19. The map is there because in the mid-fifteenth century it was recycled and part of an extensive family tree was drawn on the back of it. See the recent article by Peter Barber, 'The Evesham World Map', cited above.

99. A recent work which discusses the enduring ideal of the empire in the Middle Ages is Anthony Pagden, *Lords of All the World: Ideologies of Empire in Spain, Britain, and France, c.1500–c.1800* (New Haven, Connecticut, 1995), pp. 11–28.

7 HISTORIES WITHOUT MAPS, MAPS WITHOUT HISTORIES

1. Paolino Minorita's work, sometimes called the *Satyrica Historica*, contains not only a world map, but regional maps, city plans, and other diagrams, such as a circular diagram of the labours of Hercules. Both works are from the first half of the fourteenth century. Beryl Smalley, *Historians in the Middle Ages* (New York, 1974), 174, comments on the rarity of illustrations in histories before the thirteenth century.

2. The originator of this thesis was Richard Uhden, whom the alert reader will now recognize as a scholar who tried to associate every medieval map with someone famous. His article is 'Gervasius von Tilbury und die Ebstorfer Weltkarte', *Jahrbuch der Geographischen Gesellschaft zu Hannover* XXXVII (1930), 185–200. For more recent opinions on this thesis see Armin Wolf, 'News on the Ebstorf World Map: Date, Origin, Authorship', in *Géographie du Monde au Moyen Age et à la Renaissance*, ed. by Monique Pelletier (Paris, 1989), pp. 51–68, and his expanded version of this article in *Ein Weltbild vor Columbus: Die Ebstorfer Weltkarte*, ed. by Hartmut Kugler and Eckhard Michael (Weinheim, Germany, 1991), pp. 54–116. Von den Brincken reproduces the quotation about the map from *Otia*, II, in *Fines terrae*, p. 79.

3. For a discussion of this problem, see David Woodward, 'Medieval Mappaemundi,' in *History of Cartography*, I, 287–8. For references to maps or possible maps in medieval library catalogues, see Marcia Kupfer, 'Medieval World Maps: Embedded Images, Interpretive Frames', *Word and Image*, X, no. 3 (July–Sept. 1994), 262–88, especially p. 281, nn.15–18. *Item spera* appears in a catalogue of the library of St Emmeram, Regensburg, in 1347; *ymago mundi* in a list of the books belonging to Albert Behaim, a papal legate, at Passau in 1246. Of course, the 'ymago mundi' could also have been a book. For these references see Christine E. Ineichen-Eder, *Mittelalterliche Bibliothekskatalog Deutschlands und der Schweiz* (Munich, 1977), IV.1, 160 and 36.

4. For an extended analysis of this map see Peter Barber, 'The Evesham World Map'. Barber notes its similarity to the maps in Ranulf Higden's history, concluding that both were generic maps, not adapted as illustrations.

5. This interesting subject was first introduced by Frances A. Yates, *The Art of Memory* (Chicago, 1966), and was carried further by Mary J. Carruthers, *The Book of Memory: a Study of Memory in Medieval Culture* (Cambridge, 1990). Both focus on the teaching of memory techniques. The possibility of using a map as a 'memory palace' remains largely unexplored. See also Jonathan Spence, *The Memory Palace of Matteo Ricci* (New York, 1984).

6. Marcia Kupfer, 'The Lost Wheel-Map of Ambrogio Lorenzetti', *Art Bulletin*, LXXVIII, no. 2 (June 1996), 286–310, examines this interesting work and its wider implications. Kai Broderson, *Terra Cognita: Studien zur römischen Raumerfassung* (Hildesheim, 1995), pours scorn on the idea that there ever was an 'Agrippa World Map.' For a different account of the latter, see O. A. W. Dilke, 'Maps in the Service of the State', in *History of Cartography*, I, 207–9.

7. This is Juan Cornago, 'Missa de la mapa mundi', composed in Naples in the late fifteenth century. The mass is based on the tune of the popular song whose lyrics run: 'I have seen the map of the world and the navigator's chart, but still Sicily seems to me the most beautiful [place] in this world.' The discussion of the map in question continues. See Allan W. Atlas, *Music at the Aragonese Court of Naples* (Cambridge, 1985), p. 63.

8. Miller, *Mappaemundi*, *passim*, does a very thorough job of comparing texts and names from map to map. His work is flawed only by the misreadings which were the necessary result of his being forced to consult many manuscripts by means of poor reproductions.

9. P. D. A. Harvey, *Mappa Mundi: The Hereford World Map* (London, 1996), p. 34. For the location of Paradise, based on different exegetical traditions, see the forthcoming work by Alessandro Scafi in this series.

10. Peter Barber records the cost of making a map, which was almost certainly the Evesham map, in the late fourteenth century to be six marks or £3 13s 4d, the equivalent of the annual wage of an agricultural laborer. The Evesham map was smaller than these examples (0.94 × 0.46 m = 0.43 sq. m), so we can imagine that they cost even more. See Barber, 'Evesham World Map', p. 21.

11. Woodward, 'Medieval mappaemundi', in *History of Cartography*, I, p. 326.

12. Graham Haslam, 'The Duchy of Cornwall Map Fragment', in *Géographie du Monde au Moyen Age et à la Renaissance*, ed. by Monique Pelletier (Paris, 1989), pp. 33–49. He includes a color reproduction of the remaining piece of the map, showing the four figures and a part of a fifth one. The manuscript is to be found at the Duchy of Cornwall office, London, Maps and Plans, MS 1.

13. Woodward, 'Medieval mappaemundi', History of Cartography, I, 306–8 and fig.18.17. Kamal, no. 997. Carlo Capello, *Il Mappamondo Medioevale di Vercelli (1191–1218?)* (Turin, 1976).

14. Marcia Kupfer, who traveled to see the Vercelli map recently, reports that much of the nomenclature is now illegible. Personal communication.

15. London, B.L., Add. MS 28261, fols 9^r–9^v.

16. Peter Barber, 'Old Encounters New: the Aslake World Map', in *Géographie du Monde*, ed. by Pelletier, pp. 77–8.

17. A good reproduction of this map can be found in Birgit Hahn-Woernle, *Die Ebstorfer Weltkarte* (Ebstorf, 1987), p. 36. Kai Broderson comments on this map in *Terra Cognita* p. 53, n. 1. He associates this type of map with geographical organization by landmarks, which he sees as a form of spatial cognition for large areas, in contrast to location through an astronomically determined grid of latitude and longitude.

18. Nigel J. Morgan, *Early Gothic Manuscripts, II, 1250–1286*, in *Survey of Manuscripts Illuminated in the British Isles* (London, 1988), IV, ii, no. 114, dates the manuscript after 1262 and suggests that its place of origin is London. An excellent illustration in colour can be found in Peter Whitfield, *The Image of the World* (London, 1994), p. 19.

19. London, B.L., MS Royal 3.D.VI. See Graham Haslam, 'The Duchy of Cornwall Map Fragment', pp. 41–2.

20. Hahn-Woernle's book contains a number of excellent illustrations, including a large fold-out reproduction of the whole map in a back pocket. The latest batch of scholarly articles come from a 1988 colloquium and are published in Hartmut Kugler and Eckhard Michael, *Ein Weltbild vor Columbus: Die Ebstorfer Weltkarte* (Weinheim, 1991). Miller devoted an entire volume to this map in *Mappaemundi*, V. A large colour reproduction accompanies a complete set of his work.

21. Margriet Hoogvliet, 'The Mystery of the Makers: Did Nuns Make the Ebstorf Map?', *Mercator's World* I, no. 6 (1996), 16–21.

22. The martyrs are first mentioned by Adam of Bremen as being sixty priests who were killed during a rebellion in the reign of Otto III (983–1018). Their complex post-mortem history is traced by Hahn-Woernle, pp. 80–2. The appearance of the graves on the map, labelled *hic quiescunt martyres*, is the first evidence of their presence at Ebstorf. Soon after various miracles were reported, the site became a goal of pilgrimage, and in 1419 a chapel was built.

23. Hahn-Woernle, p. 77.

24. Paul Binski, *The Painted Chamber at Westminster* (London, 1986), pp. 16 and 44.

25. Harvey, *Mappa Mundi: the Hereford World Map*, p. 7.

26. W. L. Bevan and H. W. Phillott, *Medieval Geography: an Essay in Illustration of the Hereford Mappa Mundi* (London, 1873; repr. Amsterdam, 1969), introduction (no page numbers). Other sources for this map include Miller, *Mappaemundi*, IV; Gerald R. Crone, *The World Map by Richard of Haldingham in Hereford Cathedral, Reproductions of Early Manuscript Maps*, III (London, 1954), with a facsimile. It is briefly described by David Woodward, 'Medieval mappaemundi', in *History of Cartography*, I, 309–12 with a photograph and useful notes.

27. Noted by Bevan and Phillott, and discussed at length in the appendix to the introduction (no page number).

28. For the state of this question, see Harvey, *Mappa Mundi*, pp. 7–11.

29. Kupfer, 'Medieval World Maps', pp. 273–5 and *passim*. My account depends heavily on her analysis.

30. See her study, 'The Lost Mappamundi at Chalivoy-Milon', *Speculum* LXVI, no. 3 (1991), 540–71; also Serafín Moralejo, 'El Mapa de la Díaspora Apostólica en San Pedro de Rocas', *Compostellanum* XXXI (1986), 315–40. Both describe lost wall-paintings of world maps in churches.

31. Harvey, *Mappa Mundi*, p. 54.

32. This survey – whether it happened or not, who did it, and what happened to the information that resulted – has been the subject of much interesting scholarly work. See for example Claude Nicolet, *Space, Geography and Politics in the Early Roman Empire* (Ann Arbor, Mich., 1990), originally published as *L'Inventaire du Monde: Géographie et Politique aux Origines de l'Empire Romain* (Paris, 1988); and, most recently, Kai Brodersen, *Terra Cognita: Studien zur römischen Raumerfassung* (Hildesheim, 1995). The survey is first mentioned in the *Cosmography* of Julius Honorius (*c.* AD 400, oldest manuscript is sixth century) and has been linked to the supposed world map of Marcus Agrippa, mentioned by Pliny.

33. The text on the map is mostly Latin, but a few of the inscriptions in the margins are in Norman French. These marginal inscriptions are helpfully transcribed and trans. in Harvey's book, *Mappa Mundi*, p. 54.

34. Christopher de Hamel, *Mappa Mundi* (London, 1989). This is the paste-up for a book which was made for the Sotheby's auction and never printed. The only copy is in the Hereford Cathedral library. It is illustrated with outstanding photographs of the map and its details.

35. G. R. Crone, 'New Light on the Hereford Map,' *Geographical Journal* CXXXI, part 4 (Dec. 1965), 447–62, with illustrations.

36. Bevan and Phillott, ch. 6.

37. Crone includes a useful map in his article with several of these itineraries marked on it, 'New Light', p. 450.

38. Miller, IV, 8–9.

39. Woodward, 'Medieval mappaemundi', in *History of Cartography*, I, 309, n. 113.

8. SPIRITUAL MAPS

1. A bilingual edition in Greek and French is by Wanda Wolska-Conus, *Cosmas Indicopleustès: Topographie Chrétienne* (Paris, 1968). See I, 61 on Cosmas's identity. An English translation is by J. W. McCrindle, *The Christian Topography of Cosmas, an Egyptian Monk*, in Hakluyt Society, vol. 98 (London, 1987). Cosmas is treated by David Woodward, 'Medieval Mappaemundi', in *History of Cartography*, I, 261–3, with illustrations. Excerpts from his geographical descriptions as well as illustrations are reproduced by Youssouf Kamal, *Monumenta cartographica Africae et Aegypti* (Leiden, 1932), II, fasc. 3, 362–78. Cosmas is discussed at length by C. R. Beazley, *Dawn of Modern Geography* (London, 1897), I, 273–303 and *passim*.

2. Beazley, I, 277.

3. Prologue, 1, and Exposition, 4. Wolska-Conus, pp. 254 and 266.

4. These are Vatican Bib. Apos., MS Greek 699 (ninth century, Constantinople); St Catherine's of

Mt Sinai, MS Greek 1186 (eleventh century, Cappadocia); Florence, Bibliotheca Laurenziana, Plut. IX.28 (eleventh century, Mount Athos). There are also a number of manuscripts with fragments of Cosmas's work, including copies of some of the illustrations. See Wolska-Conus, pp. 94–116.

5. See Jeffrey Burton Russell, *Inventing the Flat Earth* (New York, 1991), especially pp. 31–5. Russell cites Cosmas's translator, J. W. McCrindle ('long night of medieval ignorance and barbarism'), whose sentiments are echoed in the twentieth century by H. J. Randall, *Making of the Modern Mind* (Boston, 1926), p. 23; and George H. T. Kimble, *Geography in the Middle Ages* (London, 1938), p. 35. Patrick Gautier Dalché says bluntly that Cosmas was 'unknown in the Latin Middle Ages.' *La 'Descriptio Mappe Mundi' de Hugues de Saint-Victor* (Paris, 1988), p.119, n.8.

6. '*Et quo falcibus haec seminis grana per agrum huius mundi, quem profetae laboraverunt et hi metent, subiectae formulae pictura demonstrat.*' *Sancti Beati a Liebana Commentarius in Apocalypsin* E. Romero-Pose, ed., (Rome, 1985), I, 193, has '*facilius*', but '*falcibus*' (sickles), the reading used by Miller and Beazley, makes more sense and conforms to the language of Revelation.

7. Book VII, Romero-Pose, II, 199–203.

8. Miguel A. García Guinea, *El Monasterio de Santo Toribio de Liébana* (Madrid, 1981), p. 18. This little book has beautiful photographs of the dramatic landscape around Liébana.

9. This is the view of Kenneth D. Steinhauser, *The Apocalypse Commentary of Tyconius* (Frankfurt-am-Main, 1987), p. 147.

10. See Peter K. Klein, *Beatus a Liébana in Apocalypsim commentarius (Manchester)* in *Codices illuminati medii aevi*, no. 16 (Munich, 1990), 11–13.

11. Romero-Pose, I, 4.

12. And unfortunately now the treasure of a thief who stole the tenth-century manuscript belonging to the Cathedral of Seo de Urgel in the mountains of eastern Spain in the fall of 1996.

13. Although it was still being copied in the sixteenth century, and two manuscripts survive from this period. See Anscario M. Mundo and Manuel Sanchez Mariana, *El Comentario de Beato al Apocalipsis: Catálogo de los Códices* (Madrid, 1976), for a complete list of manuscripts.

14. There are a number of outstanding facsimiles of Beatus' manuscripts, which enable one to appreciate the range and beauty of the illustrations. These include *A Spanish Apocalypse: The Morgan Beatus Manuscript*, ed. by John Williams and Barbara A. Shailor (New York, 1991); *Beati in Apocalipsin Libri Duodecim Codex Gerundensis 2* (Madrid, 1975), 2 vols; *Comentarios al Apocalipsis y al Libro de Daniel, Edición facsimil del códice de la abadia de Saint-Sever* (Madrid, 1984), 2 vols; *Apocalipsis Beati Liebanensis Burgi Oxomensis* (Valencia, 1992); *Beato di Liébana: Miniature del Beato de Fernando I y Sancha (Codice B.N. Madrid, Vit. 14–2)*, ed. by Umberto Eco (Parma, 1973). Illustrations from all the manuscripts can now be seen in John Williams, *The Illustrated Beatus: a Corpus of Illustrations of the Commentary on the Apocalypse* (London, 1994), 2 vols, with 3 more to come.

15. Henri Stierlin, *Los Beatos de Liébana y el Arte Mozárabe* (Madrid, 1983), with outstanding illustrations. The original title of this book in French was *Le Livre de Feu*.

16. Williams, *The Illustrated Beatus*, I, ch. 2. A stemma based on the maps was proposed by Konrad Miller (I, 25) in 1895) but has been made obsolete by the discovery of additional manuscripts and the more precise dating of others. Exhaustive work on the problem of the stemma was also done by Wilhelm Neuss, *Die Apokalypse des Hl. Johannes in der altspanischen und altchristlichen Bibelillustration: Das Problem der Beatus-Handschriften* (Münster, 1931), p. 111.

17. The only possible exception is the *Liber Floridus* of Lambert of St Omer, which includes both an Apocalypse picture cycle and a variety of maps. However, they seem quite separate in the manuscript. On the maps in Beatus's work, see Konrad Miller, *Die Welkarte des Beatus, Mappaemundi*, I; Beazley, *Dawn*, II, 549–59, 591–605; Gonzalo Menendez Pidal, 'Mozárabes y Asturianos en la Cultura de la Alta Edad Media, en Relación Especial con la Historia de los Conocimientos Geográficos', *Boletín de la Real Academia de la Historia* CXXXIV, part 1 (1954), 137–291. John Williams has generously shared with me his forthcoming article, 'Isidore, Orosius and the Beatus Map', in *Imago Mundi* 49 (1997). The following is greatly indebted to his thinking.

18. Romero-Pose, I, 191–2. This work is perhaps also the work of Isidore. See the edition of *De Ortu et Orbitu Patrum* by César Chaparro Gómez (Paris, 1985), p. 216.

19. *A Spanish Apocalypse*, pp. 16–17. It is probable that the manuscript was actually made at Tabara, rather than at San Miguel. The manuscript is now New York, Pierpont Morgan Library, MS 644.

20. This is Miller's interpretation of the passage: *Mappaemundi*, I, 58. Williams suggests 'Neighbouring desert land unknown to us on account of the heat of the sun' which is closer to the Latin of Isidore XIV.5.17, and would imply that the land is not far away and might be considered part of the *ecumene*.

21. Woodward, 'Medieval Mappaemundi,' in *History of Cartography*, I, 297 and fig.18.6.

22. See a copy of his maps in *Geography*, ed. by E. L. Stevenson (New York, 1932; reprinted, 1991), ch. VII (pp. 137–40) and sixth map of Asia.

23. These manuscripts are Cathedral of Burgo de Osma, MS 1 (Sahagún, 1086); Lisbon, Arquivo da Torre do Tombo (Lorvâo, 1189); and Milan, Biblioteca Ambrosiana, MS F sup. 105, fols 71^r–72^v. The last is discussed by L. Vásquez de Parga, 'Un mapa desconodico de la serie de los "Beatos"', in *Actas del Simposio para el Estudio de los Códices del "Comentario al Apocalipsis" de Beato de Liébana* (Madrid, 1978), I, 273–8.

24. Serafín Moralejo, 'El Mapa de la Diáspora Apostólica en San Pedro de Rocas', *Compostellanum*, XXXI (1986), 315–40. The wall painting survives only in fragments.

25. '*Hec regio ab ardore solis incognita nobis et inhabitabilis manet. Sciopodum fertur habitare singulis cruribus et celeritate mirabili quos inde sciopodas greci vocant eo quod per estum in terra resupini iacentes pedum suorum magnitudine adumbrentur.*' This text is from Moralejo, whose article examines the problem of the Sciopod at some length. See Serafín Moralejo, 'World and Time in the Map of the Osma Beatus', *Apocalipsis Beati Liebanensis Burgi Oxomensis*, I (commentary), 145–74. Miller's transcription of this inscription contains several errors, While his work is valuable for its complete listing of place-names and inscriptions, it should always be remembered that he was working in many cases from photographs.

26. The Paris manuscript is Bibliothèque Nationale, MS n.a.lat. 1366 (Navarre, twelfth century). Moralejo has also found traces of this inscription at San Pedro de Rocas: 'World and Time', 148.

27. The manuscripts are in the Biblioteca de la Academia de la Historia in Madrid: MS 25,

fol. 204^v, and MS 76, fol. 108^r. Both appear in Book XIV of Isidore's *Etymologies*. My thanks to John Williams for sending me copies of these maps. The grammatical error (should be 'terra de pedibus latis') suggests that the phrase was abbreviated from some text, but that text has not been uncovered.

28. '*Extra tres autem partes orbis quarta pars trans oceanum interior est in meridie, quae solis ardore incognita nobis est. In cuius finibus antipodas fabulose inhabitare produntur.*' (In addition to the three parts of the world, a fourth part lies in the south across the interior ocean, and is unknown to us on account of the heat of the sun. In these lands the fabled antipodes are said to dwell.) *Etymologies*, XIV.5.

29. Williams, *Imago Mundi* 49 (1997), 7–32.

30. Paris, BN, MS lat.8878. This map is difficult to study as, in the interests of its preservation, the library is unwilling to let scholars see it, and there is no good photographic reproduction of it. The one in the facsimile is too small for the inscriptions to be read, and this is truer still of the various small photographs found in books. For a sample see George Kish, *La Carte: Image des Civilisations* (Paris, 1980), pl. 29. A better idea of the map can be had from Konrad Miller's actual-size drawing.

31. *Etymologies*, XIV.5.17.

32. This is Wilhelm Neuss's conclusion, *Die Apokalypse*, pp. 62–5. His reasoning is somewhat circular – if it's a good map, it must be Roman. Most subsequent authors have shied away from this theory.

33. For the occurrence of the genealogical tables in Beatus manuscripts, see Williams, *Illustrated Beatus*, II, 283–4 (table). The manuscripts with the T-O are the Tábara manuscript, Madrid, Archivo Historico Nacional, Cod.1097B (970), fol. 0^v; Turin, Biblioteca Nazionale Universitaria, Sgn.I.II.1 (early twelfth cen.), fol. 9^v; Gerona, Archivo de la Catedral, MS 7 (975), fol. 10^v; Madrid, Bib. Nac., MS Vitrina 14–2 (1047), fol. 7^r; Paris, B.N., MS lat.8878 (Saint-Sever, eleventh century), fol. 7^r. In other manuscripts which have the genealogical tables but not the map, it is replaced by a picture of Noah with two doves (New York, Pierpont Morgan Library, MS 644 (mid-tenth century), fol. 5^v) or the picture frames are left blank.

34. Williams notes that the maps with the apostles' heads all belong to a related subgroup of

Branch I, making them less valuable as a witness to the archetype. Personal communication.

35. Steinhauser, *The Apocalyse Commentary of Tyconius*, pp. 141–64 deal with Beatus.

36. See Williams in *Imago Mundi* 49 (1997).

37. Romero-Pose, I, 603ff. As a sample of eccesiastical arithmetic, this section can hardly be improved upon.

38. Romero-Pose, I, 642.

39. Patrick Gautier Dalché, *La 'Descriptio Mappe Mundi' de Hugues de Saint-Victor* (Paris, 1988).

40. Hugh of St-Victor, *Didascalicon*, ed. and trans. by Jerome Taylor (New York, 1961), p. 121.

41. *Didascalicon*, p. 136.

42. In *PL* Series Latina, ed. by J.-P. Migne, 176, cols. 681–704.

43. *PL* 176, 699. He describes the ark as having two doors, one toward the north, where the captive people of Israel were led from Jerusalem to Babylon, and one toward the south, leading the people liberated from Egypt to the promised land.

44. Most recently, Danielle Le Coq and Jean-Pierre Magnier, in 'La "Mappemonde" du *De Arca Noe Mystica*', in *Géographie du Monde au Moyen Age et à la Renaissance*, ed. by Monique Pelletier (Paris, 1989), pp. 12–14.

45. The manuscripts are Dijon, Bibliothèque Municipale, MS 561 (322), second quarter of the twelfth century, fols 162ʳ–170ᵛ; and Escorial, Biblioteca monastica, MS f.I.12, late twelfth century, fols 765ʳ–773ᵛ. Gautier Dalché's discussion of these manuscripts appears in ch. II, 25–33. The text of the *Descriptio* appears on pp.133–60.

46. Gautier Dalché, pp. 81–6. Appendix II, pp. 193–5 contains a complete list of names from this map, which is Munich, Bayerische Staatsbibliothek, Clm 10058, fol. 154ᵛ. For a good reproduction in colour, see P. D. A. Harvey, *Medieval Maps*, 22, pl. 16.

47. Gautier Dalché, p. 133. '*Nos autem non depingere, sed describere mappam mundi proponimus in hoc opere, id est non res nec rerum imagines, sed potius significationes, non quas res ipse significant, sed quibus significantur volumus demonstrare.*' (We do not propose to picture but to describe a map of the world in this work, for it is not things nor the images of things but rather their meaning that we wish to show, not what things in themselves mean, but what is meant by them.) A circumlocution worthy of a postmodernist!

[190]

BIBLIOGRAPHY

PRIMARY SOURCES

Adamnan, *De locis sanctis*, ed. by Denis Meehan (Dublin, 1958).

Alexander, Letter to Aristotle, *Epistola Alexandri ad Aristotelem* ed. by W. Walter Boer (Meisenheim, 1973).

Ambrose, *Hexameron*, trans. by John J. Savage, in The Fathers of the Church series (New York, 1961), 1–283.

Anon., 'Notitia Galliarum', in *Geographi Latini Minores*, ed. by Alexander Riese (Heilbronn, 1878), 141–4.

Anon., 'De urbibus Gallicis', *Itineraria et alia geographica*, ed. by Frater Glorie, in *Corpus Christianorum*, series latina, CLXXV (Turnhout, 1965), 409–10.

Arculfus, *The Pilgrimage of Arculfus to the Holy Land About the Year 670*, trans. by James Rose Macpherson, *Library of the Palestine Pilgrims' Text Society*, III, no. 1 (London, 1889).

Augustine, *City of God*, trans. by Gerald Walsh *et al.*, in *Fathers of the Church* series (New York, 1950, 1952, and 1954), 4 vols.

Augustine, *Confessions*, trans. R. S. Pine-Coffin (Baltimore, 1961).

Bacon, Roger, *Opus Majus*, trans. with introduction by John Henry Bridges (Oxford, 1897).

Beatus, *Sancti Beati a Liebana Commentarius in Apocalypsin*, ed. by E. Romero-Pose (Rome, 1985), 2 vols.

Bede, *Bedae Opera de Temporibus*, ed. with introduction by Charles W. Jones (Cambridge, Mass., 1943). Includes *De temporum ratione, De temporibus, Epistola ad Pleguinam, Epistola ad Wicthedum*.

Bede, *Bedae Pseudepigrapha: Scientific Writings Falsely Attributed to Bede*, ed. by Charles W. Jones (Ithaca, NY, 1939).

Bede, *De locis sanctis*, in *Patrologiae Cursus Completus*, series latina, ed. by J.-P. Migne (Paris, 1844–91), XCIV, cols. 1179–90.

Bede, *De natura rerum*, in *Opera Didascalica*, ed. by Charles W. Jones, *Corpus Christianorum*, series latina (Turnhout, 1975), CXXIII, A, 189–234.

Bede, *A History of the English Church and People*, trans. by Leo Sherley-Price (London, 1968).

Bede, *Opera Didascalica*, ed. by Charles W. Jones *et. al.*, *Corpus Christianorum*, series latina (Turnhout, 1975, 1977, 1980), CXXIII, A, B, and C.

Biblia Sacra Iuxta Vulgatam Versionem, ed. by Robertus Weber *et. al.* (3rd edn, Stuttgart, 1983).

Burchard of Mount Sion, *A Description of the Holy Land* (1280), trans. by Aubrey Stewart, *Library of the Palestine Pilgrims' Text Society* (New York., 1971; repr. from the London edition of 1896).

Byrhtferth, *Byrhtferth's Manual*, AD 1011, ed. by S. J. Crawford (Oxford, 1929).

Capella, Martianus, *The Marriage of Philology and Mercury*, trans. by William Harris Stahl and Richard Johnson, with E. L. Burge, in *Martianus Capella and the Seven Liberal Arts* (New York, 1971), II.

Chalcidius, *Commentary on the Timaeus*, ed. by J. H. Waszink, *Timaeus: A Calcidio Translatus Commentarioque Instructus* (London, 1975).

Charlemagne, 'Admonitio generalis', *Monumenta Germaniae Historica, Capitularia Regum Francorum* (Hanover, 1883), I, 60.

Chaucer, Geoffrey, *The Canterbury Tales*, in *The Works of Geoffrey Chaucer*, ed. by Alfred Pollard *et al.* (London, 1960).

Cosmas Indicopleustes, *Cosmas Indicopleustès: Topographie Chrétienne*, ed. by Wanda Wolska-Conus, (Paris, 1968), 2 vols.

Cosmas Indicopleustes, *The Christian Topography of Cosmas, an Egyptian Monk*, trans. by J. W. McCrindle, in Hakluyt Society, old series, XCVIII (London, 1897).

Cummian, *Cummian's Letter, De Controversia Paschali*, ed. by Maura Walsh and Dáibhí O Cróinín (Toronto, 1988).

Dante, *Divine Comedy*, Italian text with trans. and commentary by John D. Sinclair (Oxford, 1961).

Dante, *Monarchy* (Westport, Conn., 1979).

Dicuil, *Liber de Mensura Orbis Terrae*, ed. by J. J. Tierney, in *Scriptores Latini Hiberniae*, VI (Dublin, 1967).

Eusebius, *Eusebii Chronicorum Libri Duo*, ed. by Alfred Schoene (orig. 1875; Zurich, 1967).

Eusebius, *The History of the Church*, trans. by G. N. Williamson (Baltimore, 1965).

Galteri de Castellione Alexandreis, ed. by Marvin L. Colker, *Thesaurus Mundi*, Bibliotheca Scriptorum Latinorum Mediae et Recentioris Aetatis, XVII (Padua, 1978).

Gautier (Walter) de Châtillon, *The Alexandreis*, trans. by R. Relfryn Pritchard (Toronto, 1986).

Herodotus, *The Persian Wars*, trans. by George Rawlinson (New York., 1942).

Herrad of Landsberg, *Hortus Deliciarum*, ed. and trans. by Aristide D. Caratzas (New Rochelle, NY, 1977).

Higden, Ranulf, *Polychronicon Ranulphi Higden Monachi Cestrensis*, ed. by Churchill Babington, in *Chronicles and Memorials of Great Britain and Ireland in the Middle Ages*, XLI (London, 1865), 9 vols.

Honorius Augustodunensis, *Honorius Augustodunensis Imago Mundi*, ed. by Valerie Flint, in *Archives d'Histoire Doctrinale et Littéraire du Moyen Age*, XLIX (1982), 1–151.

Hugh of Saint-Victor, *De Arca Noe Mystica*, in *Patrologiae Cursus Completus*, series latina, ed. by J.-P. Migne, CLXXVI (Turnhout, n.d.), cols. 681–704.

Hugh of Saint-Victor, *Didascalicon*, ed. and trans. by Jerome Taylor (New York, 1961).

Isidore of Seville, *Chronica Maiora*, in *Monumenta Germaniae Historica: Chronica Minora, saec. IV, V, VI, VII*, ed. by T. Mommsen (Berlin, 1894).

Isidore of Seville, *De natura rerum*, ed. and trans. by Jacques Fontaine, with Latin text, *Isidore de Séville Traité de la Nature* (Bordeaux, 1960).

Isidore of Seville, *Etymologiarum sive Originum, Libri XX*, ed. by W. M. Lindsay (Oxford, 1911), 2 vols.

Isidore of Seville, *History of the Goths, Vandals and Suevi*, trans. with an introduction by Guido Donini and Gordon B. Ford, Jr. (2nd edn rev., Leiden, 1970).

Isidore of Seville, *De ortu et orbitu patrum*, ed. and trans. by César Chaparro Gómez (Paris, 1985).

Jerome, *Onomastica sacra: studia et sumptibus alterum edita*, ed. by Pauli de Lagarde (Göttingen, 1887), 118–90.

Jerome, 'Prefatio', *Liber de situ et nominibus locorum hebraicorum*, in *Patrologia Cursus Completus*, series latina ed. by J.-P. Migne (Paris, 1845), XXIII, 859–60.

Josephus, Flavius, *Jewish Antiquities*, trans. by H. St-J. Thackeray (London, 1930).

Julius Honorius, *Cosmographia*, in *Geographi Latini Minores*, ed. by Alexander Riese (Heilbronn, 1878), 24–55.

Lambert of St Omer, *Liber Floridus: Codex Autographus Bibliothecae Universitatis Gandavensis*, ed. by A. Derolez and I. Strubbe (Ghent, 1968). (A facsimile of Ghent, Rijksuniversiteit Bibliotheek, MS 92.)

Lucan, *The Civil War (Pharsalia)*, trans. by J. D. Duff (Cambridge, Mass., 1928).

Macrobius, *Commentary on the Dream of Scipio*, trans. with introduction by William Harris Stahl (New York, 1950 and 1992).

'Mappa Mundi e codice Albigensi 29', in *Itineraria et alia geographica*, ed. by Frater Glorie, in *Corpus Christianorum*, series latina, CLXXV (Turnhout, 1965), 465–94.

Matthew Paris, *Chronica Majora*, in *Matthew Paris's English History*, trans. by J. A. Giles (London, 1852–4), 3 vols.

Orosius, Paulus, *Historia adversum paganos: Seven Books of History Against the Pagans*, trans. by Roy J. Deferrari (Washington, 1964).

Otto of Freising, *The Two Cities: A Chronicle of Universal History*, trans. by Charles C. Mierow (New York, 1928).

Plato, *Timaeus*, trans. by Benjamin Jowett (Indianapolis, , 1949).

Pliny, *Natural History*, trans. by H. Rackham (rev. edn; Cambridge, Mass., 1991), 10 vols.

Plutarch, 'Life of Theseus', *Rise and Fall of Athens*, trans. by Ian Scott-Kilvert (Baltimore, 1960).

Polemius Sylvius, *Nomina omnium provinciarum*, in *Geographi latini minores*, ed. by Alexander Riese (Heilbronn, 1878), 130–2.

Priscian, 'Periegesis', in *Poetae latini minores*, ed. by Emil Baehrens (Leipzig, 1880), V, 275–312.

Ptolemy, *Geography*, ed. and trans. by E. L. Stevenson (New York, 1931; repr. 1991).

Raban Maur (Hrabanus Maurus), *De computo*, ed. by Wesley M. Stevens, *Corpus Christianorum: Continuatio Mediaevalis*, XLIV (Turnhout, 1979), 163–323.

Sallust, *War with Jugurtha*, Loeb Classical Library (Cambridge, Mass.).

Strabo, *Geography*, trans. by H. C. Hamilton and W. Faulconer (London, 1854).

Thucydides, *The Peloponnesian War*, trans. by Rex Warner (New York, 1972).

Virgil, *Virgil's Aeneid, Books I-XII*, introduction by Henry S. Frieze, rev. by Walter Dennison (New York, 1902).

Virgil, *Eclogues, Georgics, Aeneid I-VI*, trans. by H. Rushton Fairclough, Loeb Classical Library, rev. ed. (Cambridge, Mass., 1974).

SECONDARY WORKS

Almagía, Roberto, *Monumenta Cartographica Vaticana* (Vatican City, 1944–55), 4 vols.

Alexander, J. J. G. and Binski, Paul, *Age of Chivalry: Art of Plantagenet England* (London, 1987).

Anderson, A. R., *Alexander's Gate: Gog and Magog and the Inclosed Nations* (Cambridge, Mass., 1932).

Andrews, Michael, 'The study and classification of medieval mappaemundi', *Archaeologia*, LXXV (1925–6), 61–76.

Arentzen, Jörg-Geerd, *Imago Mundi Cartographica: Studien zur Bildlichkeit mittelalterlicher Welt- und Ökumenekarten unter besonderer Berücksichtigung des Zusammenwirkens von Text und Bild* (Munich, 1984).

Arnaud, Pascal, 'Plurima Orbis Imago: Lectures conventionelles des cartes au moyen âge', *Médiévales*, XVIII (spring 1990), 31–51.

Aveni, Anthony F., *Empires of Time: Calendars, Clocks and Cultures* (New York, 1972).

Bagrow, Leo, *History of Cartography*, rev. edn. by R. A. Skelton (Cambridge, Mass., 1966).

Baker, Peter, 'Byrhtferth's Enchiridion and the Computus in Oxford', in *Anglo-Saxon England*, ed. by Peter Clemoes, X (1981), 123–42.

Baltrusaitis, Jurgis, 'L'image du monde céleste du IXe au XIe siècle', *Gazette des Beaux-Arts*, ser. 6, XXI (1939), 137–48.

Barber, Peter M., 'The Evesham World Map: a Late Medieval English View of God and the World', *Imago Mundi*, XLVII (1995), 13–33.

Barber, Peter M., 'Old Encounters New: the Aslake World Map,' in *Géographie du Monde au Moyen Age et à la Renaissance*, ed. by Monique Pelletier (Paris, 1989), 69–88.

Bately, Janet, ed., *The Old English Orosius*, Early English Text Society (London, 1980).

Beazley, C. Raymond, *The Dawn of Modern Geography* (London and Oxford, 1897, 1901, 1906), 3 vols.

Bevan, W. L., and Phillott, H. W., *Medieval Geography: an Essay in Illustration of the Hereford Mappa Mundi* (London, 1873; repr. Amsterdam, 1969).

Binski, Paul, *The Painted Chamber at Westminster* (London, 1986).

Bischoff, Bernhard, *Manuscripts and Libraries in the Age of Charlemagne*, trans. and ed. by Michael Gorman (Cambridge, 1994).

Blakemore, Michael J. and Harley, J. B., 'Concepts in the History of Cartography: a Review and Perspective', *Cartographica*, XVII, no. 4 (1980) Monograph 26, 17–23.

Bober, Harry, 'An Illustrated Medieval School-book of Bede's "De natura rerum"', *Journal of the Walters Art Gallery*, XIX-XX (1956-7), 65–97.

Bober, Harry 'In Principio: Creation before Time', in *Essays in Honor of Erwin Panofsky*, ed. by Millard Meiss (New York, 1961), I, 13–29.

Bolgar, R. R., ed. *Classical Influences on European Culture, 500–1500* (Cambridge, 1971).

Bonner, Gerald, ed., *Famulus Christi: Essays in Commemoration of the 13th Centenary of the Birth of the Venerable Bede* (London, 1976).

Borst, Arno, *The Ordering of Time* (Chicago, 1993).

Bosio, Luciano, *La Tabula Peutingeriana: una descrizione pittorica del mondo antico* (Rimini, 1983).

Brandon, S. G. F., *History, Time and Deity* (Manchester, 1965).

Bréhaut, Ernest, *An Encyclopedist of the Dark Ages: Isidore of Seville* (New York, 1912; reissued 1968).

Breisach, Ernst, *Historiography: Ancient, Medieval and Modern* (Chicago, 1983).

von den Brincken, Anna-Dorothee, *Fines Terrae: Die Enden der Erde und der vierte Kontinent auf mittelalterlichen Weltkarten* (Hanover, 1992).

von den Brincken, Anna-Dorothee, 'Gyrus und Spera: Relikte griechische Geographie im Weltbild der Frühscholastik', *Sudhoff's Archiv*, LXXIII (1989), 129–44.

von den Brincken, Anna-Dorothee, 'Die Klimatenkarte in der Chronik des Johann von Wallingford – ein Werk des Matthaeus Parisiensis?' *Westfalen*, 51 (1973), 47–56.

von den Brincken, Anna-Dorothee, 'Die Kugelgestalt der Erde in der Kartographie des Mittelalters', in *Archiv für Kulturgeschichte*, ed. by Fritz Wagner, LVIII (1976), 77–96.

von den Brincken, Anna-Dorothee, 'Mappa mundi und chronographia: Studien zur *imago mundi* des abendländischen Mittelalters', *Deutsches Archiv für Erforschung des Mittelalters*, XXIV (1968), 118–86.

von den Brincken, Anna-Dorothee, 'Monumental Legends on Medieval Manuscript Maps', *Imago Mundi*, 42 (1990), 9–25.

von den Brincken, Anna-Dorothee, '"ut describeretur universus orbis" zur Universalkartographie des Mittelalters', in *Methoden in Wissenschaft und Kunst des Mittelalters*, ed. by Albert Zimmermann (Berlin, 1970), 249–78.

von den Brincken, Anna-Dorothee, 'Der vierte Erdteil in der Kartographie des Hochmittelalters', in *Reisen in reale und mythische Ferne*, ed. by Peter Wunderli (Düsseldorf, 1993), 16–34.

von den Brincken, Anna-Dorothee, 'Weltbild der lateinischen Universalhistoriker und -kartographen', in *Popoli e paesi nella cultura altomedievale* (Spoleto, 1983), I, 377–408.

Broderson, Kai, *Terra Cognita: Studien zur Römischen Raumerfassung* (Hildesheim, 1995).

Brown, Lloyd A., *The World Encompassed: an Exhibition of Maps Held at the Baltimore Museum of Art* (Baltimore, 1952).

Caldwell, James R., 'Manuscripts of Gervase of Tilbury's *Otia Imperialia*', *Scriptorium*, XVI (1962), 28–45, 246–74.

Camille, Michael, *Images on the Edge: the Margins of Medieval Art* (Cambridge, Mass., 1992).

Campbell, Mary, *The Witness and the Other World: Exotic European Travel Writing, 400–1600* (Ithaca, NY, 1988).

Campbell, Tony, *The Earliest Printed Maps* (London, 1987).

Campbell, Tony, 'Portolan Charts from the Late Thirteenth Century to 1500', in *History of Cartography*, I, ed. by J. B. Harley and David Woodward (Chicago, 1987).

Carruthers, Mary J., *The Book of Memory: a Study of Memory in Medieval Culture* (Cambridge, 1990).

Coh, Robert L., *Shape of Sacred Space: Four Biblical Studies* (Chico, Calif., 1981).

Comentarios al Apocalipsis y al Libro de Daniel, Edición facsimil del códice de la abadía de Saint-Sever (Madrid, 1984), 2 vols. (A facsimile of Paris, B. N., MS lat. 8878 with interpretative essays.)

Cortesão, Armando, *Portugaliae Monumenta Cartographica* (Lisbon, 1960–2).

Cousin, P. *Abbon de Fleury-sur-Loire* (Paris, 1952).

Crone, Gerald R., *Early Maps of the British Isles, AD 1000–1500* (London, 1961).

Crone, Gerald R., 'New Light on the Hereford Map', *The Geographical Journal*, 131, part 4 (Dec. 1965), 447–62.

Crone, Gerald R., *The World Map by Richard of Haldingham in Hereford Cathedral, Reproductions of Early Manuscript Maps*, III (London, 1954), with a facsimile.

Danzer, Gerald A., *Mapping Western Civilization* (New York, 1990).

Degenhart, Bernhard, and Schmitt, Annegrit, 'Marino Sanudo und Paolino Veneto', *Römisches Jahrbuch für Kunstgeschichte*, XIV (1973), 1–137.

Delano Smith, Catherine, 'Geography or Christianity: Maps of the Holy Land Before 1000',

Journal of Theological Studies, new series, XLII, part 1 (April 1991), 143–52.

Delano Smith, Catherine, 'Maps as Art and Science: Maps in 16th Century Bibles', *Imago Mundi*, 42 (1990), 65–83.

Delano Smith, Catherine, and Gruber, Mayer, 'Rashi's Legacy: Maps of the Holy Land', *The Map Collector*, no. 59 (summer 1992), 30–5.

Delano Smith, Catherine, 'Why Theory in the History of Cartography?' *Imago Mundi*, XLVIII (1996), 198–203.

Delisle, Léopold, 'Notice sur les manuscrits du *Liber Floridus* de Lambert', *Notices et extraits des manuscrits de la Bibliothèque Nationale*, XXXVIII, no. 2 (1906), 577–791.

Derolez, Albert, ed., *Liber Floridus Colloquium*, (Ghent, 1973).

Derolez, Albert, *Lambertus Qui Librum Fecit: een Codicologische Studie van de Liber Floridus-Autograaf* (Brussels, 1978), with a summary in English on 469–79.

De Smet, J.-M., 'La mentalité religieuse du chanoine Lambert', *Liber Floridus Colloquium*, ed. by Albert Derolez (Ghent, 1973), 11–12.

Destombes, Marcel, ed., *Mappemondes, AD 1200–1500: Catalog preparé par la Commission des Cartes Anciennes de l'Union Géographique Internationale* (Amsterdam, 1964).

Díaz y Díaz, Manuel C., *Isidoriana: Colleción de estudios sobre Isidoro de Sevilla* (Léon, 1961).

Díaz y Díaz, Manuel C., *Libros y Librerías en la Rioja altomedieval* (Logroño, 1979).

Dilke, O. A. W., 'Cartography in the Byzantine Empire', in *History of Cartography*, I, ed. by J. B. Harley and David Woodward (Chicago, 1987), 258–75.

Dilke, O. A. W., *Greek and Roman Maps* (Ithaca, NY, 1985).

Dilke, O. A. W., 'Maps in the Service of the State', in *History of Cartography*, I, ed. by J. B. Harley and David Woodward (Chicago, 1987), 201–11.

Dominguez-Bordona, J., *Spanish Illumination* (orig., 1929; New York, 1969).

Duchet-Suchaux, G., ed., *Iconographie médiévale: Image, texte, contexte* (Paris, 1990).

Durand, Dana Bennett, *The Vienna-Klosterneuberg Map Corpus of the 15th Century* (Leiden, 1952).

Eastwood, Bruce S., 'The Astronomies of Pliny, Martianus Capella and Isidore of Seville', in *Science in Western and Eastern Civilization in Carolingian Times*, ed. by P. L. Butzer and D. Lohrmann (Basel, 1993), 161–80.

Eastwood, Bruce S., 'Origins and Contents of the Leiden Planetary Configuration, MS Voss Q–79, f.93^v: an Artistic Astronomical Schema of the Early Middle Ages', *Viator* XIV (1983), 1–39.

Eastwood, Bruce S., 'Plinian Astronomical Diagrams in the Early Middle Ages', in *Mathematics and its Applications to Science and Natural Philosophy in the Middle Ages: Essays in Honor of Marshall Clagett*, ed. by Edward Grant and John E. Murdoch (Cambridge, 1987), 141–172.

Eastwood, Bruce S., 'Plinian Astronomy in the Middle Ages and Renaissance', in *Science in the Early Roman Empire: Pliny the Elder, His Sources and Influence*, ed. by Roger French and Frank Greenaway (Totowa, NJ, 1986), 197–251.

Eco, Umberto, ed., *Beato di Liebana: Miniature del Beato de Fernando I y Sancha (Codice B.N. Madrid, Vit. 14–2)* (Parma, 1973).

Edgerton, Samuel Y., Jr., 'From Mental Matrix to Mappamundi to Christian Empire: the Heritage of Ptolemaic Cartography in the Renaissance', in *Art and Cartography: Six Historical Essays*, ed. by David Woodward (Chicago, 1987), 10–50.

Edney, Matthew, 'Theory and the History of Cartography', *Imago Mundi*, 48 (1996), 185–91.

Edson, Evelyn, 'Matthew Paris's "Other" Map of Palestine', *The Map Collector*, no. 66 (Spring 1994), 18–22.

Edson, Evelyn, 'The Oldest World Maps: Classical Sources of Three Eighth-Century Mappaemundi', *The Ancient World*, XXIV (1993), no. 2, 169–84.

Edson, Evelyn, 'World Maps and Easter Tables', *Imago Mundi*, 48 (1996), 25–42.

Egry, Anne D., 'O mapa-mundi do "Apocalipse de Lorvão"', *Coloquio*, no. 59 (1970), 24–8.

Endt, Johann, 'Isidorus und die Lucanscholien', *Wiener Studien* XXX (1908), 294–307.

Engelen, Eva-Marie, *Zeit, Zahl und Bild: Studien zur Verbindung von Philosophie und Wissenschaft bei Abbo von Fleury* (Berlin, 1993).

Esmeijer, Anna C., *Divina Quaternitas: A Preliminary Study in the Method and Application of Visual Exegesis* (Amsterdam, 1978).

Flint, Valerie, 'Honorius Augustodunensis Imago Mundi', in *Archives d'Histoire Doctrinale et Littéraire du Moyen Age*, ann. 57, t. XLIX (Paris, 1983), 1–151.

Flint, Valerie, *Honorius Augustodunensis of Regensburg*, in *Authors of the Middle Ages*, ed. by Patrick J. Geary (Aldershot, UK, 1995), II, no. 6.

Fontaine, Jacques, 'La diffusion carolingienne du *De natura rerum* d'Isidore de Seville d'après des manuscrits conservés en Italie', *Studi Medievali*, ann. 7 (1963), fasc. 1, 108–27.

Fontaine, Jacques, *Isidore de Séville et la culture classique dans l'Espagne Wisigothique* (Paris, 1959), 2 vols.

Fontaine, Jacques, *Isidore de Séville Traité de la nature* (Bordeaux, 1960).

Friedman, John B., *The Monstrous Races in Medieval Art and Thought* (Cambridge, Mass., 1981).

Galbraith, V. H., *Historical Research in Medieval England* (London, 1951).

Gautier Dalché, Patrick, *La 'Descriptio mappe mundi' de Hughes de Saint-Victor* (Paris, 1988).

Gautier Dalché, Patrick, 'De la glose à la contemplation: Place et fonction de la carte dans les manuscrits du haut moyen âge', *Testo e immagine nell'alto medioevo*, Settimane di Studio del Centro Italiano di Studi Sull'Alto Medioevo (Spoleto, 1994), XLI, 693–71.

Gautier Dalché, Patrick, 'Notes sur la "Carte de Théodose II" et sur la "Mappemonde de Théodulf d'Orléans"', *Geographia Antiqua*, III–IV (1994–5), 91–108.

Gilson, J. P., and Poole, H. *Four Maps of Great Britain Designed by Matthew Paris* (London, 1928).

Glorie, Frater, *Itineraria et alia geographica*, in *Corpus Christianorum*, series latina, CLXXV (Turnhout, 1965).

Gomez Pallares, J., 'Sobre manuscritos latinos de cómputo en escritura visigótica', *Hispania Sacra*, XXXIX, 25–48.

Gotoff, Harold C., *The Transmission of the Text of Lucan in the 9th century* (Cambridge, Mass., 1971).

Gow, Andrew, 'Gog and Magog on Mappaemundi and Early Printed Maps: Orientalizing Ethnography in the Apocalyptic Tradition,' in *Journal of Early Modern History* (summer 1996).

Green, C. M. C., 'De Africa et eius incolis: the Function of Geography and Ethnography in Sallust's History of the Jugurthine War', *The Ancient World*, XXIV (1993), no. 2, 185–97.

Grosjean, George, ed., *Mappamundi: the Catalan Atlas for the Year 1375* (Zurich, 1978).

Grotefend, H., *Zeitrechnung des deutschen Mittelalters und der Neuzeit* (Hanover, 1891–98), 2 vols in 3 parts.

Hahn-Woernle, Birgit, *Die Ebstorfer Weltkarte* (Ebstorf, 1987).

Hapgood, Charles H., *Maps of the Ancient Sea Kings: Evidence of Advanced Civilization in the Ice Age* (rev. ed; New York, 1979).

Harley, J. B., 'Maps, Knowledge, and Power', in *The Iconography of Landscape*, ed. by Denis Cosgrove and Stephen Daniels (Cambridge, 1988).

Harley, J. B. and Woodward, David '*Cartography in Prehistoric, Ancient, and Medieval Europe and the Mediterranean*', *History of Cartography*, ed. by Harley and Woodward, I (Chicago, 1987).

Harley, J. B. and Woodward, David, *Cartography in Traditional Islamic and South Asian Societies*, *History of Cartography*, II, book 1 (Chicago, 1992).

Harley, J. B., *Maps and the Columbian Encounter* (Milwaukee, 1990).

Harley, J. B., 'Silences and Secrecy: the Hidden Agenda of Cartography in Early Modern Europe', *Imago Mundi*, 40 (1988), 57–76.

Harrison, Kenneth, 'Luni-Solar Cycles: Their Accuracy and Some Types of Usage', in *Saints, Scholars and Heroes*, ed. by Wesley M. Stevens and Margot H. King (Collegeville, Minn., 1979), 65–78.

Harvey, Paul D. A., 'Matthew Paris's Maps of Britain', *Thirteenth-Century England*, V (Woodbridge, UK, 1992), 109–21.

Harvey, Paul D. A., *Mappa Mundi: the Hereford World Map* (London, 1996).

Harvey, Paul D. A., *Medieval Maps* (London, 1991).

Harvey, Paul D. A., 'Medieval Maps: an Introduction', in *History of Cartography*, I, ed. by

J. B. Harley and David Woodward (Chicago, 1987).

Harvey, Paul D. A., 'The Sawley Map and Other World Maps in Twelfth-Century England', *Imago Mundi*, 49 (1997).

Haslam, Graham, 'The Duchy of Cornwall Map Fragment', in *Géographie du Monde au Moyen Age et à la Renaissance*, ed. by Monique Pelletier (Paris, 1989), 33–49.

Heidel, William A., *The Frame of the Ancient Greek Maps: With a Discussion of the Sphericity of the Earth* (New York, 1937).

Heller, Johannes, 'Uber den Ursprung der sogenannten spanischen Aera', *Sybel's Historische Zeitschrift*, XXXI (1874), 13–32.

Helms, Mary W., *Ulysses's Sail: an Ethnographic Odyssey of Power, Knowledge and Geographical Distance* (Princeton, 1988).

Higgins, Anne, 'Medieval Notions of the Structure of Time', *Journal of Medieval and Renaissance Studies*, XIX (Fall 1989), 227–50.

Hillgarth, J. N., 'The Position of Isidorian Studies: a Critical Review of the Literature, 1936–75', *Studi Medievali*, ann. 24 (1983), fasc. 2, 817–905.

Hoogvliet, Margriet, 'The Mystery of the Makers: Did Nuns Make the Ebstorf Map?' *Mercator's World*, I, no. 6 (1996), 16–21.

Illich, Ivan, *In the Vineyard of the Text: a Commentary to Hugh's Didascalicon* (Chicago, 1993).

Ineichen-Eder, Christine E., *Mittelalterliche Bibliothekskatalog Deutschlands und der Schweiz* (Munich, 1977), IV, part 1.

Irblich, Eva, *Karl der Grosse und die Wissenschaft* (Wien, 1994).

Jacob, Christian, *L'empire des cartes: Approche théorique de la cartographie à travers l'histoire* (Paris, 1992).

Jacob, Christian, 'L'oeil et la mémoire: sur la Périégèse de la Terre habitée de Denys', in *Arts et Légendes d'Espaces*, ed. by Christian Jacob and Frank Lestringant (Paris, 1981), 21–98.

Jacob, Christian, 'Toward a Cultural History of Cartography', *Imago Mundi*, XLVIII (1996), 191–8.

James, M. R., *The Wanderings and Homes of Medieval Manuscripts* (London, 1919).

Janvier, Yves, *La géographie d'Orose* (Paris, 1982).

Jomard, Edme F., *Les monuments de la géographie* (Paris, 1842–62).

Jones, Charles W., 'A Legend of St Pachomius', *Speculum* XVIII (1943), 198–210.

Jones, Charles W., 'Manuscripts of Bede's *De natura rerum*', Isis, XXVII (1937), 432–3.

Kamal, Prince Youssouf, *Monumenta cartographica Africae et Aegypti* (Cairo: 1926–51), 5 vols.

Katzenstein, Ranee, and Savage-Smith, Emilie, *The Leiden Aratea: Ancient Constellations in a Medieval Manuscript* (Malibu, Calif., 1988).

Kemp, Wolfgang, 'Medieval Pictorial Systems', in *Iconography at the Crossroads*, ed. by Brendan Cassidy (Princeton, 1993), 121–38.

Kimble, George H. T., *Geography in the Middle Ages* (London, 1938).

King, G. G., 'Divagations on the Beatus', *Art Studies*, VIII, part 1 (1930), 3–58.

Kish, George, *La carte: Image des civilisations* (Paris, 1980).

Kitzinger, Ernst, 'World Map and Fortune's Wheel: a Medieval Mosaic Floor in Turin', *Proceedings of the American Philosophical Society*, CXVII (1973), 344–73.

Klein, Peter K., *Die ältere Beatus-Kodex Vitr. 14–1 der Biblioteca Nacional zu Madrid* (Hildesheim, 1976), 2 vols.

Klein, Peter K., *Beatus a Liébana in Apocalypsim commentarius (Manchester)* in *Codices illuminati medii aevi*, no.16 (Munich, 1990).

Klein, Peter K., 'La Tradición Pictórica de los Beatos', *Actas del Simposio para el Estudio de los Códices del 'Comentario al Apocalpisis' de Beato de Liébana* (Madrid, 1978), 83–166.

Klibansky, Raymond, *The Continuity of the Platonic Tradition During the Middle Ages* (London, 1939).

Knowles, David, 'The Mappa Mundi of Gervase of Canterbury', *Downside Review*, XLVIII (1930), 237–47.

Koehler, William, *Die Karolingischen miniaturen* (Berlin, 1960), 5 vols.

Krusch, Bruno, *Studien zur christlich-mittelalterlichen Chronologie: der 84jährige Ostercyclus und seine Quellen* (Leipzig, 1880).

Krusch, Bruno, *Studien zur christlich-mittelalterlichen Chronologie: die Entstehung unserer heutigen Zeitrechnung* (Berlin, 1938).

Kugler, Harmut and Michael, Eckhard, eds., *Ein Weltbild vor Columbus: Die Ebstorfer Weltkarte*, Interdisciplinary Colloquium 1988 (Weinheim, 1991).

Kupfer, Marcia, 'The Lost Mappamundi at Chalivoy-Milon', *Speculum*, LXVI, no. 3 (July 1991), 540–71.

Kupfer, Marcia, 'The Lost Wheel Map of Ambrogio Lorenzetti', *Art Bulletin*, LXXVIII, no. 2 (June 1996), 286–310.

Kupfer, Marcia, 'Medieval World Maps: Embedded Images, Interpretive Frames', *Word and Image*, X, no. 3 (July-Sept. 1994), 262–88.

Lattin, Harriet Pratt, 'The 11th Century MS Munich 14436: its Contribution to the History of Coordinates, of Logic, of German Studies in France', *Isis*, XXXVIII (1947–8), 205–25.

LeCoq, Danielle, 'La "Mappemonde" du *De Arca Noe Mystica*', in *Géographie du Monde au Moyen Age et à la Renaissance*, ed. by Monique Pelletier (Paris, 1989), 9–32.

LeCoq, Danielle, 'La Mappemonde d'Henri de Mayence, ou l'Image du Monde au XIIe Siècle', in *Iconographie Médiévale: Image, Texte, Contexte*, ed. by Gaston Duchet-Suchaux (Paris, 1990), 155–207.

LeCoq, Danielle, 'La mappemonde du *Liber Floridus* ou la vision de Lambert de Saint-Omer', *Imago Mundi*, 39 (1987), 9–49.

LeCoq, Danielle, 'Saint Brandan, Christophe Colomb et le paradis terrestre', *Revue de la Bibliothèque Nationale*, no. 45 (1992), 14–21.

Lecouteux, Claude, *Les monstres dans la pensée médiévale européenne* (Paris, 1993).

Lefèvre, Yves, 'Le *Liber Floridus* et la littérature encyclopédique au Moyen Age', *Liber Floridus Colloquium*, ed. by Albert Derolez (Ghent, 1973), 1–9.

LeGoff, Jacques, *The Medieval Imagination*, trans. by Arthur Goldhammer (Chicago, 1988).

Lelewel, Joachim, *Géographie du moyen âge* (Brussels, 1852–7), 5 vols.

Levine, Philip, 'The continuity and preservation of the Latin tradition', in *The Transformation of the Roman World*, ed. by Lynn White (Berkeley, 1966), 219–22.

Lewis, C. S., *The Discarded Image: an Introduction to Medieval and Renaissance Literature* (Cambridge, 1964).

Lewis, Suzanne, *The Art of Matthew Paris* (Berkeley, 1987).

Lindberg, David C., *The Beginnings of Western Science: the European Scientific Tradition in Philosophical, Religious, and Institutional Context, 600 BC to AD 1450* (Chicago, 1992).

McCluskey, Stephen C., 'Gregory of Tours, Monastic Timekeeping and Early Christian Attitudes Toward Astronomy', *Isis*, LXXXI (1990), 9–22.

McGurk, Patrick, 'Carolingian Astrological Manuscripts', in *Charles the Bald: Court and Kingdom*, ed. by Margaret Gibson and Janet Nelson (Oxford, 1981), 317–32.

McGurk, Patrick, 'Computus Helperici: its Transmission in England in the 11th and 12th Centuries', *Medium Aevum*, XLIII (1974), 1–5.

McGurk, Patrick; Dumville, D. N.; Godden, M. R.; and Knock, Ann, *An Eleventh-Century Anglo-Saxon Illustrated Miscellany: British Library Cotton Tiberius B. V. Part I, Together with Leaves from British Library Cotton Nero D. II, Early English Manuscripts in Facsimile*, XXI (Copenhagen, 1983).

Magoun, Francis P., 'An English Pilgrim-Diary of the Year 990', *Medieval Studies*, II (1940), 231–52.

Manitius, Max, *Handschriften antiker autoren in mittelalterlichen Bibliothekskatalogen* (Leipzig, 1935; repr. Wiesbaden, 1968).

Marques Casanova, Jaime, *et. al.*, *Beati in Apocalipsin Libri Duodecim Codex Gerundensis 2* (Madrid, 1975), 2 vols. (A facsimile with interpretative essays and text of the Gerona Cathedral MS 7.)

mas Latrie, Comte de, *Trésor de Chronologie* (Paris, 1889; repr. 1969).

Meersseman, G. G. and Adda, E., *Manuale di Computo con Ritmo Mnemotecnico dell'Arcidiacono Pacifico di Verona (d.844)* (Padova, 1966).

Melitzski, Dorothy, *The Matter of Araby in Medieval England* (New Haven, 1977).

Menendez Pidal, G., 'Mozárabes y asturianos en la cultura de la Alta Edad Media en relación especial con la historia de los conocimientos geográficos', *Boletín de la Real Academia de la Historia*, CXXXIV (1954), 137–291.

Michelant, Henri and Raynaud, Gaston, *Itinéraires à Jerusalem et descriptions de la Terre Sainte, rédigés en français au XIe, XIIe, et XIIIe siècles* (Geneva, 1882).

Miller, Konrad, *Itineraria Romana: Römische Reisewege an der Hand Schrift der Tabula Peutingeriana* (edn., repr. Rome, 1916).

Miller, Konrad, *Mappaemundi: die ältesten Weltkarten* (Stuttgart, 1895–8), 6 vols.

Mitchell, J. B., 'Early Maps of Great Britain: I. The Matthew Paris Maps', *Geographical Journal*, LXXXI (1933), 27–34.

Moé, Émile-A. van, *L'Apocalypse de Saint-Sever, MS lat. 8878 de la Bibliothèque Nationale* (Paris, 1943).

Moffitt, John F., 'Medieval Mappaemundi and Ptolemy's Chorographia', *Gesta*, XXXII/1 (1993), 59–68.

Moralejo, Serafin, 'El Mapa de la Diáspora Apostólica en San Pedros de Rocas', *Compostellanum*, XXXI (1986), 315–41.

Moralejo, Serafin, 'World and Time in the Map of the Osma Beatus', *Apocalipsis Beati Liebanensis. Burgi Oxomensis, II: El Beato de Osma: Estudios*, ed. by John Williams (Valencia, 1992), 151–79.

Morrison, Karl F., *History as a Visual Art in the 12th Century Renaissance* (Princeton, 1990).

Mostert, M. and R., 'Using Astronomy as an Aid to Dating Manuscripts: the Example of the Leiden Planetarium', *Quaerendo*, XX (1990), 248–61.

Murdoch, John E., *Album of Science: Antiquity and the Middle Ages* (New York, 1984).

Nebenzahl, Kenneth, *Maps of the Holy Land: Images of Terra Sancta Through Two Millennia* (New York, 1986).

Neuss, Wilhelm, *Die Apokalypse des Hl. Johannes in der altspanischen und altchristlichen Bibelillustration: Das Problem der Beatus-Handschriften* (Münster, 1931).

Nicolet, Claude, and Gautier Dalché, Patrick, 'Les "Quatre Sages" de Jules César et la "mésure du monde" selon Julius Honorius', *Journal des Savants*, 1987, 157–218.

Nicolet, Claude, *Space, Geography and Politics in the Early Roman Empire* (Ann Arbor, 1990).

Nordenskjold, A. E., *Facsimile Atlas to the Early History of Cartography*, with a new introduction by J. B. Post (orig. 1889; New York, 1973).

Nordenskjold, A. E., *Periplus: an Essay on the Early History of Charts and Sailing Directions*, trans. by Francis A. Bather (Stockholm, 1897).

Pagden, Anthony, *Lords of All the World: Ideologies of Empire in Spain, Britain and France c.1500–c.1800* (New Haven, Conn., 1995).

Pelletier, Monique, ed., *Géographie du monde au moyen âge et à la Renaissance* (Paris, 1989).

Philipp, Hans, *Die historisch-geographischen Quellen in den etymologiae des Isidorus von Sevilla*, in *Quellen und Forschungen zur alten Geschichte und Geographie*, ed. by W. Sieglin, XXV and XXVI (Berlin, 1912–13).

Plaut, Fred, 'Where is Paradise? The Mapping of a Myth', *Map Collector*, no. 29 (Dec. 1984), 2–7.

Poole, Reginald L., *Chronicles and Annals* (Oxford, 1926).

Price, Derek de Solla, 'Medieval Land Surveying Techniques', *Geographical Journal*, CXXI (1955), 1–10.

Raizman, David Seth, *The Later Morgan Beatus (M. 429) and Late Romanesque Illumination in Spain*, University of Pittsburgh, Dissertation, 1980.

Ramsay, H. L., 'Le commentaire de l'Apocalypse par Beatus de Liébana', *Revue d'Histoire et de Litterature Religieuses* VII, no. 5 (Sept./Oct. 1902), 419–47.

Revenga, Luis, ed., *Los Beatos* (Brussels, 1985).

Reynolds, L. D. and Wilson, N. G. *Scribes and Scholars: a Guide to the Transmission of Greek and Latin Literature*, 3rd edn (Oxford, 1991).

Reynolds, L. D., ed., *Texts and Transmission: a Survey of the Latin Classics* (Oxford, 1983).

Riché, Pierre, *Education and Culture in the Barbarian West*, trans. by John J. Contreni (Columbia, SC, 1976).

Robin, Harry, *The Scientific Image: From Cave to Computer* (New York, 1992).

Robinson, Arthur, and Petchenik, Barbara, *The Nature of Maps: Essays Toward Understanding Maps and Mapping* (Chicago, 1974).

Rohricht, Reinhold, 'Karten und Pläne zur Palästinakunde aus dem 7 bis 16 Jahrhundert', *Zeitschrift des Deutschen Palästina-Vereins*, XIV (1891), 8–11.

Rohricht, Reinhold, *Bibliotheca Geographica Palaestinae* (Berlin, 1890).

Rojo Orcajo, T., *El Beato de la Biblioteca de S. Cruz de Valladolid*, in *Estudios de códices visigóticos* (Madrid, 1930).

Romm, James S., *The Edges of the Earth in Ancient Thought: Geography, Exploration, and Fiction* (Princeton, 1992).

Ross, David J. A., *Alexander Historiatus: a Guide to Medieval Illustrated Alexander Literature* (Frankfurt-am-Main, 1988; repr. of 1963 edition).

Ruberg, Uwe, 'Mappaemundi des Mittelalters in Zusammenwirken von Text und Bild', in *Text und Bild*, ed. by Christel Meier (Wiesbaden, 1980), 550–92.

Russell, Jeffrey B., *Inventing the Flat Earth* (New York, 1991).

Salomon, Richard G., 'A Newly Discovered Manuscript of Opicinus de Canistris', *Journal of the Warburg and Courtauld Institute*, XVI (1953), 45–57.

Salomon, Richard G., 'Aftermath to Opicinus de Canistris', *Journal of the Warburg and Courtauld Institute*, XXV (1962), 137–46.

Salzman, Michele Renee, *On Roman Time: the Codex Calendar of Urban Life in Late Antiquity* (Berkeley, 1990).

Sandford, Eva M., 'The Manuscripts of Lucan: Accessus and Marginalia', *Speculum*, IX (1934), 278–95.

Sato, Masayuki, 'Comparative Ideas of Chronology', *History and Theory: Studies in the Philosophy of History*, XXX, no. 3 (1991), 275–301.

Saxl, F., 'Illuminated Scientific Manuscripts in England', in *Lectures* (London, 1957), 96–110.

Saxl, F., 'Illustrated Medieval Encyclopedias', in *Lectures* (London, 1957), 228–54.

Saxl, F., 'A Spiritual Encyclopedia of the Later Middle Ages', *Journal of the Warburg and Courtauld Institutes*, V (1942), 82–142.

Schulz, Juergen, 'Jacopo de' Barbari's View of Venice: Map Making, City Views, and Moralized Geography Before the Year 1500', *Art Bulletin*, LX (1978), 425–74.

Schulz, Juergen, 'Maps as Metaphors', in *Art and Cartography: Six Historical Essays*, ed. by David Woodward (Chicago, 1987), 97–122.

Schnetz, Joseph, ed., *Itineraria Romana, II: Ravennatis Anonymi Cosmographia et Guidonis Geographica* (Stuttgart, 1940; repr. 1990).

Sicard, Patrice, *Diagrammes médiévaux et exegèse visuelle: le 'libellus de formatione arche' de Hughes de Saint-Victor* (Paris, 1993).

Singer, Charles and Dorothea, 'Byrhtferð's Diagram', *Bodleian Quarterly Record*, II, no. 14 (1917), 47–51, with illustrations.

Singer, Charles, *et al.*, *A History of Technology* (Oxford, 1954–78), 7 vols.

Singer, Charles, 'A Review of the Medical Literature of the Dark Ages, with a New Text of About 1110', *Proceedings of the Royal Society of Medicine*, X (1917), 117–27.

Skelton, R. A., *Looking at an Early Map* (Lawrence, Kan., 1965).

Skelton, R. A., *Maps: a Historical Survey of Their Study and Collecting* (Chicago, 1972).

Skelton, R. A., ed., *The Vinland Map and the Tartar Relation* (New Haven, 1965).

Smalley, Beryl, *Historians of the Middle Ages* (London, 1974).

Smalley, Beryl, 'Sallust in the Middle Ages', in *Classical Influences on European Culture, 500–1500*, ed. by R. R. Bolgar (Cambridge, 1971), 165–76.

Stahl, William Harris, *Martianus Capella and the Seven Liberal Arts* (New York, 1971), 2 vols.

Stahl, William, *Roman Science: Origins, Development and Influence to the Later Middle Ages* (Madison, Wisconsin, 1962).

Steinhauser, Kenneth D., *The Apocalypse Commentary of Tyconius* (Frankfurt-am-Main, 1987).

Stevens, Wesley M., *Bede's Scientific Achievement* (Newcastle-upon-Tyne, 1985).

Stevens, Wesley M., 'Compotistica et Astronomica in the Fulda School,' in *Saints, Scholars and Heroes*, ed. by Wesley M. Stevens and Margot H. King (Collegeville, Minn., 1979), 27–63.

Stevens, Wesley M., 'Computer databases for early manuscripts', *Encyclopedia of Library and Information Science*, LVI, Suppl. 19, ed. by Allen Kent and Carolyn M. Hall (New York, 1995).

Stevens, Wesley M., 'The Figure of the Earth in Isidore's "De Natura Rerum"', *Isis*, LXXI (1980), 268–77.

Stewart, Aubrey, *Itinerary from Bordeaux to Jerusalem: the Bordeaux Pilgrim*, in *Palestine Pilgrims' Text Society*, I (New York, 1971; repr. 1887–97 edn)

Stierlin, Henri, *Los Beatos de Liébana y el Arte Mozárabe* (Madrid, 1983). (Original title: *Le Livre de Feu.*)

Swarzenski, Hanns, 'Comments on the Figural Illustrations', in *Liber Floridus Colloquium*, ed. by Albert Derolez (Ghent, 1973), 21–30.

Taylor, Eva G. R., 'The "De Ventis" of Matthew Paris', *Imago Mundi*, II (1937), 23–6.

Taylor, John, *The Universal Chronicle of Ranulf Higden* (Oxford, 1966).

Taylor, John, *The Use of Medieval Chronicles* (London, 1965).

Teyssedre, Bernard, 'Les illustrations du *De natura rerum* d'Isidore: un exemple de survie de la figure humaine dans les manuscrits précarolingiens', *Gazette des Beaux-Arts*, 6th series, LVI (1960), 19–34.

Thorndike, Lynn, *A History of Magic and Experimental Science During the First Thirteen Centuries of Our Era* (New York, 1923), 8 vols.

Thrower, Norman J. W., *Maps and Civilization: Cartography in Culture and Society* (Chicago, 1996).

Tibbetts, Gerald R., 'The Beginnings of a Cartographic Tradition', in *Cartography in the Traditional Islamic and South Asian Societies*, in *History of Cartography*, ed. by J. B. Harley and David Woodward (Chicago, 1992), II, 90–107.

Tibbetts, Gerald R., 'Later Cartographic Development', in *Cartography in the Traditional Islamic and South Asian Societies*, in *History of Cartography*, ed. by J. B. Harley and David Woodward (Chicago, 1992), II, 137–55.

Tobler, Titus, and Molinier, A., *Itinera Hierosolymitana et Descriptiones Terrae Sanctae* (Geneva, 1879).

Tomasch, Sylvia, 'Mappae Mundi and "The Knight's Tale:" the Geography of Power, the Technology of Control', in *Literature and Technology*, ed. by Mark L. Greenberg and Lance Schachterle (Bethlehem, Pa, 1992), 66–98.

Toulmin, Stephen, and Goodfield, June, *The Discovery of Time* (Chicago, 1977; repr. 1965 ed.).

Tristram, Hildegard, *Sex aetates mundi: die Weltzeitalter bei den angelsachsen und den iren Untersuchungen und Texte* (Heidelberg, 1985).

Tsafrir, Yoram, 'The Maps Used by Theodosius: on the Pilgrim Maps of the Holy Land and Jerusalem in the Sixth Century AD', *Dumbarton Oaks Papers*, XL (1986), 129–45.

Uhden, Richard, 'Gervasius von Tilbury und die Ebstorfer Weltkarte', *Jahrbuch der Geographischen Gesellschaft zu Hannover*, XXXVII (1930), 185–200.

Uhden, Richard, 'Specimen Terrae: Landermässe eines unbekannten Geographen aus dem I. Jahrhundert n. Chr.', *Petermanns Mitteilungen*, LXXVII (1931).

Uhden, Richard, 'Die Weltkarte des Isidorus von Sevilla', *Mnemosyne: Bibliotheca Classica Batavia*, 3rd ser., III, part 1 (1935–6), 1–28.

Uhden, Richard, 'Die Weltkarte des Martianus Capella', *Mnemosyne*, 3rd ser., III, part 3 (1935–6), 97–124, with foldout map.

Usener, Hermannus, *M. Annaei Lucani Commenta Bernensia* (repr. of 1869 edn, Hildesheim, 1967).

Vásquez de Parga, L. 'Un mapa desconocido de la serie de los "Beatos"', in *Actas del Simposio para el Estudio de los Códices del "Comentario al Apocalipsis" de Beato de Liébana* (Madrid, 1978), I, 273–8.

Vaughan, Richard, ed., *The Illustrated Chronicles of Matthew Paris* (Cambridge, 1993).

Vaughan, Richard, *Matthew Paris* (Cambridge, 1958), 242.

Vidier, Alexandre, 'La mappemonde de Théodulphe et la mappemonde de Ripoll, IX–XI siècles', *Bulletin de géographie historique et descriptive*, XXVI (1911), 285–313.

Vyver, A. van der, 'Dicuil et Micon de Saint-Riquier', *Révue belge de philologie et d'histoire*, XIV:1 (1935), 25–48.

Vyver, A. van der, 'Les oeuvres inédites d'Abbon de Fleury', *Révue Bénédictine*, (1935), 125–69.

Wallis, Faith E., 'Images of Order in the Medieval Computus', in *Ideas of Order in the Middle Ages*, ed. by Warren Ginsberg (Binghamton, NY, 1990), 45–68.

Wallis, Faith E. 'MS Oxford, St John's 17: a Medieval Manuscript in its Context,' University of Toronto dissertation (1985).

Wallis, Helen and Tyacke, Sarah, *My Head is a Map: Essays and Memoirs in Honour of R. W. Tooley* (London, 1973).

Weber, Ekkehard, ed., *Tabula Peutingeriana: Codex Vindobonensis 324* (Graz, 1976), 2 vols.

Weitzmann, Kurt, *Illustrations in Roll and Codex: a Study of the Origin and Method of Text Illustration* (Princeton, 1970).

Werckmeister, Otto-Karl, 'Pain and Death in the Beatus of St-Sever', *Studi Medievali*, 3rd ser., XIV, part 2, (1973) 565–626.

Whitfield, Peter, *The Image of the World* (London, 1994).

Wilcox, Donald J., *The Measure of Times Past: Pre-Newtonian Chronologies and the Rhetoric of Relative Time* (Chicago, 1987).

Wilken, Robert L., *The Land Called Holy: Palestine in Christian History and Thought* (New Haven, 1992).

Williams, John, *The Illustrated Beatus: a Corpus of the Illustrations of the Commentary on the Apocalypse* (London, 1995), 5 vols.

Williams, John, 'Isidore, Orosius and the Beatus Map', *Imago Mundi*, 49 (1997).

Williams, John, and Shailor, Barbara, eds., *A Spanish Apocalypse: The Morgan Beatus Manuscript* (New York, 1991). (A facsimile of Morgan MS 644.)

Wilmart, Andreas, *Codices Reginenses Latini* in *Bibliothecae Apostolicae Vaticanae Codices Manu Scripti Recensiti* (Vatican, 1945), 2 vols.

Wolf, Armin, 'Ikonologie der Ebstorfer Weltkarte und politische Situation des Jahres 1239', in *Ein Weltbild vor Columbus: die Ebstorfer Weltkarte*, ed. by Harmut Kugler and Eckhard Michael (Weinheim, 1991), 91–103.

Wolf, Armin, 'News on the Ebstorf World Map: Date, Origin, Authorship', in *Géographie du Monde au Moyen Age et à la Renaissance*, ed. by Monique Pelletier (Paris, 1989), 51–68.

Wolf, Kenneth Baxter, *Conquerors and Chroniclers of Early Medieval Spain* (Liverpool, 1990).

Woodward, David, 'Medieval Mappaemundi', in *Cartography in Prehistoric, Ancient, and Medieval Europe and the Mediterranean, History of Cartography*, ed. by J. B. Harley and David Woodward (Chicago, 1987), I, 286–370.

Woodward, David, 'Medieval World Maps', in *Géographie du Monde au Moyen Age et à la Renaissance*, ed. by Monique Pelletier (Paris, 1989), 7–8.

Woodward, David, 'Reality, Symbolism, Time, and Space in Medieval World Maps', *Annals of American Geographers*, LXXV, no. 2 (1985), 510–21.

Wright, John K., *Geographical Lore at the Time of the Crusades* (New York, 1925).

Yates, Frances A., *The Art of Memory* (Chicago, 1966).

BIBLIOGRAPHIC WORKS

Alexander, J. J. G., *Insular Manuscripts from the 6th to the 9th centuries*, in, *Survey of Manuscripts Illuminated in the British Isles*, I (London, 1978).

DeLisle, Leopold, *Mélanges de Paleographie et de Bibliographie* (Paris, 1880).

Díaz y Díaz, Manuel C., *Index Scriptorum Latinorum Medii Aevi Hispanorum* (Salamanca, 1958–9), 2 vols.

Goetz, Georg, *Corpus Glossariorum Latinorum* (Leipzig, 1888–1923).

Homburger, Otto, *Die illustrierten Handschriften der Bürgerbibliothek, Bern* (Berne, 1962).

Jeudy, Collette, and Riou, Yves-François, *Les manuscrits classiques latins des bibliothèques publiques de France* (Paris, 1989), 2 vols.

Kauffmann, C. M., *Romanesque Manuscripts, 1066–1170*, in *Survey of Manuscripts Illuminated in the British Isles*, III (London, 1975).

Ker, Neil Ripley, *Catalogue of Manuscripts Containing Anglo-Saxon* (Oxford, 1959).

Ker, Neil Ripley, *Medieval Manuscripts in British Libraries* (Oxford, 1969), vols.

Kristeller, Paul O., *Latin Manuscript Books Before 1600: a List of the Printed Catalogues and Unpublished Inventories of Extant Collections* (2nd edn, New York, 1960).

Lowe, E. A., *Codices Latini Antiquiores: a Paleographical Guide to Latin Manuscripts Prior to the 9th Century* (Oxford, 1934 ff.), 12 vols.

Madan, F., Craster, H. H. E., and Denholm-Young, N., *Summary Catalogue of Western Manuscripts in the Bodleian Library at Oxford* (Oxford, 1937), 7 vols.

Morgan, Nigel J., *Early Gothic Manuscripts, 1250–86*, in *Survey of Manuscripts Illuminated in the British Isles*, (London, 1988) IV.

Mundo, Anscario M. and Mariana, Manuel Sanchez, *El Comentario de Beato al Apocalipsis: Catálogo de los Códices* (Madrid, 1976).

Munk Olsen, Birger, *Catalogue des manuscrits classiques copiés du IXe au XIIe siècle* (Paris, 1982 ff.), 3 vols.

Pächt, Otto, and Alexander, J. J. G., *Illuminated Manuscripts at the Bodleian Library* (Oxford, 1966–74), 4 vols.

Paris, Bibliothèque Nationale, *À la découverte de la terre: Dix siècles de cartographie. Trésors du Dept. des Cartes et Plans* (Paris, 1979).

Paris, Bibliothèque Nationale, *Choix de documents géographiques conservés à la Bibliothèque Nationale* (Paris, 1883).

Ricci, Seymour D., ed., *Census of Medieval and Renaissance Manuscripts in the U.S. and Canada* (New York, 1935–40; supplement, 1962).

Sandler, Lucy F., *Gothic Manuscripts, 1285–1385*, in *Survey of Manuscripts Illuminated in the British Isles*, V. London, 1986.

Saxl, Fritz, and Meier, Hans, *Catalogue of Astrological and Mythological Illuminated Manuscripts of the Latin Middle Ages* (London, 1953), vols.

Shailor, Barbara, ed., *Catalog of Medieval and Renaissance Manuscripts in the Beinecke Rare Book and Manuscript Library, Yale University* (Binghamton, NY, 1984 and 1987).

Silverstein, Theodore, *Medieval Scientific Writings in the Barberini Collection: a Provisional Catalog* (Chicago, 1956).

Stevens, Wesley D., 'Computer Databases for Early Manuscripts', in *Encyclopedia of Library and Information Science*, ed. by Allen Kent and Carolyn Hall (New York, 1995), LVI, suppl. 19.

Temple, Elzbieta, *Anglo-Saxon Manuscripts, 900–1066*, in *Survey of Manuscripts Illuminated in the British Isles*, II (London, 1976).

Tesi, Mario, ed., *Monumenti di Cartografia a Firenze, secoli X–XVII* (Firenze, 1981).

Thorndike, Lynn, and Kibre, Pearl, *A Catalogue of Incipits of Medieval Scientific Writings in Latin* (rev. edn, Cambridge, Mass., 1965).

von Euw, Anton, and Plotzek, Joachim M., *Die Handschriften der Sammlung Ludwig* (Cologne, 1982), 4 vols.

Watson, Andrew G., *Catalogue of Dated and Datable Manuscripts, c. 700–1600 in the Department of Manuscripts, the British Library* (London, 1979).

Wickersheimer, Ernest, *Les manuscrits de médecine du haut moyen âge dans les bibliothèques de France* (Paris, 1966).

GENERAL INDEX

INDEX OF MANUSCRIPTS